# TH

# Complete Detective

*Raymond C. Schindler*

# The Complete Detective

*Being the Life and Strange and Exciting Cases
of* Raymond Schindler, Master Detective

## BY RUPERT HUGHES

*With a Foreword by* Erle Stanley Gardner

M. EVANS
*Lanham • New York • Boulder • Toronto • Plymouth, UK*

M. Evans
An imprint of The Rowman & Littlefield Publishing Group, Inc.
4501 Forbes Boulevard, Suite 200, Lanham, Maryland 20706
http://www.rlpgtrade.com

10 Thornbury Road, Plymouth PL6 7PP, United Kingdom

Distributed by National Book Network

**Library of Congress Cataloging-in-Publication Data Available**

ISBN 13: 978-1-59077-454-0 (pbk: alk. paper)

♾™ The paper used in this publication meets the minimum requirements of American National Standard for Information Sciences—Permanence of Paper for Printed Library Materials, ANSI/NISO Z39.48-1992.

Printed in the United States of America

# CONTENTS

FOREWORD by ERLE STANLEY GARDNER          9

1. THE DETECTIVE IN FACT AND FICTION          15
2. THE SERIAL MURDERER          30
3. BEAUTY IN DISTRESS          67
4. RAY'S MOST FAMOUS CASE          87
5. HIS HARDEST CASE          116
6. THE WOMAN OF TOO MANY PASTS          135
7. CINEMA SHAKEDOWN          143
8. BLACKMAIL AS AN INDUSTRY          151
9. A FEW HORS D'OEUVRE          170
10. EVEN HIS INITIALS WERE R O B          180
11. THE DICTOGRAPH AS A PUBLIC DEFENDER          196
12. THE DICTOGRAPH AS A PRIVATE EAVESDROPPER          208
13. CRIME AGAINST CRIME          222
14. THE KOREAN MIND AND FACE          231
15. THE TYPEWRITTEN KIDNAPPER          242
16. PAINTINGS VANISH, JEWELS REAPPEAR          247
17. HE BUILDS A RAILROAD          261
18. VANISHED WEALTH          269
19. A RAID ON FAIRYLAND          275
20. GRAND (SOAP) OPERA          282
21. HE PLAYS SANTA CLAUS          288
22. PRETEXTS AND THE PASSION PLAYERS          292
23. THE LIE DETECTOR DETECTS THE TRUTH          300
24. THE LOST GIRL          312
25. WHO WAS THE RED KILLER?          313

# A Foreword
# THE CASE OF THE
# DETERMINED DETECTIVE

*by* ERLE STANLEY GARDNER

# THE CASE OF THE
# DETERMINED DETECTIVE

*by* ERLE STANLEY GARDNER


I first met Raymond Schindler in 1943 at Miami Beach.

It was just before the opening of the famous de Marigny trial in the Bahamas. I was to cover that trial for the *New York Journal-American* and some of its affiliated newspapers. Raymond Schindler was acting as consulting criminologist for the defense, employed by de Marigny's beautiful wife, the former Nancy Oakes.

Tom Ferris, the incomparable publicity man of Miami Beach, arranged the meeting at the Versailles Hotel, and Tom saw there were plenty of cameramen along. We sat at a sun-swept table against the background of the beautiful hotel swimming pool with its overhanging cocoanut palms. Flash bulbs blazed and shutters clicked while Ray and I got acquainted.

Not too well acquainted, because Ray was embarking upon one of the most difficult jobs of his entire career and he was playing them very, very close to his chest.

A few days later, the scene shifted over to Nassau in the Bahamas.

There I had an opportunity to see Ray Schindler in action. Bit by bit, he began to warm up to me and let down the bars.

Before I became a mystery writer, I was a trial lawyer. During that time I had occasion to employ quite a few private detectives, and I employed some good ones. Therefore, my appreciation of Ray Schindler's technique was founded upon a pretty fair knowledge of what he was up against.

9

Only those who were in the Bahamas during the trial of Alfred de Marigny and were familiar with the terrific tension, the behind-the-scenes developments, can appreciate the magnitude of Ray Schindler's task.

Almost immediately after the murder of Sir Harry Oakes, the Duke of Windsor, then the governor of the island, had personally called in Captain Edward Melchen, of the Florida police. Melchen and Captain James L. Barker, also of the Florida police, arrived on the island. Apparently their status was never fully clarified. They may or may not have thought they were helping the island police. The island police apparently thought they had been superseded. In any event, the investigation of what is perhaps the most mysterious and baffling murder of all time devolved upon these two Florida police officers who were dealing with a strange legal procedure in a strange land and trying to pull a rabbit out of the hat in a matter of hours.

The officers discovered, interpreted or encountered evidence which led to the arrest of Alfred de Marigny.

By far the most significant part of that evidence was the fingerprint produced by Captain Barker, a fingerprint which was concededly made by one of de Marigny's fingers, and which Barker insisted he had removed from a wooden screen which had been within a few feet of the bed where the body of the murdered millionaire had been found.

For some time prior to the murder, Sir Harry Oakes and de Marigny had been estranged. De Marigny insisted he had not been in the house where the murder was committed for a long time, and, quite obviously, if his fresh fingerprint had actually been found on that wooden screen, the case against him would have been as black as the deepest cell in a dark dungeon on a cloudy night.

It is a mistake to assume that Ray Schindler was ever employed to solve the murder of Sir Harry Oakes. He was employed to see that de Marigny wasn't convicted on evidence which wouldn't stand up to the searching analysis of modern criminology.

The fact that this fingerprint, unquestionably that of de Marigny's little finger, authenticated by police testimony as having come from that wooden screen, didn't put the noose right around de Marigny's neck is one of the greatest investigative triumphs of modern times. I know of no detective who has ever faced a tougher assignment or discharged it more triumphantly.

Rupert Hughes, famous for his biographical technique as well as for his fiction, gives the reader in a special chapter in this book Ray Schindler's story of the de Marigny case and discloses facts which have hitherto not been available to the public.

There is, therefore, no point in discussing at this time how Ray Schindler did the thing that he did. I only mention the case because, for several long weeks, each day of which was packed with enough excitement to make a dime novel seem anemic in comparison, I watched Ray Schindler in action.

Feeling was running high on the island. There was intense prejudice against de Marigny. There was prejudice against American sensationalism. There was wild excitement. There were rumors. There were even rumors of threats.

Against that background, Ray Schindler, quietly, competently, aggressively, vigorously, went about his work. He surrounded himself with some of the best men in the business. He directed their efforts with the talent of a born executive.

But the thing which impressed itself upon my mind was the fact that in all of this atmosphere of wildly distorted rumors, fantastic speculation, prejudice, heat, haste, uncertainty and doubt, Ray Schindler never for a moment lost his mental perspective. He listened to everything, saw everything, investigated everything, and sifted facts out of the chaff of rumor and speculation. Always his mind was as cold, calm, detached and deadly efficient as though the man had been some calculating machine.

Gradually, bit by bit, the remorseless energy of his mind drove that fingerprint farther and farther from the screen until at the time of trial the thing simply couldn't be identified with any specific area on the screen. Up until a few days before he was to go on the stand, Captain Barker had the place marked on the screen where he claimed the fingerprint had been before he "lifted" it. When he got on the stand, he had decided he couldn't be sure.

De Marigny was acquitted.

Since that time I have seen a great deal of Ray Schindler. I have learned now something of the background of the man. the reason for those qualities which made him stand out so sharply during those hectic days on the Bahamas.

It is a remarkably interesting character, and the things which have made it what it is are analyzed in Rupert Hughes' book. Here the reader can meet one of the most outstanding of all of the real detectives. Here he can follow him through case after case, watching a man who can't be excited, can't be stampeded, and can't be frightened. A man who matches the ingenuity of crime with an even greater mental resourcefulness and who has in addition a dogged determination and a big fighting heart.

The history of Raymond Schindler is far more fascinating than fiction. His biography is the story of a great investigator, of a life that is packed with exciting adventures and of criminals who are outwitted, outfought and smashed.

It is a great story.

# THE

# Complete Detective

# 1.

## THE DETECTIVE

## IN FACT AND FICTION

*"If you will save my husband from being hanged as the murderer of my father, I will pay you all the money you may ask."*

*It was a beautiful, young American Marquise who threw herself on the mercy of Raymond Schindler. She appealed to his—shall we say, cupidity?—but he answered warmly:*

*"I will do my best, my dear child—but on one condition. If my investigations turn up evidence that your husband is guilty, I will turn that evidence over to the prosecution."*

*The desperate girl had to consent. All the world read in the newspapers of that time how Ray Schindler not only saved her husband from execution but won an almost instant verdict of "Not Guilty" from the jury. He tore the case against the Marquis to shreds by new methods of dealing with fingerprints.*

*"We haven't much money but we believe that this worthless Negro, who is about to be railroaded to his death, is innocent of the ghastly murder of that poor young girl."*

*The case against the Negro seemed to be absolutely unbreakable; the financial rewards were almost nil; yet Ray gave his utmost art to that case.*

*Few things in detective fiction are more complex and ingenious than Raymond Schindler's discovery and trapping of the real murderer, and the extraction of a full confession from him. Ray's immensely modern methods included the*

15

*publication of false copies of three leading newspapers, the simulation of a murder, the use of the dictograph, and elaborate and subtle psychological devices.*

*"If you tell my husband what you have found out, I will kill myself."*

*A beautiful wife was on her knees to Ray Schindler. It was the detective who pleaded.*

*"But, my dear lady, I have no choice. I must tell him."*

*"Then go ahead and tell him," she cried. "And I will kill myself. I mean it!"*

*How Ray Schindler saved her and did his duty by his client is as fantastic a series of facts as any imaginary story any fiction writer ever concocted.*

The writer of mystery stories can, and sometimes does, show great invention in working up plots and characters. But, in a pinch, an author can make any changes he may find necessary, or convenient, or exciting.

The detective in real life needs just as much imagination as the fictionist, and often more. The real detective has to take a ready-made plot, find out the hidden characters, take them as he finds them and deal with them as they change their efforts to elude him.

It is not enough for a paid detective to keep a reader awake or scare one to sleep with a thrilling bed-time story. The detective has to work out his plot until it will convince a jury that it could not possibly have happened otherwise. He must be ready to confront expensive criminal lawyers of equal imagination who aim to persuade emotional juries that the accusations are entirely false; or, even if they are true, that the guilty ones should not be punished for them.

The story of Ray Schindler's life and works is not only a cyclopaedia of enthralling stories, but also a travelogue through nearly every phase of human life.

Having known the man for many years, I have come to

feel an affection for him as great as my admiration. He deserves a biography far more than most of those whose lives are set forth in pretentious tomes; for he has been the protector of the weak and the savior of the guiltless as well as a preventer of crime and an avenging fate on the heels of the wicked.

He has invoked and developed the newest scientific devices of every sort, and collaborated with the highest experts in every field of medical, chemical, and electric discovery.

Most of his adventures far outrun in ingenuity and suspense the masterpieces of detective fiction; and they have the added value of genuine human documents.

I have tried to recount these stories faithfully as they first came to Ray Schindler's office in all their cloudy mystery; then to show how, with inspired imagination and unwearying skill and science, indomitable pertinacity and ingenuity, he penetrated the fogs and jungles, overcame the conspiracies of obscurity and villainy, brought home the true truth, and served the high offices of justice and mercy, making life safer for everybody.

This may not be popular fiction; but if it is not popular fact, it is my fault, not his.

Few people realize how important to the public safety is the activity of the private detective. Fewer people knew that this same Ray Schindler devoted far more time and genius to saving a drunken, disreputable, ex-convict Negro from being hustled off to the electric chair for the horrible murder of a little girl, than he spent in rescuing a rich Marquis from prosecutors determined to execute him.

The high sense of pure justice that led Ray Schindler to save the life of a worthless derelict is one of the qualities that inspire him. His exceedingly busy life has done much to lift the name and trade of the private detective into the realm of high art, and the high dignity of public protection.

Many criminal lawyers, though sworn to act as allies with the courts as officers of the law, gain wealth and fame by defeating justice and saving the guilty from punishment. And there have been more than enough evil detectives, both private and public. But Ray Schindler feels that he is a part of the administration of the law.

The clearing of that trapped Negro and the discovery and the conviction of the true murderer of the little girl, won from Dorothy Dix the phrase: "the most brilliant piece of detective work in American history." One would search far to find another that involved such elaborate and patient toil and such imagination. It invoked the invention and perseverance of the dramatist, and the scientist. The relentless siege of the guilty mind until it gave up its own secret was a superlative feat of psychology in action.

In this case he made the only use he ever made of a fictional story; for he took a hint from Conan Doyle's "Hound of the Baskervilles" and had for his collaborator a dog, as in another of his cases he found a most useful ally in a monkey.

Among the triumphs of Ray Schindler's creative and analytic genius which are to be recounted in this story of his life, many of the most exciting to read about never reached the glare of publicity till now. He often forswore the advantages of advertisement for the sake of poor creatures entangled in meshes of circumstances from which he alone could release them without exposing them.

What could be more dramatic or horrifying than the experience of the emotional millionaire who accidentally stumbled on the fact that the wife of his bosom, whom he had loved and adored for years, had tricked him into matrimony and concealed an almost unbelievably wicked past of many marriages and the crassest blackmail?

He called on Ray Schindler to rescue him from the claws of the unscrupulous harpy and to get her out of his life and his home without a prodigious scandal. Ray Schindler managed it by pitting his skill and stubbornness against her relentlessness; but he had to visit many European capitals before he won the battle.

Then there was the big hotel that appealed to Ray to save it from an enormous damage suit threatened by a pretty girl who was growing rich by pretending to swallow broken glass in successive hotels. Then the grafting woman whose celluloid combs exploded in her hair—

On one occasion he built fourteen miles of railroad to convince, and so unseat, a crooked railroad president. And he made the railroad pay a profit!

On another, he opened a bank to persuade a banker to disclose his own dishonesties.

He laid out the plans for a gigantic radio program in order to save the product of a soap manufacturer who was helpless to protect his own field from invasion by powerful rivals.

In his early days he had a large share in putting behind bars San Francisco's mayor and so many other officials that the city had to be run by an "elisor" designated by the courts.

He saved Atlantic City from enormous municipal robbery, and imprisoned grafters in high places.

One of his noblest achievements has been his collaborations with Erle Stanley Gardner in their "Court of Last Resort," which investigates the cases of men convicted of murder and claiming innocence. The Court, at vast expense of time and money, has already released three guiltless wretches who had already served twelve or more years' time at hard labor in penitentiaries. The proof of their innocence had been as difficult as it was divinely merciful.

He has kept abreast of, and taken constant advantage of the ever-increasing resources of science. His clever adaptations of radio have been startling. He was perhaps the first detective to employ the dictograph in his work. After making use of the first gropings towards mechanical discovery of the truth, he was closely allied with Leonarde Keeler in the employment of his widely known, widely misunderstood and underrated marvel, the polygraph, generally called "the lie detector."

Another partner of his has been the eminent expert in

the chemistry of crime, Dr. Lemoyne Snyder, formerly med-ico-legal director of the Michigan State Police.

In fact, Ray Schindler and Dr. Snyder have joined with the famous handwriting expert, Clark Sellers, and William Harper, the physicist, to form a sort of court of appeal called "Scientific Evidence Inc.," to which individuals or officers of the law in need of the highest criminological skill can refer difficult problems.

Though the private detective of fiction, like the black sheep among private detectives in fact, works against the legal police forces, Ray Schindler always cooperates with them.

Homer Cummings, while he was Attorney General of the United States, wrote: "In my judgment, Raymond C. Schindler is a great detective. He has at his fingertips the techniques of his craft. He never evolves theories of his cases until the last scrap of evidence has been developed and ana-lyzed. I never knew a man to move more swiftly or with surer touch. He is loyal to the most exacting and ethical standards."

How the Federal Bureau of Investigation values him is shown by this excerpt from a letter written by its chief, J. Edgar Hoover:

"I am looking forward to shaking hands with my friend, Ray Schindler, so that I may be able personally to tell him how much I appreciate his ardent support of the F.B.I. One always likes to know who his friends are, and it is good to know that I have such a friend in Ray."

As I have gone about with him I have been astonished by the number of people who know him and greet him with affection. It seems that half the people in the country must call him "Ray."

In the usual detective fiction, the sleuth is an eccentric character of strange habits and quaint dialect. When he is called in to repair the stupidity of the dull-witted and blun-dering constables of Scotland or other Yards, he puts on his fore-and-aft cap or other quaint costume, takes a shot of his favorite narcotic, lights his pipe, arms himself with his trusty magnifying glass, and sallies forth to perform a miracle by way of analyzing cigarette ashes or penetrating the mind of the occult murderer. When he has astounded the public and humiliated the bumbling officers of the law, he goes back to his Dr. Watson, or his private hobbies and awaits the next appeal to his uncanny intuitions.

But Ray Schindler is more of a syndicate than an individual. Instead of waiting for an emergency call, he goes to his main office in the morning and inspects a daily work-sheet that may contain fifty current cases on which he is working with his staff. These are of every imaginable and picturesque variety. He has associated offices in twenty important cities and cooperative arrangements with other bureaus everywhere.

His brother and associate, Walter Schindler, spent the whole summer of 1949 travelling Europe and reestablishing connections with foreign agencies in the principal capitals abroad.

His clients are not merely victims of blackmail threats, thefts, forgery, mayhem, murder, arson, sabotage, but also great banks, hotels, department stores, insurance companies, railroads and other corporations.

At any moment a telephone call or a telegram may lead him to throw out, like an alarmed fire department, a swarm of twenty or thirty operatives, whom he sends scurrying forth in all directions. He may dash to a plane, a train, a steamer or an airplane for Europe.

Ray Schindler himself, though he is constantly wandering into danger, has never worn a disguise or carried a firearm. He has never been engaged in a fight, though on one occasion he did vault over a rail and drop fifteen feet onto the shoulders of a man who had been eluding the police of half a dozen cities for half a dozen years.

Ray's principal weapons are his extraordinary intuitions as to human nature, his genius for inventing ways to uncover its workings and outwit it; his acquaintance with every known scientific implement, and the patience and perseverance that may keep him at work on a case day and night for years on end.

Yet there is something so human about him that even the criminals he overtakes and delivers to trial are ordinarily more angry at themselves than at him. He often promises his friendship and a job to some man whom he has been instrumental in sending to prison. More than one murderer whose conviction has been due to Ray Schindler has gone to his death with expressions of affection for him.

He has an enormous acquaintance everywhere in all walks of life from the highest to the lowest and can count on friendly collaborators wherever he needs them. He finds time, too, for much social activity and has been president of the Adventurers Club three times, as well as one of the leading figures in the hilarious festivals of the Circus Saints and Sinners. He is also an ardent worker for the Boys' Clubs and the Future Presidents' League. He lectures widely. In 1939 he founded, and became President of, International Investigators, a worldwide organization.

Ray Schindler is a made detective, not a born one. In his early life he showed none of the love of sleuthing that gives so many boyhoods an aura of imaginary melodrama.

It took the San Francisco earthquake to shake Ray Schindler down into the detective business.

He was born in the town of Mexico, New York, on November 11, 1882. His father was John Franklin Schindler, a graduate of St. Lawrence University, and a minister in the Universalist Church. A month after Ray's birth, a new church was offered in the near-by city of Oswego. A few years later the family moved to a parsonage in Marshalltown, Iowa. Later, the roving pastor took over the Universalist Church in Stillwater, Minnesota.

The state prison there was in charge of a warden who was

a pioneer in many prison reforms nowadays more or less generally practiced. There, perhaps, Ray acquired his first realization that criminals are human beings; the prey of their own natures and environments. He has pursued them but he has never persecuted them.

His mother founded the prison library and served without pay as the librarian at the penitentiary. She also conducted Sunday School classes for the prisoners. She was assisted by Henrietta Younger, sister of three inmates famous as the Younger Brothers, later closely allied with the James Brothers in the annals of American crime.

The Schindlers moved next to Whitewater, Wisconsin, where Ray began a schooling, which was continued in later stopovers at Racine and Milwaukee. At this point, his father, having accumulated four sons and three daughters, left the profession of saving souls in the hereafter for that of insuring lives in this world. Long afterward he followed his sons into the detective business.

Outside his school hours, Ray was industrious in delivering papers for 25 cents a day, then special delivery letters. At night he was a theater-usher and played small parts in a stock company. On one occasion he spoke three lines in Richard Mansfield's production of "Cyrano de Bergerac."

In 1900, he spent a summer vacation as night clerk in a hotel in Escanaba, Michigan.

He finally saved enough money to buy into a Californian gold mine and later, with a new capital of a thousand dollars, decided to go West and look into his gold mine, which rejoiced in the name of "Sky High." This journey took Ray into an odyssey of adventures. Cut-rate railroad ticket sharks sent him and a buddy of his on a roundabout journey via Denver and Cheyenne, at which point their money all but gave out.

The kindly brakeman on a freight train smuggled them for five dollars each into a refrigerator car where they perched on crossbeams in a crouching position. They had no food and a December blizzard combined with the freezing temperature inside nearly delivered the young men as frozen meat.

At Laramie their faint cries were heard and they were removed from the ice box. After thawing out for a day and a half, their gluttony for adventure led them to bribe another brakeman to let them "ride blind baggage." This put them outside on the front platform of the first baggage car immediately behind the engine and the snowplow, which had to buck heavy drifts and a continued blizzard.

Choked and blackened by soot and smoke and congealed with blown snow, they managed to live a few hours till the fireman noticed them, hauled them over the top of the coal car and warmed them with ten hours of shoveling coal into the firebox of the engine.

Ray's further mishaps were too harrowing to relate, but he reached his gold mine on an icy Christmas Day. The horses actually wore snowshoes! The supplies were brought in on skis, and the inhabitants left their houses by second-story windows to get out on top of the sixteen-foot-deep snow. Ray worked under frightful hardships twelve hours a day, seven days a week until spring came. Then the mine was abandoned.

He arrived in San Francisco just in time to find the town in ruins from the famous earthquake. He slipped through the lines while the fire was still raging and secured a job with a refreshment stand in the burned-over area. After a month of this his eye was caught by a want advertisement beginning with the word "Historians" of all words! It read:

"Historians. Wanted men with college education to record the greatest catastrophe that ever occurred on this continent. Good salary. Apply G. Franklin Mc-Mackin Historical Society."

Ray had never had a college education, but the words "good salary" inspired him to talk around the subject and he became an "historian."

Unconsciously and unintentionally he had also become a detective. At last the wanderer had found his path of destiny.

The word "historians" was the subterfuge of a New York private detective. He had been sent to the stricken city by some of the big fire insurance companies, whose very existence was threatened and in some cases snuffed out by the enormous losses. The mission of the sleuth was to prove that most of the houses had been wrecked by the earthquake before the fires broke out. Since the earthquake was interpreted as "an act of God," the insurance companies preferred to leave the compensation to Him.

So the sleuth hired forty-two investigators to call upon persons who had visited the region before the fire followed the quake, and wheedle out of them statements as to the condition of the buildings before they were attacked by the flames. It took some skill to elicit this information without rousing suspicion. That was why the investigators were called "historians." They were merely compiling a history of the cataclysm.

As one of the forty-two, Ray was so zealous and so ingenious that, at the end of a month, the private detective was sent back to New York and Ray was promoted to his post.

The investigation kept him busy for a year and a half, during which time he had his headquarters in an apartment house where a rising young lawyer, Hiram Johnson, had taken up temporary offices while his burned-out building was being rebuilt.

All this while San Francisco had been suffering from political termites, who were wrecking the city like a slow earthquake. The boss was Abe Ruef, one of the most picturesque, clever, and tenacious criminals in all the ghastly history of American municipal corruption. His tool and confederate was the violinist and orchestra leader, Eugene Schmitz. He was one of the countless contradictions of Shakespeare's beautiful lines:

"The man that hath no music in his soul
Is fit for treasons, stratagems and spoils."

Mayor Schmitz had plenty of music in his soul and in his fingers, but his soul had also room for treasons and stratagems and all the spoils his clever fingers could pick up.

The gang that owned San Francisco took money from licensed pickpockets, licensed prostitutes, licensed criminals of every sort. They collected wholesale graft from street car companies, telephone and gas companies and every other activity. A small army of collectors went about gathering in all the traffic would bear and hunting down every imaginable source of revenue.

One day Hiram Johnson, who had taken a liking for young Schindler, told him that President Theodore Roosevelt had sent out an Assistant U. S. District Attorney and a U. S. Secret Service detective to San Francisco to work secretly. This was at the request of Fremont Older, the newspaper publisher, who loved his city well enough to uncover its shame and so to rescue it from its degradation and slavery. He had the financial backing of the wealthy Rudolph Spreckels.

The U. S. Attorney was Francis J. Heney, and the Secret Service man was William J. Burns. Hiram Johnson was assisting Heney and, at his recommendation, Burns took Ray Schindler as his right hand man. With Ray he took over sixteen of the "historians." And now Ray was aide and pupil to one of the greatest of all American detectives.

The investigation and the trials lasted for three years. The U. S. Attorney Heney was shot through the head in open court; but Hiram Johnson took his place on the firing line, refused all remuneration and fought the case through. Jurors were shamelessly bribed. When the dishonest Police Chief was removed, his successor was promptly taken out in the police boat and drowned. The chairman of the Board of Supervisors turned State's evidence, and his house was blown up with dynamite, he and his family narrowly escaping death.

It would take volumes, and volumes have been written, to tell of that incredible battle against embattled crime. Some of the worst crooks were acquitted; but, after exhausting all the wiles and loopholes available, Mayor Schmitz went to jail and Abe Ruef finally landed in San Quentin Penitentiary. After a few years of decent and honest administration San Francisco grew weary of virtue, and when Eugene Schmitz was released from prison, he shamelessly ran for mayor and came within a few thousand votes of being shamelessly re-elected.

On other occasions, to be described later on, Ray Schindler aided in ridding other American cities of monstrous grafters and sending them to prison. In these cases, on their return from prison, they ran again for the offices they had befouled, and were triumphantly re-elected.

While Ray has never hesitated to do a good deed because there was no money in it, he soon learned not to belittle his art by putting a low price on it. He owes this to Hiram Johnson, who, on learning that Ray had charged a man ten dollars for a service, scathingly rebuked him for not asking a hundred dollars.

During their association, William J. Burns gained complete respect for Ray's abilities. When at length Burns resigned from government service and prepared to open a huge agency, he offered Ray the post of chief assistant. They came to New York together in 1909.

While Burns has been violently abused by many critics for his achievements in a field where it is extraordinarily easy to make both mistakes and enemies, Ray Schindler has paid him tribute in the following words:

"Burns had imagination. He was a stickler for details. He taught his men to work from 15 to 18 hours a day. It was perhaps this training, particularly in the art of setting up a pretext that was foolproof, that caused me to make this my life's work. The challenge to outsmart, analyze the workings of a guilty mind and cause that person to assist you in obtaining evidence against him, is fascinating."

While he was with Burns, the office was called on to clean up Atlantic City, which was another lesser San Francisco as a stinkhole of political graft, bribery, licensed and heavily taxed gambling, thievery, and prostitution. By a fascinating wonderwork of detection and what is technically known as "roping," and the use of a hundred thousand dollars in actual cash for a pretended bribery, eleven city officials were caught and indicted. Seven were convicted. But later the prodigal leader came out of the penitentiary and was so welcomed home that he was elected to his old post and served for years.

About the same time, a Governor of one of the Carolinas was the victim of the office's skill. He was impeached and thrown out of office for the odious business of selling pardons. But, after a brief period of rustication, he also was lovingly forgiven and elected to the United States Senate for many terms.

Three years after joining William J. Burns, Ray decided to strike out for himself. In 1912, he opened his own business. It has grown steadily in importance and good works ever since. His father (recently deceased) and his brother Walter joined forces with him, and added an efficiency and conscientiousness to his own that have kept the name of Schindler amazingly free from either the suspicions or the accusations that usually cloud the very name of detective.

A catalogue of Ray's achievements would include nearly every imaginable kind of crime and criminal, along with every imaginable kind of victim. This book is therefore a sort of cyclopaedia of human life as it is really lived. And it gives a hint as to the enormous number of people who have had reason to look upon Ray Schindler with profound gratitude for saving them from evil men and women who were outwitted and thwarted only because Ray Schindler and his aides were cleverer than they were, and far more patient, far, far more unfaltering.

# 2.

## THE SERIAL MURDERER

The managers of big New York hotels have strange complaints and stranger requests heaped upon them by strangers from out of town. One day the manager of one of the tallest hotels in town was called by a newly arrived guest who gave his name and room number and asked:

"Could you come up here at once?"

"Of course! I'm on my way now."

He found a parson and a physician from Grand Rapids. They looked as tame as it is possible to look, but frightened.

The parson said, "We want a good detective in a hurry."

"Do you think you've been robbed here? I'll call our house-dick."

"No, we believe that two murders have been committed and a third is about to be, unless something's done in a hurry."

"Have you tried the police? The District Attorney?"

"No. They couldn't and wouldn't move. Who's the best detective in town?"

"If you believe their advertisements, there are a hundred bests. But for my money, I'd choose Raymond C. Schindler."

"Get him, please. It's a matter of life and death. The man we think is twice a murderer is due here on a train tomorrow with the third victim."

The manager's eyes looked exclamation points, but the rule was, "The customer is always right." So he bestirred himself.

If he had been looking for Sherlock Holmes, he would have gone to Baker Street, London, where he would expect to

find the great man smoking his pipe while he analyzed cigarette ashes, and emptied a hollow needle into himself; but
knowing Ray Schindler's gregarious habit of studying hu-
manity in the mass, he began with the night-clubs. At the
very first on the manager's list he found his man.

Joe E. Lewis, the comedian, had just remarked to his audience:

"There sits Ray Schindler. He pretends to be a detective,
but—why, he doesn't know who killed Cock Robin! As Gil-
bert White put it, Ray Schindler couldn't follow an elephant
with a nosebleed around Central Park after a heavy snow."

Nobody laughed harder than Ray, who loves jokes and
caricatures of himself almost as well as he loves to do elaborate foot-work in the rhumba. Joe E. Lewis had finally torn
himself away from his insatiable audience; the orchestra had
just called the sitters from their tables to that form of agitated
mucilage which is called dancing nowanights; and Ray was
just beginning to match his finest footwork with that of his
pretty partner when the hotel manager wormed his way
through the jelly-like throng, apologized for cutting in and
dragged Ray to the edge of the floor. He said: "Ray, this is
serious! In my hotel I've got two doctors waiting—a parson
and a medic. The murderer gets in on a morning train, and
you've got to meet him and take his prey away from him."

In this proposal there was the challenge of the impossible.
Ray nodded. Like a doctor dragged away from revelry, he
bade his guests a regretful goodnight, told the head-waiter
to charge everything to him, and went with the hotel man
to a taxicab.

At the hotel he found two middle-aged men of the least
imaginable dramatic aspect. They were introduced to him
as Dr. Perry Schurtz and the Reverend Dr. Alfred Wishart,
both just arrived from Grand Rapids. Dr. Wishart began at
the beginning.

"I have a parishioner named Percy Peck. He called on me
to say that his father, John Peck, a very wealthy manufac-

turer, had died in New York the day before, and his body was being brought home by Percy's sister and her husband. The father had died of a heart attack while visiting his daughter.

"Percy was hardly out of mourning for his mother, who had died six weeks before, also of a heart attack, while on a visit to that same daughter in New York. His sister and her husband had brought the mother back for burial and the sister's husband, Dr. Waite, had sorrowfully stated that the poor woman's last wish had been that we should have her cremated. This was done, and the dead woman's husband, Percy's father, was crushed with grief for his beloved wife. So Dr. Waite had suggested that it might be well if the poor old man went back to New York to be with his daughter so that they could console each other. And he thought the change of scene would help.

"The old man went to New York and stayed a long while. Now Percy gets word that his father has also died of a heart attack, brought on by mourning for his wife. Once more the daughter and her husband were making a melancholy trip to Grand Rapids. As if the double blow were not heavy enough for Percy, his grief was interrupted by a mysterious telegram that came to him. This is it":

Dr. Wishart produced, and Ray read, this message:

SUSPICION AROUSED. DEMAND AUTOPSY. DO NOT REVEAL TELEGRAM. K. ADAMS

Lifting his eyes from the yellow sheet, Ray asked the obvious question:

"And who is K. Adams?"

"That's mystery Number One," said Dr. Wishart. "Percy has not the faintest idea who he—or she—might be. Percy does not know and has never heard of anybody of that name."

Dr. Schurtz broke in: "The mere thought of an autopsy is revolting to the layman."

The clergyman took over again: "Poor Percy, now doubly orphaned, was horribly shocked. Into his sorrow was injected this poison of suspicion—but suspicion of whom? Of what? He had no more respect for an anonymous sender of a poison telegram than anybody else would have; but he was tormented by the strange coincidence. His mother had visited his sister and come back dead; his father had visited his sister and was coming back dead. Percy naturally turned to me, his pastor, for help and advice. I called in the family physician, Dr. Schurtz here. Go on from there, Perry."

The physician went on: "Of course, it was natural enough that an elderly father should follow an elderly mother into the grave that gets us all; but I had been the family doctor for years and had never noticed a trace of heart trouble in either of them. Yet the mother's death had been certified as due to heart failure by a New York physician—who was not, of course, Dr. Waite. He is actually a dentist and a distinguished one.

"I said to Percy, 'An autopsy can do no harm. If it proves that your father did die of a heart attack it will put your mind at ease and it will be the best answer to that peculiar telegram. If you don't have the autopsy, you will be tormented with suspicion all your life. Your sister can surely have no objection. You owe it to both of them to clear them of any doubt. It's just possible that the sender of the telegram really had some information that you ought to have.'

"That's what I told Percy, and he agreed with me. He gave me authority to arrange the necessary formalities, and I got permission from the authorities for an autopsy. We all went to the train to meet Dr. and Mrs. Waite. The body was in the baggage car of the same train."

He waved to the clergyman, who proceeded: "Percy's sister threw herself into her brother's arms and they wept together, while Dr. Waite, who is a tall, finely preserved man, put an arm about each of them and did his best to comfort them, though all he could say was, 'Be brave! He is at peace. He has gone to join his beloved wife.'

"When she was calmer, Percy's sister asked if arrangements had been made for the funeral and Dr. Waite added: 'Your father wanted to be cremated so that his ashes could rest beside the urn of his beloved.'

"It took no little courage for Percy to say to his sister: 'I have arranged to have father's body sent to the undertaker's first.'

"His sister gasped: 'But why, dearest? Why?' Percy did not want to let Dr. Waite know of his plan to have an autopsy performed, so he did not mention the matter, but stubbornly insisted on the removal of the body to the undertaker's."

Ray broke in: "How did Dr. Waite take this news?"

Dr. Schurtz answered: "I kept my eye on him and though I think he suspected our purpose, he made no objection except to say: 'Percy, your poor father died peacefully. Here is the certificate of a New York doctor that he died of a heart attack, just as your poor mother did.'

"He produced a certificate in the regular form, but it was signed by a different physician from the one who had certified the mother's death.

"Percy was shaken, but he held firm and went home with his sister and her husband, leaving me to take care of things.

"The autopsy revealed not even the faintest trace of any heart disorder. But the intestines were in a state of acute contraction and they were fiery red. There was also evidence that the victim had undergone violent spasms of vomiting."

Ray Schindler's long practice and experience had taught him all too much about autopsies, and he had been closely associated with Otto Schultz, a leading expert in medical criminology. So Ray forestalled the doctor's next remark:

"You suspected poison, of course. Which form of poisoning was it?"

Shaking his head with regret, Dr. Schurtz answered: "I am sorry to say I am not an expert in that field. Nor is there one in Grand Rapids. So I removed the vital organs and sent them by special messenger to an expert in the neighboring city of Ann Arbor."

"And what did he report?" Ray demanded.

His face fell when Dr. Schurtz answered: "I haven't had his report yet. But I returned the body as nearly as possible to its former appearance, without letting anyone know of what I had found. Dr. Waite tried to open the coffin to see if an autopsy had been performed, as he suspected, but he was not permitted to lift the lid. The funeral was held and the body was cremated. When we learned that Dr. Waite and his wife were to return to New York at once—owing to important engagements—Dr. Wishart and I—at Percy's request and expense came at once to New York. And here we are. Dr. and Mrs. Waite are taking a midnight train to-night for New York and are due in the forenoon. And now you know as much as we know. What do you propose to do?"

Ray's first answer was a profound silence; but his brain was clicking on all six cylinders. Dr. Schurtz felt that a little further justification of his act might be called for. He said:

"The autopsy on the father was justified by that telegram. I couldn't perform one on the mother because she was by now only a little heap of ashes in a little urn. But I was further worried by a remark of Dr. Waite's when he said to me: 'Dr. Schurtz, I wish you would take a special look at my poor wife while she's here. You've known her since infancy. She's so prostrated by losing both her mother and her father that she says she doesn't want to survive them long. And I am afraid for her. When there's little will to live, you know, the battle for life is already half-lost.'"

All these coincidences combined to arouse suspicion. But a motive is of vital importance in any theory that a crime has been committed. Ray looked up from the notes he was making to ask a very natural question:

"Do you know anything about a will? Did Mr. Peck have any important money to leave to his son and daughter?"

"More than a million dollars," was Dr. Wishart's startling answer. "That is the estimated estate. The dear old man once mentioned to me the fact that he had willed his estate in equal shares to his son Percy and his daughter Clara, and in her grief Clara told me how good her husband was to her and said that she had made a will leaving her share to her dear husband, Dr. Waite."

And now, whether a crime would be revealed or not, a possible motive was clear. A million dollars is a lot of motive.

One thing was plain and undeniable: it was evidently dangerous to be closely associated with Dr. Waite. His mother-in-law and his father-in-law were dead already. Only his wife's life stood between him and perhaps a million dollars. And he had said that he was "afraid" of his wife's reluctance to survive them long.

There was no scintilla of legal evidence that Dr. Waite had murdered either of his wife's parents, or had anything but love for his wife. Yet it could do no harm to protect her against an off-chance. An anonymous—at least a pseudonymous—telegram had caused an autopsy to be made, and this had disclosed that Dr. Waite had told a lie, or had been misinformed, when he telegraphed that his father-in-law had died of a heart attack. Even the death certificate had been shown to be false.

So, without delaying to analyze the situation, Ray glanced at his watch and said:

"Call the son at once. Percy, isn't it?"

"Yes."

"Get him on the long distance telephone right away. Tell him he must keep his sister with him at all costs, and let Dr. Waite come on alone."

"What excuse can he give for holding her there?" Dr. Schurtz asked. Ray improvised a pretext.

"Tell him to tell Waite that Clara must remain to—to sign certain legal documents so as to hurry up the settling of the probation of the will. I think that will satisfy Waite. He's sure to be interested in getting the will probated as soon as possible."

Immediately Dr. Schurtz put through the call and luckily found Percy at home. He introduced Ray, and Ray gave Percy instructions, finding him entirely willing to cooperate, for terrible suspicions were now festering in his heart.

When the conversation was finished, Ray turned to the two elderly men, who were as helpless and as terrified by mysterious bogies as the two Babes in the Woods. He spoke with sympathetic serenity and an authority that won their respect and trust.

"You two gentlemen must realize that you have no evidence that a district attorney would even look at. So you come to me. What do you want me to do?"

The clergyman spoke up: "Find out if Mr. and Mrs. Peck were murdered. If so, who murdered them. Then save their daughter's life. Percy empowered us to engage you at any reasonable fee."

Waiving this matter, Ray said: "That midnight train takes a little less than twelve hours. It should bring Dr. Waite here before noon. The first thing to do is to go over his apartment —if we can get into it."

His clients looked at Ray in amazement. Dr. Schurtz said: "Do you propose to use a jimmy? Or skeleton keys? Or what?"

"I'll try a little persuasion first," Ray smiled. "You'd better come along."

The two men had the number and the street, and Ray took them down to a taxicab. While Ray and his clients are on their long midnight ride, it might be well to apprise the reader of just what sort of adversary Ray was planning to confront. It was not easy to find out all the details of Dr. Waite's picturesque biography, and some of them took a long while in their disclosure: but it will help to bring the suspect's life up to the point where he first impinged upon Ray Schindler's consciousness.

Dr. Waite had known only success. Sometimes his obstacles seemed insurmountable, but he had topped them all. He was tall, dark and handsome; and he had charm enough to have won stardom on the stage, the screen, radio, or in high society. He had begun poor. As a boy in Grand Rapids he had worked his way through high school by delivering papers, of which he stole great numbers; and kept the subscription money. In college he had paid his way by his assiduity in playing poker and his cleverness in cheating at cards. He had perfected his pious appeal by acting as president of the Christian Endeavor chapter.

For his chosen career he had selected the art and science of dentistry. He stole a plate made by another student and turned it in as his own handiwork, thus graduating with distinction. Still not satisfied, he had gone abroad—to Oxford University, no less—for further prestige. There, by forging credits, he had shortened his course and gained his diploma with almost unprecedented speed. Easily he persuaded an English dental firm to send him to South Africa as an office manager. There he had added to his income by travelling about as a dental surgeon.

By his skill at tennis, he had ingratiated himself into the most polite and wealthy circles. In his impatience for quick and easy riches, he had spared neither himself nor the spare parts of automobiles. When he needed any gadgets for his car, he would go to big receptions, then slip out and steal what he needed from cars parked about the home of his host.

Incidentally, of course, he was constantly cheating his employers by manipulating the books, lifting gold fillings and expensive instruments and selling them outside. But even such genius as his had its moments of bad luck, or overconfidence. Eventually his employers stumbled on a shortage of about $20,000 in his accounts. Though he had sent it to

a bank in the United States, he was inspired to pretend that
he had been lured into speculation and had lost it all. He was
actor enough to weep and "repent" and so escape prosecution. He was allowed to leave South Africa with no stigma
on his fair name.

Returning to America and his old home town, Grand Rapids, he soon encountered a former schoolmate, the daughter
of wealthy John Peck. He soon enchanted her, and he told
her parents so many stories of his high achievements that
they were glad to welcome him into the family as a son-
in-law. They even furnished him capital when he expressed
an ambition for removal to a wider field in New York. There
he wrote back such glowing accounts of triumphs of dentistry
and such distinctions that his mother-in-law visited him and
her daughter. His fascinations were such, indeed, that his
wife's aunt, Katherine Peck, begged him to handle her fortune for her. And he invested it so well that it was soon paying her heavy dividends. But, curiously enough, the dividends came to her, not in checks from the corporations, but
in Dr. Waite's own personal checks.

He often told his wife, her sister and their mother how he
loved to steal away to Long Island for the fresh air and to
satisfy his love for stray dogs. But he never took his family
along with him. It came out later that he used his dogs in
certain experiments with various poisons until he decided
at last that he was ready to try his skill on a human subject.

Since Katherine Peck loved and trusted him so well and so
enjoyed going to church with him, he may have decided that
she was near enough to heaven to be helped over the stile.
But while she experienced certain strange ailments, she recovered from all of them, and her suspicions were never
aroused.

And now the reader knows what there is to know about
Dr. Waite up to the death of his dear mother-in-law from a
"heart attack."

When Ray arrived at the apartment house where Dr. Waite

lived in state, he had no key, of course. But he learned from the elevator boy that the owner and manager of the apartment house lived in the building and was at home. So, though the hour was late, Ray prepared his most winning smiles and most persuasive speeches and rang the bell.

There was no answer. He rang again. Again no answer. While the two Grand Rapids doctors shifted wearily from one foot to another, Ray rang that bell for fifteen minutes without getting the door opened by so much as a crack.

Suddenly he heard in back of him the cold voice of a policeman:

"What do you fellows want here?"

Naturally, Ray could not explain the nature of his errand, and he and the two highly respectable visitors from Grand Rapids were soon being hustled along the dark street for several blocks to the police station.

When Ray expressed his polite surprise at this treatment, the police captain who knew him by reputation, divulged the fact that the owner of the apartment house had lost $5,000 in a poker game and had paid his losses with a check; but later, suspecting the probity of the players and their cards, had stopped payment on the check. The winner had promptly called him on the telephone and offered him the choice of forking over the five grand or having his heart cut out.

In a stubborn effort to retain both his blood-money and his blood-pump, the owner of the apartment house had locked himself in. When Ray and his two companions appeared in the black of the night and rang his bell, he had assumed that they had come for his money or his life. And he had let them ring while he telephoned to the police to come and get the mobsters before they broke in and got him. It had taken the police only fifteen minutes to arrive and steal up on the gangsters—three of the tamest gangsters the disappointed coppers had ever collided with.

The police captain accepted Ray's disclaimer of criminal

intent, and the clergyman and the doctor carried papers that satisfied him of their innocence. But he insisted on knowing why Ray's errand could not wait till morning.

Ray could hardly confess: "I plan to break into the apartment of a total stranger without warrant or permission and go through everything I find there."

So he refused to explain his visit to the apartment house as anything except something concerning the owner himself. He was so eloquent that he actually persuaded the captain to call the owner on the telephone and say:

"Say, I got those three guys here who've been buzzing your bell, and they ain't the men you thought they were. Fact is, one of them is the well-known deteckatiff, Ray Schindler, who means you no harm. He's a good guy for you to know and might come in handy to you. The other two guys are a sky-pilot and a medico. Schindler says he's got something you'd ought to know and you'll find it very interestin'. So leave 'em in, will you, when they come back?"

The gambling landlord's relief at having a famous detective at his door instead of a trio of murderers must have had something to do with the cordiality of the welcome he now extended. But it took the last drop of Ray's practically irresistible resources of persuasion to induce him to take out his passkey, admit Ray to Dr. Waite's apartment, and then go back to bed and ask no questions.

Stealing into an unknown home was no novelty to Ray, but the parson and the doctor were as nervous as cats on hot tiles.

Dr. Waite's apartment was luxuriously furnished, but Ray was not interested in the comfortable divans, though his footsore clients sank deep into them with sighs of relief and watched in wide-eyed wonder while Ray went through that home of mystery with the practiced skill of a second-story worker wielding a fine-tooth comb. He studied the pictures on the walls, not as a connoisseur of art, but with interest only in what was in back of the canvas. Behind the twentieth frame he found at last a small wall-safe.

He took a chance on the careless custom of some safe-owners and, finding the dial turned a little to the left, turned it very slowly to the right. The steel door obligingly swung open.

In the safe he found: first, a small red notebook of addresses and telephone numbers; second, a copy of a power of attorney signed by John Peck's Aunt Katherine Peck, giving full legal power to Dr. Waite; third, rental receipts for three safe deposit boxes in a New York bank. Among the other contents were glass slides that seemed to have been used for cultivating bacteria. Ray handed them to Dr. Schurtz, who noted them with interest. He exclaimed, "Why, they're all labelled 'typhoid!' I wonder why on earth a dentist should be experimenting with such a disease."

He continued to wonder and to worry while Ray was jotting down a large number of names and numbers he found in the address book. Then he went on with his search of the apartment. On the top shelf of a closet he found several books and, tucked in behind them, a volume on Pharmacology. In it was a bookmark set at a page containing a minute discussion of the effects on the human system of several slow poisons, with a subheading: "Alternatives—Arsenic."

In the apartment Ray also found a few photographs of the handsome Dr. Waite. He pocketed one of the photographs for future use.

It had been half-past two in the morning when Ray entered the apartment. It was seven o'clock and broad daylight before he had finished his study of its contents and what they disclosed or insinuated concerning their owner. His clients had watched him with a consuming interest, and helplessness to aid. They were glad to be put to some use when he asked them to do their best to restore the apartment to the state in which they had found it, so that when Dr. Waite returned he would not suspect that anybody had visited him during his absence. When they had finished, Ray showed his photographic memory by finding several mistakes they had made.

Before he left, he went to Dr. Waite's telephone and dialed his own office, where there was always someone on duty, day and night, Sundays, holidays, always. He talked to his brother Walter and set many wheels in motion, summoned many aides to many tasks.

And now the men from Grand Rapids found how different is the approach of a Schindler from the classic procedure of that Sherlock Holmes, of whom they had expected to see a poor imitation. Ray had taken up an untouched case which, as he had said, no district attorney or police detective would even look into. In fact, a little later Ray would be practically thrown out of the New York District Attorney's office by that indignant official, who would further promptly inform the suspect that private detectives were surrounding him.

Ray Schindler has rarely worked alone. He not only keeps a large staff of detectives on salary the year round, but he has an almost unlimited number of detectives on call. His bureau has branches in many other cities and correspondents and associates in practically every city at home and abroad. These can be added to his force on receipt of a telephone call.

Before this day was over, Ray would have a small army of skilled assistants going over certain districts of New York as carefully as he had gone over that apartment.

Returning with the doctor and the preacher to their hotel, he found his brother Walter waiting for them. Walter reported that he had already arranged to have an operative in a car posted at every entrance to the Grand Central Terminal. Ray gave Walter the photograph of Dr. Waite and asked him to have it photographed in a hurry and many prints made of it. A copy of it would be given to each of the watchmen outside the station, so that the man could be recognized at sight. This was managed with expert speed. But Ray did not rely on such identification and such coverage as infallible.

He took Drs. Schurtz and Wishart to the railroad station half an hour before the train was due, so that they could identify Dr. Waite the moment he stepped off the train. They were to signal Ray, who would tail Dr. Waite to whichever of the many exits he might take. Then Ray would signal whichever operative might be waiting outside in a car.

When the three took posts in the station, Ray decided that it would be best if Dr. Waite did not recognize Wishart or Schurtz and take alarm. Having no disguise for Dr. Schurtz, Ray gave the clergyman his own great fur coat and hat in exchange for Wishart's raincoat and hat. Ray does not in the least resemble a lean ascetic and the slender Dr. Wishart's raincoat would neither button nor reach Ray's hips. The clerical hat was three sizes too small for Ray's commodious skull.

A glance at Ray might have given Dr. Waite a smile, but he would hardly have guessed that the grotesque figure was a famous detective. Dr. Wishart was just as funny with Ray's big hat reposing on his ears and Ray's huge fur coat engulfing his ankles.

The train was posted an hour and a half late, but trains have a way of either losing more time or making up a bit; so the three had to keep their eyes open and watch the bulletin board.

At what is well called long last, the express lumbered in; the passengers poured out from every car, and suddenly Dr. Wishart began wig-wagging at a tall handsome man who looked like Dr. Waite's photograph.

Now came a demonstration of the importance of leaving nothing either to chance or to rule. Instead of going to any of the carefully covered exits, Dr. Waite suddenly slipped into a telephone booth. Ray, who was close on his heels, found the adjoining booth providentially empty, and slipped into that. The telephone was not a dial instrument and Ray could overhear the number the dentist called. His elephantine memory recognized it as that of the Plaza Hotel. His excellent ears also caught the dentist's every word, as he asked for room 1105 and greeted warmly the woman who answered, saying:

"Darling, I've just got in. But I can't talk to you now. Something has happened that I can't explain over the public telephone. But you must pack up at once, pay your bill, and check out with all our things. I'll get in touch with you at the School as soon as I can. Do just as I say, darling, and ask no questions. G'by!"

The unbelievable luck of such eavesdropping was cancelled by the sudden whim of Waite to go to the one exit where Ray had been unable to post a man in a car. He chose the underground corridor to the Biltmore Hotel. Heeled by Ray, Waite walked up the steps into the hotel lobby, through it and down the steps to the front door. There he dived into a waiting taxicab and ordered it off in a hurry.

Ray could not catch the address Waite gave to his driver; but he made a mental note of the number 61708 on the rear plate of the cab, and promptly stepped into the next cab up. He murmured the classic line of the detective-fiction writers, who know no better:

"Follow that car!"

The driver answered: "Sorry, mister, but it's against the rules for us to follow our own company cars."

Ray knew this as well as the driver did, but he was desperate. He had extra cars of his own everywhere but at that point. He had no other means of locomotion now but his own legs. And Ray is no champion of the cinder-path. Nor was he dressed like one. But he did his best.

Few who saw him could have guessed that the ridiculously garbed clown, madly knocking people aside as he darted through the throngs, was America's most famous detective in hot pursuit afoot of some one of the countless taxicabs that make New York streets one almost continuous yellow streak. Clinging to his hat, Ray panted and puffed up Madison Avenue all the way to 48th Street. There luck caught up with him for a moment. He saw Dr. Waite's cab two blocks ahead. He bunted aside another man about to enter an independent cab and dived in. The driver made no demur to Ray's demand:

"Ignore traffic lights! Close up on that taxi ahead. And stick to it. And I'll do right by you."

The cabdriver was in a mood for romance. And the traffic lights held up Waite and not him. But the upshot of all this good luck was that Waite's cab suddenly stopped at a garage. He paid off his cab and entered the garage, while Ray instructed his driver to pull to the curb just beyond and hold it. In due time, Waite whirled out of the garage in a car of his own and drove to his own apartment.

Ray's ideal is an operative waiting at every conceivable spot in the world. It is an unattainable ideal, but he does his humble best. So he had instructed two of his own men that, if they missed Waite at the station, they were to speed to the apartment house and take up observation posts there.

While Waite was parking his own car outside his home, Ray, who had followed closely on his wheels, had a chance to point him out to his operatives in their cars and signal them to keep him under observation wherever he might go. It was understood that they would report to the office whenever they got the chance.

Leaving his prey to the observation of his two watchdogs, Ray hurried back to his office, and arrived just in time to receive a telephone call from one of the operatives in one of the two cars he had left outside Waite's apartment. He reported that Waite had come out almost at once and driven to a bank, perhaps to draw money; then he had come out and driven to another garage, which he entered. He could still be seen in there, talking to a tall man in black, who seemed to have no connection with the garage, and was apparently there to keep an appointment with Waite. The operative suggested that he and his partner separate, one following the stranger, the other tailing the slippery dentist. Ray approved the plan and the operative went back to his post.

Now Ray felt sure that Waite had taken alarm at the curious interference of young Peck in the funeral plans and his insistence that Mrs. Waite remain in Grand Rapids. The telephone call to the girl, whom he had warned to vanish at once, proved, not only that he was frightened, but that he was also carrying on a clandestine love affair.

Successful criminals, like successful detectives, have to keep their suspicions alert; but Ray believed, and hoped, that Waite had not yet got wind of the fact that a detective bureau was after him.

The bigness of Ray's bureau was seen in his first act. His brother Walter had already set ten operatives combing all drug stores in widening circles to see if Waite had bought any poison anywhere. This was, of course, because of the books Ray had found in Waite's apartment with marks at the pages treating of poisons.

Now Ray dispatched an experienced operative to the Plaza Hotel to interview that woman, if she had not already disappeared. If she had, he was to try to find out where she had gone and collect all the information he could glean about her. At the same time, Ray and Walter were collecting another large force to hunt down Waite's standing with his profession and to learn his connections, if any, with hospitals or patients.

By this time Ray had about thirty assistants hot at work all over the town. They were none too many, and it is difficult to imagine what the solitary Sherlock Holmes could have accomplished in such a situation. Of course, the captivating Conan Doyle made up his stories backwards and controlled his criminals as well as his crimes. Ray had to take what he found as he found it.

While his far-flung cohorts were multiplying Ray, and taking him everywhere at once, he decided to visit in person that Katherine Peck, Mrs. Waite's aunt, whose power of attorney he had found in Waite's wall-safe. As the reader has been told, she was the woman whose investments Dr. Waite had been handling to her complete satisfaction.

Ray found her a fashionable lady, living in a fashionable hotel. She proved to be an elderly woman of charm and authority, and more than willing to talk about her dear nephew-in-law, Dr. Waite. Needless to say, Ray did not tell her what his true purpose was.

Miss Peck told him how attentive Waite had been to her; how piously he had accompanied her to church every Sunday, how he brought her flowers, and personally took care of her whenever she was ill. Suspicious of poison, Ray did not feel so easy about these illnesses and attentions as she did.

He was hardly surprised when Miss Peck told how great an interest Dr. Waite took in her investments. He had advised her, she said, to put a hundred thousand dollars in a certain stock and soon brought word that it had nearly doubled in value. He sent her his own checks whenever dividends were due without keeping her waiting for the slow bank. Incidentally, she tossed in the name of the bank she dealt with. Ray said he was delighted to learn so much about so charming a man. When he finally bowed out, he went to the bank where Waite had his safe deposit boxes and talked frankly with the president—a friend of his, of course.

He was so persuasive that the president actually went to the vault with him and had the box opened. There they found the original of Miss Peck's power of attorney and a great deal of jewelry.

Thanking the most obliging bank president, Ray left him and called next on a famous doctor whose name he had found in Waite's address book. To this man Ray unbosomed himself as, frankly, a detective investigating a man suspected of a double murder.

The physician told him how charming and straightforward he had found Dr. Waite. And yet, he confessed, he had been disturbed a bit when Waite once actually asked him to write a prescription for arsenic. He had done Waite that favor and now, at Ray's request, he looked up his copy of the prescription and lent it to Ray.

When Ray said that Waite seemed to be interested in cultivating certain bacteria, the doctor gasped; for he remembered that Waite had told him of studying typhoid germs and had asked where he could buy such cultures. The doctor had wondered then. Now he shuddered to think that Waite might have been planning to use typhoid bacteria for murderous purposes.

Leaving Waite's unintentional collaborator to his own resources, Ray went back to his office. There Walter told him that one of his operatives had followed the man whom Waite had met in the garage, and telephoned to say that the fellow was named "Kane," and he ran an undertaking parlor. This turned out to be the very parlor where Waite had had the bodies of his wife's father and mother embalmed before he took them to Grand Rapids.

Odd wasn't it? that a dentist should meet an undertaker in a lonely garage?

Also, the other operative, who had stuck to Waite, had telephoned in that Waite had visited the bank where his safe deposit boxes were, and had drawn out $15,000 in cash. Then he had visited the Berlitz School of Languages. After that, he had driven his car through various Harlem streets, stopping now and then as if looking for a house, but finally returning to his apartment.

Ray remembered that, when Waite had slipped into the telephone booth at the Grand Central Station and called up his "Darling" at the Plaza Hotel, he had promised to meet her at "the school." Was it the Berlitz School?

The operative's report that Dr. Waite had driven up and down certain streets in Harlem reminded Ray that, when he had talked the night before to the owner of the apartment house, the owner had mentioned the little detail that Waite had a Negro cook, whom the owner had secured for him. The man had even told Ray the woman's address in Harlem. Ray had noted down the address and now he guessed that Waite had forgotten the exact number and had been hunting for it —perhaps to warn his cook not to talk.

Information was pouring in now from all directions. One of the ten operatives sent out to study Waite's professional life reported in that the "famous dentist" was not even registered as a practicing dentist, and had no office! This information was received from the telephone company, which had no record of a telephone in his name, listed or unlisted. Even the electric light company had been visited, and had reported that nobody of Waite's name had purchased any electricity for light or heat. Plainly he used the apartment house telephone, light and heat; and had no separate office.

All this gives a hint of the minute thoroughness of the Schindlerian technique. A further glimpse of it can be seen in the fact that other operatives had already visited not less than twenty hospitals and learned that the great Waite was known at not one of them. Yet he had given his dead father-in-law and young Peck the impression that he was one of the busiest surgeon dentists in New York. He had certainly been busy; but not with other people's teeth.

And now, to pile confusion on confusion, and work on work, the man Ray had sent to the Plaza Hotel telephoned in that he had arrived there too late to intercept the girl; but had managed to learn that she had been registered there with her "husband" as "Dr. and Mrs. A. W. Walters of New Rochelle."

The operative had taken with him a copy of the photograph of Dr. Waite, and the hotel clerk had said that he recognized it as that of "Dr. Walters." He also let fall the statement that "Mrs. Walters," on her abrupt departure, had left a package to be picked up later by a messenger. Since the clerk would not disclose the address, the operative had to haunt that hotel lobby until a messenger called at the desk and picked up that parcel.

Then the operative had to follow the messenger until he delivered it to a "Mrs. Von Palmenburg" at an address in West 72nd Street.

Isn't there something rather hair-raising or breathtaking, or whatever sensation you experience, in realizing how much knowledge of all these total strangers had been acquired since Ray had been called at ten o'clock the night before to talk to two strangers from Grand Rapids?

There had followed in dizzy sequence a telephone call to the dead man's son, the entry into Waite's apartment, secured with great difficulty in after-midnight hours, the collection of vital documents there, a train met, a telephone call listened in on, a taxicab chase, a rendezvous with a man who turned out to be Waite's pet undertaker, a talk with a bank president, a visit to a safe deposit vault, a conference with a famous physician, visits to thirty hospitals, to the telephone company, the electric company, to numberless drug stores, the Plaza Hotel—what not!—whom not?

All these things had been ordered, conducted, reported, and acted on in about sixteen hours' time.

Never pausing to congratulate himself on a busy day and a successful one, nor refreshing himself with even thirty winks of sleep, Ray now called on the City Medical Examiner, Dr. Otto H. Schultz, whom he knew. Ray told him a bit about the case, and asked him to be ready to make a train trip. Then he gathered up Dr. Schultz, Dr. Schurtz, and Rev. Mr. Wishart and motored down to the office of the District Attorney.

The night before, Ray had told his clients from Grand Rapids that they had not an iota of legal evidence which a district attorney would even look at. He was soon proving his point up to the hilt; for, even when he laid all his accumulated facts before the District Attorney of New York, that official found them invisible.

Ray told the then District Attorney, Edward H. Swann, that Waite was a liar about his hospital activities as consulting dental surgeon; that he was enriching himself by handling the funds of his wife's aunt, and paying alleged dividends with personal checks; that he had almost certainly murdered his mother-in-law and his father-in-law and was studying typhoid germs in order to murder his wife, and thus inherit her estate of perhaps a million dollars. Finally, as a bit of an anti-climax, Ray announced that Waite was living in a hotel under an assumed name with an assumed wife.

District Attorneys live in such a welter of crime that they are hard to excite. Mr. Swann took all this with skepticism as to its absolutely conclusive legal value. Now he handed Ray what Ray had handed to his clients when he first heard their unsupported story. Mr. Swann said, icily:

"You have no proof positive that all these facts can be explained only as the deeds of a murderer."

This was not the first time in his life that Ray had been rebuffed, and he retorted:

"You want more evidence before you will even entertain a suspicion or lift a finger to defend a poor woman against a cold-blooded liar and double murderer. This family physician, Dr. Schurtz, found evidence that Waite's father-in-law had not died of a heart attack. He sent the vital organs to an expert in Ann Arbor for final examination. Will you allow the City Medical Examiner, Dr. Otto Schultz, to go to Ann Arbor and take part in the final tests?"

"That's asking a lot," the D.A. protested. But finally he yielded to the plea of Dr. Schurtz and gave a reluctant consent.

For fear he might change his mind, Ray hurried away and put the City Medical Examiner on the first train for Ann Arbor along with Ray's own office manager.

Even now the indefatigable, indestructible Ray, who had been dragged from his rhumba the night before, did not pause for breath. He sped to Harlem and the address of Dr. Waite's cook. She was in, and she loved to talk when she had an appreciative audience. Never had she had a more interested listener, nor one who made her feel more important.

"When was the last time you saw Dr. Waite?" Ray asked.

"When was a las' time I seen mah boss?"

Ray nodded.

"Why, a las' time I seen mah boss was when him and mah missus took off for de Gran' Rapids wid de corpus of po'

Mistoo Peck what done die on 'em. He say I could take time off till he git back. I'm awaitin' now for his call."

"Did you ever give any medicine to Mrs. Waite's mother and father when they were alive and ailing?" Ray asked casually.

"Did I done give 'em any med'cine? Whah, yes, I 'member givin' po' ol' Miz Peck some white powda now and den. It was at Dr. Waite's orders, o'cose. He tol' me to put a mite of it in her vittles when I was cookin' up somethin' special for her."

Arsenic is a white powder. Ray went on: "Did you ever put any of the white medicine in Mr. Peck's food?"

"Nossa! I ain't nevva put no white powda in po' ol' Mistoo Peck's vittles. But sometimes Doctah Waite would come into mah kitchen and sprinkle a little on de ol' man's vittles. He say de old gemman so pernickety abote takin' his med'cine he had to slip it into de old man's vittles kind of secretious like. But it didn' seem to do no good, for de po' ol' soul done die all on a suddens."

Suddenly her luxurious sense of importance ended in a jolt of uneasiness as if she realized that there might be some connection between that white powder and Mr. Peck's death, and some connection between her and Mrs. Peck's death. Sweat fairly shot out of her pores and she glared at Ray as she demanded:

"Say, man, who's you anyway? How you git up here? Why you want to know so much abote me and mah boss and his med'cines?"

Ray did his best to calm her fears without diminishing her sense of importance.

"You have no cause for the slightest uneasiness. You have an excellent reputation as a wonderful cook. Nobody suspects you of anything wrong. But the District Attorney may ask you to—"

"De Districk Attunney!" she gasped. "What I done dat dat ol' debbil wanna see me?"

"You've done nothing wrong. But you're an important woman and you may be of great help to the great city and county of New York."

She grew queenly again. "Me? I could maybe be of he'p to be Districk Attunney? Wait till mah boss hears of dis!"

"You could be of help only if you don't mention it to Doctor Waite that you have talked to me or to anybody."

This bugged her eyeballs almost out of their sockets. Her loyalty to her employer was at war with her hunger for importance. Her importance—or let us say her sense of civic duty—won, and she promised Ray to keep her big mouth shut.

Leaving her to her palpitations, Ray called next on that "Mrs. Von Palmenburg," to whom the package from the Plaza Hotel had been sent. Here he ran into a shower bath of good luck.

In a dazing coincidence, the door was opened by a pretty young woman for whom Ray had recovered some stolen jewels a few years before. She welcomed him warmly, and told him that she had now a new name and a new husband.

But her face fell when Ray said: "I didn't call on you, my dear. I came to see Mrs. Walters."

"Don't tell me that you've been engaged by Dr. Walter's real wife to investigate poor Margaret, who's been foolish enough to pretend that she was Mrs. Walters. What fools love makes of us poor women! It's going to be tough for Margaret, because she has a legal mate of her own. He's a well-known actor, but I don't like him any more than she does now. Well, of course if you're on the case, it's hopeless and I wash my hands of it. I warned her a dozen times. Please keep me out of it, won't you?"

"There's no reason to drag you into it, my dear, and your friend may be mighty glad if I drag her out of it."

"I'll call her in, and leave her to your tender mercies."

And soon Ray was in the presence of the woman of whom, a few hours earlier, he had learned by an overheard telephone talk only that she was a somebody in a certain room at the Plaza Hotel.

Margaret was pretty and well poised and she made no denial of her liking or her liaison with Dr. Walters. She, too, said: "I warned him of the danger of discovery. But I was afraid only of those enemies of love, the newspapers, with their screaming scandals. Dr. Waite—I mean Walters—is so prominent that he rates headlines."

She spilled the beans with enthusiasm. She boasted rather than confessed to the receipt of some jewels and other gifts from "Dr. Walters," and she let slip a startling bit of information: "Dr. Walters is going to take me to Paris as soon as he has settled up a large estate he came into by the death of a rich aunt. That's why he had me studying French at the Berlitz School. As soon as we get to Paris, Dr. Walters will secure a French divorce from his wife and get me one from my good-for-nothing husband. Then Dr. Walters and I will get married and live happily ever after. I do pray to high heaven you're not planning to spoil our lovely romance. He's such a wonderful man! Shh! Here comes my husband now. You can see for yourself what a rat he is."

No fictioneer would dare overwork coincidence as Mother Nature sometimes does. And now she actually brought Margaret's actor husband into the scene. There, in Ray's presence, Margaret was emboldened to tell him what she had just told Ray of her plans. The husband was just as frank. He sighed:

"I knew you were having one of your flirtations with that Walters fellow, but I never guessed how far it had gone." He turned to Ray: "Ain't women a scream? I've given the dame a good home, a maid, and a swell new car. What more can a woman want? I guess they're all just like Mother Eve. Give 'em the whole Garden of Eden and a good Adam for a husband and they holler for something forbidden, if it's only an old apple."

This ancient generalization on her sex did not distress his

wife. She was shedding comfortable crocodile tears and over-looking her husband in her anger at Ray.

"How can you be so mean? What won't men do for money? Here you are working for that old Mrs. Walters to get evidence so she can sue for a divorce and drag poor me in as a co-respondent. It's cruel! It's shameful!"

Ray was not even tempted to tell her that, instead of hating him, the poor, pretty idiot might soon be thanking him for saving her from being perhaps the future victim of a modern Bluebeard.

Content with his harvest in that field for the moment, Ray rolled back to his office.

There he received some of the dizzying blows he had been dealing out all day, with a few added punches that would have knocked out anyone who was less of a glutton for punishment.

He learned that two of his operatives had actually been led by Dr. Waite to the District Attorney's building in Center Street!

Waite had walked right into the lion's den and spent an hour there with the District Attorney. Then he had come out of the building, walked right up to the operatives, and laughed in their faces.

"You boys don't have to follow me any longer. Go telephone your boss that the District Attorney has just given me a clean bill of health."

Then Waite had driven away. One of the operatives had continued to follow him. The other came back to the office to deliver the dynamite in person.

This was enough to make even the patient Schindler see red. He went promptly to Swann's office and asked him:

"Did you tell Waite that I had men following him?"

The District Attorney answered: "Yes, I 'phoned him to come down to my office. Your suspect came at once and laid his cards on the table. He told me a straight story and frankly admitted he was having an affair with a girl. But his very candor convinced me he is innocent of anything criminal. I told you that you had no case against him."

When Ray grew sarcastic, Swann grew ugly. He said:

"After all, Schindler, you're only a private detective trying to earn some big money. Waite is an eminent dentist and he has a right to know that he is being spied on by a gang of private dicks."

Ray laid before him what he had learned from Waite's cook about the white powder, and told him Margaret's story about the big estate Waite was soon coming into. But Swann would not be impressed. In fact he finally announced that he had telegraphed the Medical Examiner who was now in Michigan, to come back at once from his fool's errand without delaying for any silly tests.

It is always bewildering to find such cases of infatuation in high officials. But even a private detective has emotions; so Ray walked out and went on about his business, realizing that he had two powerful adversaries to contend with: the clever Waite and the stubborn District Attorney.

In sudden exhaustion and bitter despondency he called his office on the telephone and invited further bad news. But there was a bit of good. His operatives had found the very drug store where Waite had been buying arsenic. He had seen the actual prescription carrying Waite's signature. It was at a great distance from Waite's apartment and had been reached only after a search of dozens of drug stores.

Furthermore, one operative had found the assistant of the undertaker Kane (whom Waite had visited soon after he reached town) and he informed Ray that both men were in the shop. So Ray sped to the undertaker's. He was now almost in a mood to turn himself in as a customer.

Instead, he questioned Kane about his secret meeting with Waite, and suggested that Waite was a murderer. This seemed both to relieve and to shock the undertaker. After a bit of swallowing hard and fidgeting about, he decided to come clean. He said:

"I don't want to get dragged into nothing. I might as well tell you I suspicioned the same thing. I kind of had a hunch that there was dirty work going on, but I never suspicioned that Mr. and Mrs. Peck had been murdered till Dr. Waite came back to New York and asked for a private meeting somewhere outside my shop.

"He suggested that vacant garage for a meeting place, and as soon as Waite got there he had the nerve to say, 'Look here, Kane, you might be asked if you used arsenic in your embalming fluid,' he says. And I says, 'Why it's against the law to use arsenic! I'd lose my license if I did.' Then Waite says, 'Well, in case you're called on to testify, I'll give you five thousand dollars if you'll say you did use arsenic in this one case.'

"I looked at him and wanted to punch him in the jaw. But business has been very poor for me lately and I was about to have to shut up shop anyway, so I says to Waite, "If you'll make that $10,000 I'll testify I used arsenic—or any damn thing you say.' Well, would you believe it? the next thing I know, he slaps ten one thousand dollar bills in my hand. I didn't have no intention of committing no perjury like he said. But—well, I needed the money something awful, so I took it.

"The worst of it was, that my assistant was listening in and, when Waite had left, he said if I didn't give him a third of the loot, he'd spill the story to the D.A. So I promised him. And now I've told you all I know and I hope you'll keep me out of trouble."

Ray was grateful for the information, but he would make no pledges even to the man who did not believe in keeping pledges.

He returned to his office in a strange complex of moods. Everybody in town seemed to be confirming Waite's guilt; yet the adamantine District Attorney would not even aid the investigation.

It was about time for sportive Fortune to give her wheel

another spin. As Ray carried his load of glum frustration into his office, his secretary greeted him. She was waving a telegram like a banner of triumph. It was from the Medical Examiner in Ann Arbor. He had not obeyed the District Attorney's order to return till after finishing his tests. The message ended:

"We found enough arsenic in the vital organs of John Peck to kill forty men."

This was triumph enough to atone for all the insults Ray had endured. He was tempted to dash down to the District Attorney's office and shake the telegram under his snooty snoot. But just then there came a telephone call from the operative who was sticking like a burr to Dr. Waite. He said:

"I'm kind of puzzled. I tailed my man all over town and back to his apartment house. Instead of dashing out again at once, he's still stickin' up there. He's been quiet so long he's got me worried. There's no back way for him to get out without my seeing him. What do I do? Stay put?"

"I'll be with you as soon as I can get there," Ray said, and gave up gloating over his friend Swann in a mood of strange uneasiness, an unreasonable but alarming intuition of foreboding.

He hastened to the apartment house and after ringing the bell repeatedly, had the owner open the door. And now he found the elusive dentist, who had just secured the D.A.'s clean bill of health, lying on his bed in a complete stupor. He had taken a big dose of his own opiates.

Ray had hardly laid a hand on the man's ominously clammy skin when the telephone rang. When Ray answered it, he heard the voice of the District Attorney:

"Hello, Ray, I found out from your office where you were, and I thought I ought to be the first to inform you that I've just got a telegram from Ann Arbor. The Medical Examiner wires me—I quote: 'We found enough arsenic in the vital organs of John Peck to—' "

"To kill forty men," Ray broke in. "You'd better come up

here and pick up your man. He's taken enough of his own medicine to kill one man if you don't hurry."

As quickly as possible the District Attorney in person, with a retinue of policemen, photographers and reporters, burst into the apartment. The unconscious Waite was rushed to a hospital instead of a cell, and pumped out. In a few days he was ready to talk. His own brother persuaded him to make a full confession. From hints he let fall, further investigations were made that brought out the biography of almost incredible villainies and successes which the reader was apprised of earlier in this history.

A man of such perverted cleverness is sustained in such a life of assiduous evil by a certain twisted pride, a kind of Mephistophelean humor. Like any other veteran, when failure comes, he finds consolation and redemption of self-esteem in balancing a long line of successes against this one final failure. So Dr. Waite loved to talk, especially to Ray, whom he respected and liked as one who was almost as clever as himself, and a little luckier.

He told Ray that he had first planned to kill his wife's brother, Percy, so that his wife would inherit the whole estate. Then if she did not behave, he would poison her. But, first, his restless soul had turned to his mother-in-law because she came in handier, when she came to live right in the house. He practiced on her with various disease germs; but, though she weakened, she did not, as they say, pass on.

Finally he called in a prominent New York physican, who found that Mrs. Peck was suffering from a kidney condition but said that it was not at all dangerous to her life. At last Mrs. Peck began to blame the New York climate for her ill health; and decided to go back home to Grand Rapids. Since that would remove her from Dr. Waite's reach, he gave her arsenic in her food till she died. Then he called in the physician whose diagnosis had been kidney trouble, and announced that Mrs. Peck had died quietly in her sleep. The physician made no difficulty about a death certificate from heart failure.

Wearing deep mourning, Waite went home with his dead mother-in-law and her daughter, and wretchedly told how the poor woman had been converted to cremation. He was able to see to it that her "last wish" was fulfilled.

Next, he invited his inconsolable father-in-law to visit him in New York, and there Dr. Waite "consoled" him with all sorts of disease germs, which he put into the old man's food, his throat spray, and his medicines. Old men are sometimes tough, and John Peck survived these germs, as well as long rides in rain storms and the use of icy wet sheets for pretended reasons of health. Dr. Waite's hope that pneumonia would carry off the old wretch was disappointed. Then he released chlorine gas in the old man's bedroom. Vainly.

Dr. Waite laughed aloud as he told Ray how he had wasted on the old man, "Oh, millions and millions—maybe billions of germs."

The indestructible father-in-law proved so irritatingly immune that Dr. Waite was forced back on his old ally, arsenic. Yet, first, he called in a physician who admitted that there might be a mild heart-trouble and some intestinal looseness. But all he prescribed was rest and soft diet.

This treatment resulted in such apparent improvement that, sorrowfully, once more Dr. Waite called in the physician to say that his dear father-in-law had risen from his bed and started for the bathroom, only to collapse on the way. Dr. Waite feared that the poor man was dead.

The physician hastened over and found that his patient was indeed no more. He also made no trouble about issuing a death-certificate from heart disease.

Dr. Waite gave what he could of his strength to uphold his poor wife, who had now lost both her parents in her own home within six weeks. Then he kindly saw to it that the poor old man's body was sent to the undertaker who had embalmed Mrs. Peck's body. He arranged to ship the body to Grand Rapids and go with it to see to the cremation. He arranged for a drawing room on the train and left his dear dear wife nothing to do but weep.

Then his long line of almost unbroken luck had come to a short stop. He did not know of the mysterious telegram or the autopsy it had led to, but he had been puzzled by Percy's insistence on keeping his wife in Grand Rapids. It had forced him to come on alone and walk into the net Ray had spread for him.

Most of his confession was made to Ray while Dr. Waite lay in a half coma on his bed in his apartment. He was alert though and bewildered enough to write in an unsteady hand an order to his brother to give Ray a check for One Thousand Dollars. He begged Ray to use this money to bribe the colored cook and others to forget what they might testify against him. Ray cherishes the photograph of that note as a quaint thing: a caught criminal trying to bribe the detective who caught him!

Ray did not tell him of the mysterious telegram but he was still frantic to know who had sent it and why. When at last he learned, the mystery was rather increased than solved. It was one of those things they call "womanly intuition"—that instinctive cunning which so often goes astray, but now and then seems almost superhuman. This was the story as Ray finally uncovered it.

After the death of her father, Mrs. Waite was so overcome with loneliness while killing time before the train left for Grand Rapids on her second funeral journey that she cast about for some relation to talk to. She telephoned to her cousin, Mrs. Elizabeth Hardwick, who lived in New Jersey and whom she had seen so rarely that Mrs. Hardwick was a stranger to Dr. Waite.

Mrs. Hardwick came over at once and did what she could to comfort Clara till they left for the train. Then she returned to New Jersey and called her family doctor. She was in a state of wild excitement and told how she had rung the door bell and been admitted by Dr. Waite. She exclaimed:

"When that man saw me standing there in the doorway, his eyes were the eyes of a criminal—or a madman."

Her mood was so fierce that her doctor was startled. "You don't think there could have been anything wrong about the deaths of that mother and father, do you?" he asked indulgently, knowing the strange whims of his patients.

Mrs. Hardwick answered, "I've no reason to think it. But I know it!"

He could not quiet her. She insisted on summoning various members of her family to talk it over. The doctor warned them that any false accusation against Dr. Waite would provoke a ghastly scandal and render them liable to a suit for libel. Since she would not be silenced, he suggested that she might send Percy a telegram under a false name and give it to her young daughter to take to the telegraph office. Then, even if Waite learned of it, he could only sue the daughter; and she had no funds to levy on.

Finally they concocted that telegram and made up a name to sign it with:

SUSPICION AROUSED. DEMAND AUTOPSY. DO NOT REVEAL TELEGRAM. K. ADAMS

So we come back around the circle to the beginning. A woman's whisper of intuition had started an avalanche that rolled down on the perfection of Dr. Waite's plans and smashed them. Such little meddlings of odd people or circumstances are always spoiling otherwise perfect crimes.

Dr. Waite's highly intellectual and artistic work had been upset because the son of his two victims, suspecting nothing in the first case, had in the second obeyed a mysterious telegram from nowhere. His doctor and pastor had called in Ray Schindler and his army. In a whirlwind of energy they had saved the third candidate for death and frightened the lifelong criminal of all trades into trying to add himself to his catalogue of murders.

Science saved Dr. Waite for Justice. After the usual delay there was a trial. There had to be a defense; but the best that Waite's lawyer could do was to try to prove him a "moral imbecile." This was difficult after the amiable monster had sat in the witness box and chattily recounted to a fascinated jury how clever he had been till he became a little too clever. His charm mysteriously failed to sway the twelve and he was sentenced to death. As he was taken from the courtroom, an admirer in the crowd called out:

"Tough luck, Doc!"

"Don't waste sympathy on me," was the answer. "I took a chance and lost."

He was the perfect gambler. He would not even let his lawyers appeal for the usual chain of new trials, or even for a commutation to life imprisonment.

Ray tried to salvage what he could from the ruins. The $10,000 Dr. Waite had paid to Kane, the undertaker, had really come from the money entrusted to him by Katherine Peck. So the District Attorney called on Kane to deliver it. The undertaker had suffered no little notoriety from the trial, in which his connection with the case was revealed. So he consented to surrender the money and went to his home on Long Island, attended by the District Attorney, and a flock of reporters and photographers.

He said that he and his partner had buried the sum in the backyard. And he did indeed dig up a cigar box, open it and find, not $10,000, but $6,666.67. Kane recalled his promise to give his partner one-third of the money for his silence; and he alleged that the partner had quietly collected his exact share while Kane was not looking.

But when Ray and Kane called on the partner, he blandly denied that he had ever seen the money or heard of the deal. And there was no way of disproving his statement, or of proving Kane's. Yet Katherine Peck was lucky to get back even the $6,666.67, and still luckier to be allowed to live and enjoy it.

As an appendix to this life sketch of a gorgeous villain, Ray Schindler has written for me the following commentary:

"An interesting thing about many of the persons that we have arrested and sent to prison or death for all types of crimes including murder, is the fact that, after their conviction, they often solicited my friendship.

"Dr. Waite had a family consisting of mother, father, sister and brothers. They were all fine, well educated, honorable people. But, after his sentence, Waite would not allow any of them to call to see him.

"When I visited him in Bellevue Hospital, he admitted his guilt, but without remorse. He claimed that he had a Jekyll-Hyde personality. He said there was a little imp that jumped around in his brain and caused him to commit illegal acts, including murders. He called it his 'little green devil.' That was his main point of self-defense.

"While in Sing Sing awaiting the day of electrocution he again sent for me. There were certain messages he wished delivered to his family and he talked them over with me. He was most friendly with me, and I finally persuaded him to allow his brother to make one visit to take care of any family matters."

The crimes of Dr. Waite were avenged and at least one murder thwarted. Such crimes are even now being carried on all about us. Thousands of murderers have been released and are at large. Some of them will try again, and countless others will make their débuts in murder. But the Waite case has one important significance. It is an answer to a question often asked:

"Are private detectives of value to the general public?"

Imagine those two bewildered men from Grand Rapids, that doctor and that preacher, calling on the district attorney of Grand Rapids or of New York for help. Even when Ray Schindler spread before the New York official the evidence he had collected with such tremendous swiftness and efficiency, he was dismissed from the office as a money-grafting nuisance. The District Attorney—and a good, honest one he was—not only gave the murderer a clean bill of health, but information as to Ray Schindler's investigations.

If it had not been for a private detective, and one with a huge force, there can be little doubt that Waite would have murdered his wife in due time, and perhaps her rich aunt as well. Thus he would have accumulated perhaps a million or more as a climax to a life that had been one long succession of successful crimes. He might have married that other man's wife, taken her to France and tired of her there. Then what?

A private detective not only outwitted and captured that most intelligent and ruthless fiend, but he did so in spite of the active opposition of the forces of the law. He undoubtedly prevented the murder of at least one heart-broken and devoted wife. How many further crimes that accomplished villain would have committed if left alone is a matter for the imagination. Dr. Waite's case seems to justify Ray Schindler's motto:

"A private detective is a public servant—a protector of people who have no other protection."

# 3.

## BEAUTY IN DISTRESS

"If you tell my husband, I'll kill myself!"

The detective stared at the beautiful, desperate, sobbing woman, and felt that she meant what she said. The crime of which he suspected her was not a capital offense; and he was a private detective, not a public executioner.

It was the most harrowing situation that had ever confronted my friend, Raymond Schindler, in all his years of dealing with multitudinous crimes and criminals. His head and his experience told him that the guiltiest people are often afterward utterly unable to believe their own guilt. It is a rare murderer who does not, in all solemnity, even in the face of the last Judgment Seat, protest his innocence of a killing proved beyond the doubting even of a sentimental American jury.

Ray had long since learned that a woman can be beautiful as heaven and false as hell; that, with the wide eyes of guilelessness, she can plead for belief in the most conscienceless lies; that she can dodge and double like a cornered fox trying to escape the hounds.

Yet this woman was so peculiarly persuasive that Ray's heart told him she was guiltless. And yet again, the facts he had discovered in spite of her were beyond dispute; and she had not told him everything as she had insisted she had.

Many caught criminals threaten suicide merely as a last trick. But Ray was convinced that this exquisite creature would really take her own life if he did his inescapable duty.

And so the detective sat imploring the trapped criminal to spare him! Call her, for convenience and mercy, "Mrs.

67

Carrington." That will be the only untrue thing in this crowded history of a most unusual crime and criminal with a sudden conclusion that surprised the detective as he had never been surprised before during a long life in which the unexpected is the expectable routine. So Ray pleaded:

"Mrs. Carrington, my dear lady, you know that I want to help you. I'll do anything I can to help you. But you must help me to help you. Even if I were not in duty bound to tell your husband what I have found out—with no help from you, my dear—it is too late for me to keep your secret to myself. I have already told the man who employed me what I discovered. I asked him to wait for further action; but I cannot ask him to suppress the facts. If I did ask him, he would think me as crazy as you're driving me by your unwillingness to take me into your confidence and tell me everything.

"I was called into the case, to my eternal regret, by an official of an insurance company. Your husband demands forty thousand dollars to cover the loss of the jewels he gave you. You say they were stolen. You did not tell your husband, or the insurance adjuster, or me, that on the very day you reported the so-called theft you made up a package that could have contained those very jewels and sent it by registered mail to a woman in Kansas City. Since suspicion is my trade I assume that the woman is a cover for a man. But I don't know yet, though I have instructed some Kansas City detectives to find out all they can and telephone me.

"When I turned up the sending of that mysterious package you denied that the jewels were in it. You still deny it; but you won't tell me what was in it; or why you sent it, or anything about the woman you sent it to. And yet you ask me to believe you, and be as false to my employer who trusts me as—as—"

She grimly finished the difficult sentence for him: "As I was false to the husband who trusted me?"

She was deathly calm now and she spoke to Ray with a kindliness and understanding that pierced his heart.

"I don't blame you for thinking me doubly guilty—a thief and a faithless wife. I can see now why you have to tell the insurance people and why you have to tell my husband. I can't expect them to spend forty thousand dollars to save my life. So I guess there's nothing left for me to do but take it myself. I couldn't live to face my dear husband when he knows what you have found. It's a pretty sad finish to a life of such devotion and happiness as we've had, but—"

A sudden storm of protest swept through her tortured soul and she cried: "It doesn't matter about me, but oh, for God's sake, find some way to spare him. He is so good! He was so good to me! He loved me as I always loved him. In God's name, don't tell him!"

She flung herself to her knees before the detective and lifted to him a face beautiful even in its agony and its reek of tears. And there were tears in the detective's eyes.

Beautiful women—or homely women—do not have to throw themselves at Ray Schindler's feet to make him eager to be kind. In his eyes, the private detective's whole business is one of benevolence, a protection of people's rights and properties and good names, often their very lives, from the thieves, blackmailers, murderers, all the forms of vermin that infest our existence and cannot be stopped or caught by the police or the detectives of the law.

But now Ray was baffled. Sent to find a criminal, he found himself confronted with the choice between disloyalty and dishonesty. He caught Mrs. Carrington's frantic hands in his own and tried to coax her back to a life she found unendurable if some mysterious, unguessable truths were known. He argued with her as with a frenzied child; but all in vain. She wept herself into such a state of exhaustion that she sank to the floor, and only her pitiful upward palms begged him to grant the impossible.

Up to this point the case had been familiar enough in the work of the Schindler Bureau of Investigation. The man we call Carrington was a Brooklyn manufacturer, successful enough and devoted enough to have given his wife, during their sixteen years of happy life together, jewelry valued at fifty thousand dollars. For some years he had carried an insurance policy of forty thousand dollars covering them.

The Carringtons had lived for years in an old and unpretentious house in Brooklyn. Though he was wealthy enough to have given his wife such a fortune in gems, she preferred to keep only one servant in the house, a rather belligerent old German cook, though a cleaning woman came in three times a week. She must have had quite enough to do, for the house was not only a home but a menagerie and an aviary. Canaries sang and parrots screamed. An even dozen cats wandered about purring, meowling, or spitting, while an impudent and chittering monkey tried to be everywhere at once. The house even included that old-fashioned trade mark of wealth, a glassed-in conservatory filled with potted plants and caged birds.

Against such a background of cacophony and color, Mrs. Carrington, knee-deep in cats, had given the first account of her loss to Ray Schindler, who was also knee-deep in cats and under minute investigation by that father of all detectives, a monkey.

According to Mrs. Carrington, she had that morning given her jewels the thorough cleaning they required every few months. She had washed them in soap and warm water and vinegar and dipped them in alcohol, then spread them out across a towel and left them to dry on her dressing table for an hour.

She had spent that hour downstairs in dusting and straightening things. Then she returned to put her jewelry away. When she got there, the towel was bare and all her dear jewels were gone.

In a frenzy of alarm, she had telephoned her husband. He had hurried home and joined her in a vain search, then notified the police and the insurance company. Immediately an insurance executive had visited the house, but had been so baffled that he engaged Ray Schindler to investigate the evaporation of the gems.

When Ray had heard Mrs. Carrington's story, he made the routine patrol of the house. Though many of the windows were open, they were all fitted with screens so newly painted that any attempt to force one of them open would have left an impression. Ray's careful inspection showed that they had not been touched by any second-story worker, even if one could have ventured to climb up to the windows in broad daylight in full view of neighbors and passers-by. A woman who sat sewing at a window on the other side of the garden said she had seen nobody there.

A stroll around the gardens revealed no sign that a ladder had rested on the soft ground. So burglary was ruled out.

Next came the possibility of sneak-thievery. But Mrs. Carrington assured Ray that she always kept the front door bolted. She said she had opened it at nine o'clock that morning to take in some mail, and bolted it again. An hour later she had begun cleaning her jewelry.

The back door was kept locked and was furthermore under the eye of the cook, who was a good deal of middle-aged German matron in a highly bellicose mood when Ray interviewed her. The most amiable of cooks is not hospitable when her castle is invaded, and Frau Bechtel's kitchen had been raided too often already. She had been cross-examined by the frantic Mrs. Carrington, by her suspicious husband, by the cynical police, by the more cynical insurance executive —and now by a detective, yet!

Mrs. Bechtel conceded that she had let in a grocery boy; but, when Ray asked if she had let him out of her sight, she snapped:

"You mean maybe, did I send him up the beckstairs to steal the choolery? My answer is Nein! Nein! Nein! Nobody goes the beckstairs up!"

Ray retreated in good order and began a thorough search of the house. The police had already gone over it with a fine-tooth comb, but Ray had learned that second combings are often successful. In this case they were not.

He called his office and instructed one of his operatives to investigate that grocery boy, while two others called on everybody in the block to learn if anyone had noticed any strange loiterer about the place.

A day and a half of thorough work merely provided the grocery boy with a good character and an alibi. The neighbors reported nothing unusual.

On retiring from the kitchen, Ray had asked Mrs. Carrington if she had any suspicions of the cook. Her denial was so faltering that Ray pressed the question and learned that the cook had a young son, who was permitted to lunch now and then with his mother in the kitchen. But Mrs. Carrington was quite sure that he had not visited the house that day, though she admitted that the cook had begged her not to mention the boy to the police.

This gave Ray an important lead, and he had the lad hunted up and brought in to his office. The young fellow was overgrown and truculent, but Ray soon had him frightened and submissive. He was, however, a complete disappointment. Not only did he insist that he had not been near the house, and had not left the school grounds all day, but his teachers and a number of his fellow-students confirmed his story beyond further question.

The next day Ray had gone back to Mrs. Carrington and found her haggard and worn from lack of sleep. This was puzzling since her jewels were not irreplaceable heirlooms, and their loss would be almost entirely reimbursed by the insurance company.

Everything pointed to an inside job. Since the wife was admittedly alone in the house, she was logically guilty. Her emotional panic emphasized the suspicion.

In the normal program of procedure, Ray insinuated that someone might have visited the house whose name Mrs. Carrington was withholding. This threw her almost into hys-

terics. She repeated that nobody had called except the post-
man and the grocery boy, and the cook, who came in of
mornings and went home of nights.

In spite of itself, Ray's mind resisted the manifest evidence that the woman herself had made off with the jewels,
and was only pretending that they were stolen in order to
collect the insurance. That sort of thing is only too commonplace an experience with insurance companies, but it seemed
unlikely here.

Mrs. Carrington's torments of uncontrollable fear were
very touching and pitiable; yet what else could they mean
but guilt?

The third day Ray took one of his best men on what he
calls "one of those drab, dogged hunts that can sometimes
make a detective's day a plain hell of boredom." They split
the neighborhood into two parts, and each of them set about
visiting every single business establishment, however small,
within half a mile of the Carrington home. Everywhere they
asked if the Carringtons were known or dealt with, and if any
messenger or repairman had been sent to the house on the
day of the jewels' disappearance.

That old system of "Thorough, Thorough!" was rewarded
with a startling and undreamable disclosure. The operative
brought in not one word of helpful information; but Ray had
an astonishing bit of luck. It seemed foolish to waste time investigating a telegraph office; but wishing to omit nothing he
went in and repeated his dreary query. At the name of the
woman, the manager brightened:

"Oh, yes, Mrs. Carrington is a valued customer. Only last
Tuesday morning she telephoned me to send her a messenger
boy to take a sealed package to the postoffice and register it.
The boy called. She gave him the package and he did as he
was told."

This jolted Ray out of his boredom and confirmed his rule
not to be influenced by a pretty woman's copious tears and
fears.

He persuaded the manager to look into the records and he learned both the size of the package and the address in Kansas City to which it was sent—and on the very morning she reported the robbery! The package was just about the size required to hold Mrs. Carrington's missing jewels. The addressee was a woman.

Ray almost staggered out of the office, and hurried to the insurance office where he reported what he had turned up. Norman Morey, the insurance executive who had called him into the case, gave him the accolade of a cuff on the shoulder and the warm testimonial: "One of these days, my boy, if you don't watch out you will be a real detective—a genuine slouch-hound. You have already earned the company forty thousand dollars. I'll call up the husband and tell him what you've told me and ask him to withdraw his claim."

He reached for the telephone, but Ray put out a hand to check him:

"Give me a day or two more, Norman. I want to learn more from Kansas City. I want to call up my correspondent there and have his bureau look into the woman and her probable boy friend, and also search the pawnshops. They might recover the jewels and, in any case, turn up enough evidence to scare off a law suit."

"All right, my lad," said Morey. "I'll keep my mouth shut till you tell me to open it. But you look to me like a man who has gone soft-headed over a pretty dame."

"I admit she's got me worried," Ray confessed. "I can neither believe her nor disbelieve her. I'd like to turn her in for holding out this fact on me, and fooling me with her baby stare, and yet I can't help feeling there's something more here than meets the eye."

He telephoned his man in Kansas City and set the wheels of inquiry rolling there, then made his way again to Brooklyn.

Deeply humiliated at being so easily fooled by the light that lies in woman's eyes and lies and lies; and feeling more like a rank amateur than a professional sleuth, Ray slunk back to the menagerie and made his way through the uproar of the birds and cats and the monkey to Mrs. Carrington, who had made a monkey of him.

Seeing the ominous ice in his eyes she waited for the blow to fall. As gently as he could he reproached her for lying to him and concealing the fact that she had called a messenger and sent a sealed and registered parcel to Kansas City. This was a thunderbolt to her. She went into a paroxysm of weeping; but Ray watched her with the cold anger of one who had been duped once and would not be again.

She was cried out before he could even get her to listen to his advice. He warned her that she could be arrested and jailed for the attempt to defraud the insurance company; but if she would make a frank confession and persuade her husband to drop the claim, Ray thought he could persuade the company to forget the matter.

The mere mention of her husband threw her into a renewed and more complete panic. She took her oath that the jewels were stolen, and that they were not in the package she had sent to Kansas City. But when Ray asked what the package actually contained she blenched with guilt and trembled with shame, yet hysterically refused to tell him.

It was then that she sobbed:

"If my husband learns of this, my life will be ruined. And I'll kill myself."

The pitiful frenzy of her appeal almost shattered Ray's conviction of her guilt and his wrath at her deception. But he told her that he was helpless. The insurance company already knew the truth. It would, of course, refuse to pay out forty thousand dollars to protect her. Her husband would inevitably persist in his demand. The company would inevitably explain its reasons for the refusal. It would have to tell him about the registered parcel.

Now it was the woman who grew calm and icy. But what she said was:

"Then I'll take poison."

It was Ray's turn to get on his knees, figuratively at least. He implored her to let him help her. He begged her to tell him what was in the package, so that he could devise some protection for her. She refused with a grim calm, and his repeated prayers were unavailing.

At last he left her. He hated the profession that had led him into revealing such a tragedy, and he felt that, though he had entered the case to look for a thief, he was leaving it perhaps as the slayer of a beautiful creature who, for some unimaginable reason, preferred death to the revelation of what could only be proof of her lies and her guilt.

He went back to his office, and reached there just in time to receive a call from Kansas City, from the private detective he had called into the case. William Furlong had handled several cases for Ray in his earlier days as manager of the New York office of the William J. Burns detective bureau. Ray had found Furlong completely reliable and efficient, and he was already able to furnish Ray with the fruits of a long and anxious day and night of research in the slums of Kansas City. He gave the mystery a new and more startling twist. He said:

"That address you gave me is in the red light district. And the girl the parcel was addressed to is a—a streetwalker."

As if this were not earthquake enough, Furlong told the shaken Ray that the Kansas City strumpet had been receiving just such a parcel every six months from Mrs. Carrington.

This was completely maddening. The exquisite Mrs. Carrington could not have been sending her jewels to a Kansas City prostitute every six months. What had she been sending?

There was more to come, and worse. Furlong went on to say that the girl was being kept by a bad boy named Dwyer. Or, rather, she seemed to be keeping the fellow, who had an ugly police record as a procurer, a pimp.

"And every time that package comes from Brooklyn," Furlong said, "the girls at that address say that Dwyer dolls himself up in expensive new clothes and throws a party."

Feeling a grave need for an ice-cap and something to steady his battered nerves, Ray made his way to Norman Morey to report progress—but what progress!

It was all plain as day to Morey. Mrs. Carrington had been sending her jewelry in installments to her girl friend, who gave them to her boy friend, who pawned them and bought himself glad rags. When the last of her jewels had given out, Mrs. Carrington had cooked up the robbery story in the hope of getting forty thousand dollars more so that she could continue her payments to her girl friend. Just what hold the girl and her boy friend had over Mrs. Carrington must be dirty business; but it was none of the insurance company's. This was Morey's conclusion.

When Ray dolefully reiterated that Mrs. Carrington had taken her oath that she had sent no jewels to Kansas City— Morey said—and said it to Raymond C. Schindler of all people on earth:

"My boy, when you've had a little more experience with life and livers you won't be so innocent and so gullible. It's an unfortunate fact that a man cannot believe everything every pretty woman tells him. Wait till her husband hears of this!"

Ray faltered. "But if he does, she swears she'll kill herself."

Morey laughed him to scorn:

"Are you such a softie that you fall for the oldest bluff in history? Forget it, son. You've finished the case for us, and earned your fee for once. Send me your bill and go on home."

Ray merely oozed out of the office. He was torn between remorse for what he had done, and terror for what might yet come of his hateful meddling. The thought of that sweet woman in such an agony of fear that she would kill herself to be rid of it, was unbearable.

He was no longer working for the insurance company. He was on his own now. He let his conscience be his guide. He went back to the woman.

What followed was one of those everlastingly renewed proofs that truth is stranger than fiction. In fact, if any fiction-fumbler, in desperation for money or under the influence of foolish water or hasheesh, had been insane enough to cook up such a solution for a Whodunit, he would have been thrown out of the Mystery Writers' Guild and flung into an asylum.

When Ray rang that Brooklyn door bell, and his sad eyes met Mrs. Carrington's sadder eyes, she knew that something was wronger than ever. She took him up to her room, where the piercing shrieks of the parrots and the fluting of the canaries were muffled. But the monkey came along.

Mrs. Carrington sank into a chair and faced Ray with the look of a doomed woman awaiting her death warrant. That sub-human imp of a simian leapt to her shoulders and tried to snatch the bright buttons off her blouse, till even she thrust him away. Then he began to pester Ray, who did not need that extra torment or the temptation to throw the sharp-toothed devil downstairs. Brushing the little monster away as best he could, Ray told Mrs. Carrington all that he had learned from Furlong and had reported to the insurance man.

There was no panic left in Mrs. Carrington. She was drained of expression. She mumbled:

"It's all over, then. You know everything. And my husband will know it soon."

Ray was now a private citizen, and he could afford the luxury of being himself instead of a bloodhound. He said:

"Your husband doesn't have to know. If you would tell me the whole story, maybe I could find a way out for you. I'd be glad to. But you won't let me help you!"

And then she told him the whole story:

"It's not easy," she began, "but I'd like to get it off my mind before I— You've been very kind and I have no one else to confide in. Perhaps you will tell my husband—afterward. It may help him in his grief, and ease the shock and convince him that I really did love him all the while."

She spoke almost as if she were already dead. To Ray it was like reading the posthumous memoirs of someone.

"I come of a good and respectable family in a small Missouri town. I had the usual girlhood—school, Sunday school, picnics, prayer meetings, the love affairs that kids have, then a serious one. When I was twenty, I became engaged to a young fellow working in a bank. To be near him and help him, I learned bookkeeping and took a job in the same bank.

"I didn't know it, of course, but my lover, my future husband, kept giving me false bookkeeping entries to make. I trusted him and entered them with no inkling of suspicion. One day the police came in and arrested him as an embezzler. And they took me along. He was tried, found guilty and sent away to the penitentiary. I came near following him, for they accused me of being his accomplice. But somehow the jury believed in my ignorance and I was acquitted.

"It was a frightful experience, of course, and I was so wretched that I could not bear to go on living in the town. So I went to Kansas City and took a course in a business college. While I was studying there in the depths of gloom, a gay young man named Dwyer began to pay attentions to me. He taught me how to laugh again and—if you can help it, you might leave out this part of it when you tell my poor husband. Well, I was young and desperate, and he was handsome and clever and we became engaged to be married. And then—well—I—he—well, anyway, in the intimacy of being engaged, he—oh, what's the use of blaming him for my own fault! I gave in to his demands and we were man and wife before the ceremony—which he kept putting off for lack of money.

"When my landlady grew suspicious of the hours we kept, he took me to what he said was the home of a woman who would keep me till the wedding took place.

"I didn't know much, but I was so puzzled by the strange boarders and the goings-on that at last he told me the place was a bawdy house.

"What a hopeless little fool I was then, even for one so young. My first lover was an embezzler and they put him in the penitentiary. My second was a—don't they call such a man a 'procurer'? Well, whatever he was, he told me that he had no money and we would have no money unless I earned it for him by entertaining—he called them 'customers.' And he said he could bring me rich men about town and we could shake them down for a lot of money.

"It all seems so far away after sixteen years of life with a good man in a good home that I seem to be talking about some far-off person I've read about in a cheap novel. I'm horrified to think that even then I could have been such a trusting, unsuspecting little fool. But I was. I was not altogether a bad girl, though. I didn't rob the bank and I didn't entertain any customers.

"But I was as afraid of that man Dwyer as if he had been a rattlesnake—if a rattlesnake could be so vile. So I promised I'd do my best. Then, the minute he went out to find a man I packed my suitcase and skipped out of the house. I ran to the station and luckily I had money enough to pay my fare to New York and keep me alive for a day or two.

"I took the first job I could find and by and by a better one, and finally my training in the business college enabled me to get a position as stenographer with a big concern in Brooklyn. I was rather pretty then; but I think it was really my devotion to my work that attracted the attention of the head of the firm and I became private secretary to Mr. Carrington. I fell in love with him and he with me. He asked me to marry him and I did. And we have been happy as happy could be for sixteen years. They have been heaven to me—but now the old hell has come back. And that same man dragged me into it again.

"My husband and I have had every success and every happiness except children. We have tried to replace them with pets, with birds and parrots and that curious old infant, the monkey. They like us and we love them. We laugh and enjoy ourselves in this zoo we keep."

She was actually smiling again, and Ray was so convinced of the truthfulness of her story to this point that he said:

"Would you mind if I took a few notes so that I won't forget what you tell me?"

"I wish you would," she said. "They will prove to my husband that I was sincere when I gave you this—you might call it my Farewell Address."

Her lips began to quiver, and her eyes to glisten, and she went on in haste to escape another onset of despair. Ray took from his pocket some sheets of loose paper, and detached from his keyring a silver pencil with which he jotted down a few words now and then as she went on with her ancient history.

"For thirteen blessed years, my husband and I lived in perfect happiness. Then I guess the fates thought they had neglected me long enough. They brought Dwyer to Brooklyn on some errand, and took me past him on my way home from the market. Suddenly he stopped me and said, 'Hello, my dear! Fancy meeting my little runaway sweetheart in Brooklyn of all places.'

"I nearly fainted with fright and surprise. I tried to hurry past but he gripped my arm. I begged him to let me alone and told him I was a happy and faithful wife, and he laughed at the idea. He said he couldn't believe it. Still, he said he would play my game, whatever it was—on one condition. Since I had cheated him out of all the money I could have earned him in Kansas City, I could pay it back in installments. He settled on the sum of five hundred dollars twice a year. He had always earned his living from terrified women and he agreed to rent me out to my husband at that price. But he warned me never to be late with his salary for silence.

"I knew what he was capable of, and I knew how it would break my husband's heart and end our happiness if Dwyer were not hushed and kept hushed. What I was most afraid of was that, if my husband ever learned of what Dwyer had done to me in my girlhood and was doing now, he would kill the wretch. Then there would be a trial. He would have been acquitted, of course; but his life would have been ruined and his heart broken because of the exposure of my past. And so for three years I—well I have kept Dwyer quiet. And now the whole thing is coming out after all, and my poor darling's life will be wrecked. But thank God I'll not be here to see it. I'm a coward to kill myself, I suppose. But I can't stand *everything!*"

Once more she steeled herself against a frenzy and went on:

"I followed Dwyer's orders faithfully to send the money in small bills to the address of one of the girls who was working for him. I kept my promise. My husband was always so generous with me, both in money and in gifts, that I was able to pay blackmail to Dwyer every six months for three years. Sometimes it was not easy to raise the money and I was always in terror of some slip-up; but I felt I had a right to buy my husband happiness and peace of mind even at such a price.

"But now my time is up. Low dog that he is, Dwyer has kept his word and kept out of my life. The very day my jewels were stolen, I put five hundred dollars in small bills in a small box, wrapped it, sealed it, addressed it to Dwyer's girl, called for a Western Union messenger and paid him to take it to the post office and register it.

"Then I went upstairs and washed my jewels, left them to dry and went downstairs about my work as I told you. When I went back in an hour, the jewels were all gone.

"I called my husband home. You know the rest. And now

you know all there is to know. I ought to have told you everything, I suppose, about Dwyer; but I think you will understand why I didn't."

"I understand," said Ray with a sigh of regret that he had
himself unwittingly dragged her tragedy to the light, and
without coming any nearer to the solution of the robbery.
He knew that she was telling him the truth, the whole truth
and nothing but the truth. He had been proud of his skill in
running it down, but now he felt guilty of ruining her life and
perhaps of ending it.

He longed to find some way to redeem her happiness. All
the while she was wretchedly pouring forth her story, his
brain had been in a fury of thought for some way out.

And he found it.

If I were writing fiction, even my poor old shameless pen
would balk and rear up and refuse to put on paper such impossible nonsense. But the historian is always chronicling the
impossible nonsense of actual fact; so my pen plods on to
the all-but-unbelievable yet undeniable conclusion. It came
with a crashing suddenness.

Ray had been calling on heaven for help. Heaven sent
him a helper. And what a helper! That diabolical little monkey. His name, by the way, was Mingo.

When the grotesque brat had snatched at the shining
buttons on Mrs. Carrington's blouse, a thought, a mad hope
had come to Ray. He had only pretended to take notes as an
excuse for waving that bright silver pencil about. He had
noted how Mingo's greedy eyes followed it.

When Mrs. Carrington finished her story and turned her
dull funereal eyes on Ray to hear her sentence spoken, Ray
laid his silver pencil down on a little table at his elbow, and
folded his notes.

Mrs. Carrington started up with a cry:

"Mingo! Mingo! Stop it! Drop it! Mr. Schindler, he's stolen
your pencil!"

The monkey had, indeed, snatched up the shining object

and fled with it into the next room. Ray followed him quickly. At the door Ray paused and watched Mingo dancing up and down before one of those huge Chinese vases of majolica ware. This one was as tall as Mingo. He guarded it with jealous ferocity when Ray approached, and thrust him aside. Mrs. Carrington held him to keep him from using his teeth. Ray looked into the jar, and saw on the top of its contents his silver pencil. He showed it to Mrs. Carrington.

"Thank heaven, you got it back," she cried.

Ray tilted the huge dice box and shook it. A score of silver coins rolled out and scattered everywhere.

"For heaven's sake!" gasped Mrs. Carrington. "Why, Mingo, you're a little thief!"

She didn't know the half of it. With no slight effort Ray lifted the heavy jar and turned it mouth down. There was a gleaming cataract of objects, including diamonds, emeralds, rubies and other gems.

Mrs. Carrington fell in a heap beside them. She wept and wept again. But now her aching eyes were cleansed and soothed by those miraculous pearls, the tears of happiness, of lost happiness regained.

When she grew calm enough, still on her knees, she stammered her infinite gratitude to Ray. Then she ran to the telephone and called her husband.

"Oh, darling, darling!" she cried. "Brace yourself for a shock! There's been a miracle! A miracle! That wonderful Mr. Schindler has found every one of the blessed jewels you gave me. I'd rather have them than a million dollars.

"And he found the thief, too! And who do you suppose it was? It was an inside job after all. What's that you say? Who? Was it Mrs. Bechtel? Oh heavens, no. No! Nor her boy. Nor anybody. Wait! Wait!

"The thief was our own darling child, that imp of the devil, Mingo. While I was downstairs cleaning up, he was upstairs stealing all our jewels and hiding them. He's such a kleptomaniac that he stole Mr. Schindler's silver pencil, and we followed the little demon to the one place nobody ever dreamed of looking—that big majolica jar. We'll have to send Mingo to the monkey penitentiary for life. Oh darling, darling, hurry home and let me give you the jewels so that you can give them to me again."

It is wonderful how many things women can express with tears! Whatever would they do without them? Mrs. Carrington had shed floods of tears when her heart was broken and she was mourning herself as already dead of a broken heart and a broken life. Now she shed even more tears, when everything was suddenly heavenly happy. And the hardboiled detective was rainy about the eyes as she poured out on him her blessings. His eyes were dry by the time Carrington reached home and thanked him for his work. Ray bowed himself out in good order and said he would report to the insurance company.

But he had not finished his work of restoring what he had so nearly wrecked.

First he made a supplementary report to Norman Morey. And he did not have to beg Morey not to tell Carrington what he had learned. That was none of the insurance company's business. Morey was human, too, and had done his duty in saving the company's forty thousand dollars.

"I owe you an apology, Ray," he said, "for calling you a softie who believed everything a pretty woman told him. Life is very confusing. Now we see that even the light that lies in woman's eyes doesn't always lie."

That odious menace of blackmail still remained to poison Mrs. Carrington's sufficiently tormented soul. So Ray called Furlong on the long-distance telephone again, and gave him another commission. He was to go to that house where Dwyer kept the girl who kept him. And, without of course impersonating an official, he was to kind of sort of give the impression that he maybe might be an officer. Then he was to tell the girls that he had the goods on Dwyer for blackmailing a woman in Brooklyn and receiving hot money by mail, the sort of thing that the Post Office Department took a great interest in. Furlong was to ask the girls to tell him where he could find Dwyer. Of course they would never tell him. But they would undoubtedly tell Dwyer.

Ray finished his instructions by asking Furlong to leave his telephone number with the woman of the house so that she could call him up the moment Dwyer appeared, so that Furlong could come and nab him. For which cooperation madame would receive a handsome reward. Furlong listened and said:

"Well, Ray, you're the boss. But I'll lay heavy odds that, instead of turning Dwyer in, the woman will be so afraid of him and the law that she'll warn Dwyer to disappear. He'll get out of town so fast and so far he'll never be heard from again."

Ray had a good long laugh at that—a laugh long enough to reach from his New York office to Furlong's office in Kansas City. Ray's only comment was:

"If Dwyer disappeared forever—would that be bad?"

"I get you," said Furlong, returning the long-distance laughter all the way. "You can consider him gone."

Dwyer has never been heard from since. A monkey had made a monkey out of an ancient kind of man who had reached a lower degradation than any so-called "lower animal" ever reached.

The latest word Ray had of Mrs. Carrington was that she and her husband were living happily ever after.

The moral of this uninventable story seems to be: there are times when it is actually a good idea even for a detective to yield to the so-called tyranny of tears, and let his heart argue it out with his head.

# 4.

## RAY'S MOST FAMOUS CASE

Few murder stories have been more picturesque, or had more publicity. Few have been more complex or confusing. Baffling as the mystery was before the trial, it has grown more baffling since. Even more mysterious than the murder itself was the conduct of the prosecution before, during, and since the trial. The Oakes case is probably a permanent mystery of more than one fantastic facet.

This is the way it came to Ray Schindler: the newspapers had blazoned the story all around the globe about the knighted multi-millionaire, Sir Harry Oakes, found gruesomely murdered in his bed in his mansion in the Bahamas; his beautiful young daughter, Nancy, had married a fortune-hunting French Count in spite of her father's fierce protests and warnings; there had been many quarrels; finally the father was viciously slaughtered.

The finger of suspicion pointed straight at the son-in-law. And many circumstances indicated his guilt. To the ignorant, he was only a conscienceless adventurer anyway, and hanging was assumed to be too good for him even without the added excuse of a bungled killing.

The public wanted to believe him guilty. The public prosecutor was convinced of his guilt and eager to prove it.

To Ray Schindler came the grief-stricken daughter. Her fond young heart was torn in two by love for her father and love for her husband. She seemed to be the only one on earth who believed her husband innocent. There seemed to be only one man on earth able to save him from the gallows—the man who, she had heard, was the best detective on earth. She threw herself on his mercy.

Though his heart was touched by her misery, Ray had his standards of honor as well as of mercy. From what he had carelessly read in the newspaper reports, the husband was guilty almost beyond question. In any case Ray would have to go to a distant island under foreign rule with British rules and procedures and no love for American meddlers. The ground had been combed over once and the evidence impounded under guard.

So Ray said to the beautiful, weeping Nancy Oakes:

"I will take the case on one condition: that if I find evidence of your husband's guilt I will not conceal it or twist it. I will turn it over to the prosecution."

That was a hard saying. But where else could Nancy turn? She accepted the conditions. But the prosecution had called in the help of another prominent American detective, and he had turned up a fingerprint in the very vicinity of the murder, *a fingerprint of the husband!* Nothing is more damning than fingerprints and no one has greater faith in them than Ray Schindler.

Also, by the time he arrived on the scene, the prosecutor had built up a case and persuaded the public of the guilt of the accused. In a murder trial, public opinion, though based on hearsay and prejudice and ignorance, is almost all-powerful. The average jury is so swayed by it that the most heinous murderers are often acquitted and received with ovations fitting heroes returning from the wars. Now and then an unfortunate innocent is convicted by acclamation on the flimsiest evidence.

But Ray Schindler's motto is to avoid making up his mind before the evidence is all in. Above all things, he fights shy of intuitions and inspirations. He goes after his clues with the single-mindedness and deadly concentration of a bloodhound following the scent where it leads and paying no heed to the ideas or the desires of the mob, or the pulling of the leash. The bloodhound lets the scent lead the leash.

As everybody knows who knows anything about that famous trial, it ended in an acquittal. But the accused was still so unpopular that he was ordered out of the Bahama Islands as an undesirable character. And nothing can make a man more unpopular than to get himself acquitted when the public wants to see him swing or sizzle.

In the course of the trial, Ray's evidence not only discredited the famous detective brought in by the prosecution, but it left the prosecution completely prostrated.

Long afterward Ray Schindler wrote an article in which he stated that, if he were given a little official encouragement and help, he could put his finger and the evidence on the actual murderer. He even wrote a vain appeal to the Duke of Windsor, then Governor of the Bahamas, to reopen the case. The Duke's secretary replied coldly that the Nassau police would handle any further investigation. This was an icy way of saying: "This is our business; mind your own. No trespassers allowed."

As the story unfolds, the reader may also acquire a theory as to who really killed Sir Harry Oakes. But an effort will be made to tell it as it disclosed itself beneath the keen eyes, the microscopes and the chemical tests of Ray Schindler, his associates, and the practiced analytical mind of Erle Stanley Gardner, the great detective story writer who was also on the spot.

If you like high life with your murder mysteries, here you have it. A king of England gives up his throne to marry "the woman I love." She was an American woman, too. He takes the title of Duke of Windsor and is made Royal Governor of the Bahamas.

There in the capital city of Nassau, Sir Harry Oakes, whose fortune was estimated at over one hundred million dollars, is found slain and seared by fire in a most grisly manner. The murderer-elect, by popular vote, is a French Count who had married the beautiful American daughter of Sir Harry Oakes as soon as she reached the age of eighteen and could wed without her father's consent. Even that wedding was later put in question by her suit for an annulment on the ground that the Count was not fully divorced from his first wife.

Mixed with the murder are hints of savage superstitious practices like the voodoo rites of Haiti, and a theory that the actual murder was committed by a native hired for the job.

Who could ask for a murder mystery in more gorgeous surroundings? What writer of Whodunits would dare pile up in fiction such melodramas as fate and the facts heaped together here?

Sir Harry Oakes, born an American, later transferred his allegiance to the king and was knighted. He had begun humbly and built a huge fortune seemingly more for purposes of revenge than ambition. He had made enemies all the way along his long, long trail from the Klondike to the Congo and finally to Nassau in the Bahamas. The legend was that, as a rugged young man, he had once begged a merchant of mining equipment to stake him to some machinery by way of a loan. He was ordered out of the store. Long afterward, when Oakes was rich, he opened a rival establishment and cut prices till the man who had ordered Oakes out of his store was ordered out of his own store by the sheriff.

In his more prosperous days, Oakes, it was told, entered a restaurant and asked for a certain table. The headwaiter, not knowing him, refused it. Sir Harry promptly bought the hotel and threw the headwaiter and his whole staff out into the street.

Such revenges have a touch of poetic justice, but they do not make for popularity. Sir Harry had been so fierce, so violent and so ruthless that when he was found slain and the usual first question was asked: "Who was his enemy?" the answer was easy: "Who wasn't?"

Such a son-in-law to such a father-in-law did not suggest filial love; and the dullest private detective instantly "put the bee" on Alfred de Marigny. But Ray Schindler likes to demonstrate step by step what must be demonstrated and be able to put a real mathematical Q.E.D. at the end of every problem.

After Sir Harry Oakes had settled in the Bahamas and built his sumptuous residences, he formed a water company that drilled many wells in the islands. He was a frequent visitor to South America, where he had made such large investments that there was talk of his establishing a residence there. He was about to make another tour and had secured a passport with visas for various South American countries. If he had not delayed his departure for two days to confer with his engineers concerning a water project, he would have left the island before his murder.

But even that is guess work, for, according to Ray Schindler's theory, he was murdered for revenge; and perhaps the murderer might have just moved the killing forward. Even that is uncertain. Perhaps the motive for the assassination was based on something that happened after he had postponed his sailing.

Or, even if he had sailed, he might have died on the ship; he might have been murdered in one of those Spanish American countries. Or he might not have.

Speculation is as fruitless as it is fascinating. In ancient Egypt, about two thousand years B.C., among the delightful short stories written by the brilliant inhabitants of that so modern and so ancient a country, there was a popular novelette about a man who travelled North and encountered a savage crocodile. He wished that he had gone South, and was given the privilege of retracing his steps; but again he was confronted by a crocodile. He turned back and travelled East, then West. Always there lay in wait for him a fatal crocodile. Almost four thousand years later, O. Henry, who doubtless never read the Egyptian fiction, rewrote exactly the same plot in modern terms.

Many people, fatalists, would say that Sir Harry's death

was in the books. That we shall never know; and perhaps it will never be proved in open court who really did kill him.

What concerns us is that he was killed. At the time his wife and his daughter, Nancy, were in the United States. His son-in-law, Alfred de Marigny, was in the Bahamas; but he lived at a distance from Sir Harry and shared a small house with a man friend, who joined him that night in giving a small party. The party lasted till a late hour, and de Marigny drove two women guests to their homes at such distances and returned so late that he would have had precious little time in which to commit the long and laborious murder. Furthermore, as Ray Schindler found out and pointed out, since de Marigny's roommate also drove a guest home, returned later than de Marigny and left his car in the narrow driveway behind de Marigny's, the Count would have had to get his friend's car out of the way, drive a long distance, commit the murder, return home, drive his car in, then drive his friend's car in after it, and go to bed—all without attracting the attention of the man who occupied the house with him. Such things as that, and the utter absence of anything like a reasonable motive that could have impelled the Count to kill his father-in-law, made the case against him so flimsy that it offended the presiding judge.

But to return to the beginning and start all over:

On the night of the murder, Sir Harry did not sleep in the home he occupied when his family was with him, but in another of his residences, called "Westbourne." An addition was being made to Westbourne in the form of a long two-story building connecting it with a golf club house also belonging to Sir Harry.

Two night watchmen guarded the building material and were near the scene of the murder, but were not called as witnesses in the trial. They were also kept from any conversation with Ray Schindler.

Sir Harry's own servants went home at night; but in the

lot adjoining Westbourne, and separated from it only by a fence, was a neighbor's house. Two Negro maids slept there. One of them, hearing a voice in the early morning, peered out of her window and recognized a man who was running up and down the porch calling "Help, help!" The other maid, from the opposite end of the house, recognized the same man when she saw him running to a neighboring home occupied by some people named Kelly. (The maids were never called as witnesses, though they would have contradicted the testimony of the man they identified.)

Yet it was some time after his murder before Sir Harry Oakes' death was reported. This was on the morning of July 8, 1943. His head had been beaten in and then his bed had been set on fire.

It was a most peculiar kind of fire. The apparent attempt was to let the fire be blamed for his death, after it had consumed him and his bed. But, for some reason, this plan did not succeed, and the murderer left the room. He probably assumed that the fire would blaze up and devour all, and dared not return to complete his work.

In any case, Sir Harry's body was horribly burned but only partly consumed. The fatal wounds on his head immediately in front of his left ear had penetrated the skull for about an inch and an eighth. The mortuary photographs show that the blood flowed down over his nose, proving that he was lying on his right side when struck. But his body was found lying on its back. It must have been turned into that position after the blows were stuck. Otherwise the blood would have flowed down into his hair and the back of his head.

The murder weapon was never found. So far as Ray could learn, no search was ever made for it, and no reward offered for its discovery.

Even more mysterious than the behavior of the murderer were the deeds and omissions of the prosecution. As the former Attorney General of the United States, Homer S. Cummings said, "The police found their suspect and then proceeded to search for the facts to fit him."

After Sir Harry had been struck by the fatal weapon, and his body turned, the bed was set on fire. The bedclothing and his pajamas were quite consumed. A flame had been played over the lower part of his body as if in the sexual rage of a murder for revenge. Also his eyes had been deeply burned.

The room was in a dreadful state. The rug was badly burned, also a screen that stood near the bed. The prosecution claimed that an inflammable fluid had been sprayed about the room and the body, and a match applied. But there was also a strange pattern of burns about the room and even on the stairway. It led Ray to believe that something like a blow-torch had been brought upstairs and used.

The strange omissions and commissions in following up the crime were not due so much to the Nassau police as to the activities of certain detectives brought over from the United States. The actions of one of them provoked a scathing condemnation from the judge and led an American society of detectives whose standards are of the highest to convict him of conduct unbecoming a member.

As soon as the murder was discovered, the Nassau police, aware of the notorious feud between Sir Harry and de Marigny, promptly threw the Count into jail. They were at first satisfied of his guilt but before they could prove it conclusively they were forced to stand aside helplessly watching the activities of two American detectives whom the Duke of Windsor imported. These detectives seemed to Ray to have made no effort to approach the case without prejudice, but to have overlooked everything that indicated de Marigny's innocence. They actually destroyed much evidence that might have proved him guiltless, and the prosecution forbade de Marigny's attorneys and Ray Schindler access to everything that might controvert the theory of his guilt.

When Ray found in various places the imprints of a bloody hand he was calmly told:

"The fingers were stubby and de Marigny's were not, so we dismissed them."

They not only dismissed them, but tried to erase them! And succeded so far that Ray could not use them for identification of one who seemed to him the far more probable murderer.

Even in Nassau the importance of fingerprints had been heard of, and a desperate hunt was made for some evidence that de Marigny had been in the room. No trace of him was found till an American detective alleged that he had lifted a print of de Marigny's little finger from the scorched screen that stood by the bedside.

"Lifting a fingerprint" means, of course, dusting it with a powder, laying a tape over the powder and lifting away the tape.

The defense proved to the satisfaction of the judge, that the fingerprint could never have been taken from that screen, and the case was thrown out of court, while the detective himself was, as already told, censured by an American society of fingerprint experts.

In sharp contrast to the inquisitional mistreatment of de Marigny (whose alibi was as convincing to any unprejudiced judge, as to the presiding judge and the jury) was the tender consideration shown for the rights of the man who occupied a bedroom on the same floor with Sir Harry and adjoining the empty bedroom between them.

Another puzzling feature of the case was that Sir Harry had apparently feared some attack. For, though he had never been known to carry a weapon, a pistol was found in the drawer of the bedside-stand. Beneath it was a pile of bills that he had evidently put there when he undressed; after which he carefully placed the gun within reach.

Did he expect a possible attack? By whom? No effort was made to find out. The weapon itself was not even kept by the police but turned over to the caretaker of the buildings. Ray, when he arrived, was not able to see the weapon or learn if it had ever really belonged to Sir Harry. If it were borrowed, he could not learn from whom Sir Harry had borrowed it, or why, or if he had given a reason for suspecting a possible attack, or if he had ever mentioned to anybody that he thought he was in danger of one.

Ray wanted, and still wants, to put a number of Sir Harry's acquaintances on the lie detector and ask them a few questions as to the situation at the time of the murder. Such action was forbidden to him then and has since been denied to him.

Nassau wants to forget the murder. It was so eager to be rid of it that Sir Harry's body was shipped to the United States for burial in such haste that the airplane carrying it had to be recalled for even such casual examination as those hurried police cared to make.

No X-ray was ever taken of his skull beneath the wounds.

But to turn back to Ray's appearance on the scene: As he says, he left for the island "with the thought in mind that I would probably help hang the fellow." When Nancy Oakes, in her frantic wifely eagerness to save her husband from execution for murder, turned to Ray Schindler as her last and best hope she cried:

"Whatever else he is, he is not a murderer."

Her own mother was convinced of de Marigny's guilt; but Nancy fought for him and saved him by appealing to a man who, after a long lifetime of enormous activity as a detective, could say:

"I have never taken an assignment to clear a guilty man." He could also say: "I do not enter a case with my mind made up, no matter what facts are presented to me. I do not accept the statements of others as facts. I prefer to make my own investigation and, if I come to the same conclusion, it is because of double-checking, which is a good rule to follow in any murder case. I have never been able to understand how officials investigating a crime can disregard evidence that does not fit in with the evidence needed to convict the person whom they have decided to be the guilty one."

Ray had read the early accounts of the murder in the newspapers and had vaguely assumed that de Marigny was probably guilty. He seemed to be the most natural suspect. This was his third marriage to a wealthy woman. He had a reputation for working neither steadily nor often.

His first marriage was with the daughter of a Paris banker. After a divorce, he married a rich widow, who was much poorer when she divorced him.

Though he was born in a French province, it was taken over by the British and he became a British subject.

But Ray would not even accept de Marigny's word that he was truly a Count. He searched the records and found his title registered officially long before the Oakes case. This disposed of the frequent charge that de Marigny was wearing a bogus title, as a decoy for foolish women.

His second wife, Ruth Fahnestock, was an American woman but became a British subject by marrying him. She made heavy investments in the Bahama Islands. During the second World War British subjects were forbidden to remove more than a small amount of money from British possessions. So she went to Florida and secured a secret divorce in order to regain her citizenship and claim her funds as an American. But she kept the divorce a secret, and returned to Nassau and to the Count, intending to remarry him as soon as her money was safely returned to the United States.

The Count had meanwhile acquired other ideas. He had sold some of the Nassau holdings, lent a thousand pounds to a local banker, and invested about ten thousand pounds in a large chicken ranch. He then went to New York to marry Nancy Oakes on her eighteenth birthday.

It is not necessary to defend or denounce these jugglings with the marriage sacrament. They are not evidence in a murder trial, though much was made of them by the prosecution in an attempt to picture the defendant in as despicable a light as possible.

It was known that Sir Harry Oakes did not approve of his daughter's marriage with the Count. He had forbidden it. But the moment she was eighteen she had married the man of her choice. The relationship of her father and herself had never been very cordial. The wedding naturally did not enhance it.

Nancy's mother did not approve of the marriage any more than her father did, but she spent most of her time at a distance. Sir Harry and his chicken-rancher son-in-law did not get along well together. Hardly anybody got along well with Sir Harry. The prosecution claimed that the Count had threatened the life of his father-in-law. It claimed also, as a motive for the murder, that de Marigny wanted to secure the great Oakes fortune as an inheritance for his wife, so that he could control it. The prosecution also insisted that de Marigny was in dire need of money.

But Ray Schindler disproved this last charge by evidence that the Count owned a valuable chicken ranch, as well as two homes on the island, and had a considerable deposit in the bank.

They say that "a man who marries for money earns it," so de Marigny might be said to have earned his fortune before he married Nancy. In any case, evidence was produced to show that, once he was a father-in-law, Sir Harry had offered to buy de Marigny a large ranch and a beautiful home in Nassau. The Count had spurned the gift.

He was not at all the impecunious Count of fiction and fact with no skill except in the conquest of vain women and the spending of their fortunes. He had graduated from college with high honors, especially in agriculture. He had pride enough to refuse both Sir Harry's handsome gift house and an offer to set him up in business and make him president of a Nassau bank that Sir Harry owned.

"I'm not a banker. I'm a farmer," the Count had said.

He was so independent, indeed, that he openly defied the autocratic Sir Harry and quarrelled bitterly with him in public. Though he lived at some distance from Sir Harry's home, he admitted that on the night of the murder he had driven two young women guests at his party to their home and had passed within a block of Westbourne.

The Count's young wife, Nancy, was not with him at the time. She was attending college in Bennington, Vermont, taking an advanced course in dancing. Her mother and the other children were at the Oakes summer home in Bar Harbor, Maine.

When Nancy appealed to Ray Schindler for help, he consented to make his investigations and report the truth and nothing but the truth, though it might mean the hanging of his client's husband.

He flew to Nassau and studied the case as best he could. He had several interviews with the Count in his cell. He was surprised to find the man a splendid athlete. He had never sailed a boat till he went to Nassau; but he had taken up the sport and had soon become a winner in the Star class. He won races also in Cuba and at New Orleans, Palm Beach, and on Long Island Sound. His chicken ranch impressed Ray as one of the finest he had ever seen, and, even while the Count was languishing in a cell, his ranch was selling eggs and chickens to the Government that was calling him a murderer.

The Nassau prosecution had not welcomed Ray's cooperation. In fact, he had been formally informed that there was no need for private investigators. He was kept under observation constantly. Even on the golf course or at dinner, his guests were telephoned to and warned against him, as well as asked for information concerning his plans. Ray was hampered in every way; but he does not blame the Nassau police. They confessed that they were frankly humiliated and hamstrung by their subjection to the American detectives. The defense counsel was Sir Godfrey Higgs. He was efficient and eloquent, and when at last he placed the facts before the court, in open trial, they shocked the Nassau judge and jury. Even the local chief of detectives had been suddenly taken off the case and transferred to another island. It is Ray's belief that this was because his testimony would not have been what the prosecution wanted.

Important witnesses were forbidden to speak to Ray, and others came to him in great terror, secretly.

After a brief preliminary scouting, Ray flew back to the United States, thoroughly convinced both of de Marigny's complete innocence and of the appalling bungling of the case; also of the prosecution's determination to throw every possible obstacle in the path of any defense.

First, Ray went to Washington, D. C. to call on Homer S. Cummings, the former Attorney General of the United States. As prosecuting attorney, Cummings had once investigated a case against a most suspicious little defendant named Israel. Not only had the police produced witnesses to identify him but had secured from him a confession of murder. Cummings, however, like Ray Schindler, believed in double-checking, and he persuaded the very identifying witnesses that they could not have identified the defendant. When he had completed his investigation, and rose in court to open the case against the defendant, he startled the nation by avowing the defendant innocent and calling for his immediate release. This famous case was later made into the dramatic motion picture called "Boomerang."

The research Cummings made into the evidence against de Marigny, his study of the preliminary court hearings and his interviews with some of the witnesses convinced him of de Marigny's guiltlessness.

Ray also consulted and secured the advice and cooperation of dozens of lawyers, scientists, prosecutors. Everything and everybody confirmed his belief that de Marigny could not have committed the murder. This faith made him indomitable in the following battle for the man's life against the entrenched determination of the British prosecutors.

Among other scholars on criminal evidence whose aid Ray invoked was that of Judge Max Spelke.

To offset the peculiar fingerprint business that had been accepted in Nassau, Ray travelled to New Orleans and engaged the help of Maurice O'Neill, one of the greatest fingerprint experts. He secured also the cooperation of Leonarde Keeler, whose knowledge of criminology was not limited to his lie detector. Ray found him of infinite help.

Powerful aid came to him also from that most successful of mystery story writers, Erle Stanley Gardner, engaged by a syndicate to attend the trial and describe it for the press.

Before he became an author, Gardner had had long experience as a lawyer both for defense and for prosecution. It was his knowledge of the complexities and dramas of the legal labyrinth that had led him to write the first of his famous Perry Mason stories. Before he would even visit Nassau he had sought out Ray Schindler. The two men struck up a friendship that has grown with the years.

In Nassau the two men worked together as well as a private detective could work with a famous reporter whose daily stories were being exploited on the front pages of many American newspapers. Ray has said of that association:

"I was happy and honored to receive Erle's counsel and advice. It helped a lot. For example, we learned through Erle of an effort that had been made to doctor some of the testimony."

The murder of Sir Harry Oakes was a crime that had been almost incredibly easy for anyone who wanted to commit it. He had spent the night in a very large bedroom in a large house. There were twin beds, but he slept alone; and he had a revolver at hand.

The only other person known to have slept in that house was Harold Christy, a partner of Sir Harry's in many business affairs and his agent in many large real estate transactions.

He testified that he had slept through the long stormy night, unawakened by the long and noisy activity of the murderer. But testimony was given in court that he had been seen in town at a time when he swore he was asleep.

Christy stated on the stand that it was the custom for Sir Harry to have breakfast with him every morning at seven A.M. on the wide porch; but that on this particular morning when he went to the table and did not find Sir Harry waiting he looked into his bedroom and found Sir Harry bleeding and burned. As he told it, the first thing he did was to take a pillow from the adjoining bed and put it under Sir Harry's head. Next, he ran to the bathroom, filled a glass with water and forced it down Sir Harry's throat.

One who has seen the ghastly photographs of the dead man might well wonder how anyone could open those seared lips and pour in water. Next, Christy testified, he ran back to the bathroom, wet a towel and returned to wash the dead man's face. He did this a second time. The face revealed some slight evidence of this strange action.

It was only after all this that he appealed for help. But the first call went to Christy's brother. It was some time before the police were notified.

Between the room occupied by Christy and that of Sir Harry there was an unoccupied bedroom and bath. These were on the second floor of the house and opened on a large porch, whose roof was wide enough to keep out of the rooms the torrential rain that kept up most of the fatal night. To this porch there were three outside stairways and Sir Harry slept with the windows and doors of his room wide open. Anyone could have walked up any of those stairways and walked into his bedroom without unlocking a door, or breaking a window.

Though Ray's investigations did not begin till several weeks after the murder, which took place between 1:30 and 4:30 A.M., July 8, 1943, he was permitted to make numerous visits to the bedroom.

The most astounding of his discoveries was that somebody

with bloodstained hands had peered out of the windows on both sides of the room and left red palm and fingerprints on the walls. Instead of photographing and shielding these prints to identify the owner of those bloody hands, the investigating officers had dismissed them and erased them because they were different from de Marigny's. The almost incredible explanation for this all-but-incredible deed was that de Marigny was undoubtedly the murderer and the red prints might confuse the issue by involving some innocent person!

Ray Schindler has known of many astounding actions by investigators who do not investigate, but this baffling behavior led him to exclaim:

"I shall never understand how any honest investigator could have permitted this to happen. In my opinion it is criminal negligence."

To other people "negligence" might seem a polite understatement.

Furthermore, Ray found that the telephone book in the bedroom had been handled by bloody hands, and fingerprint bloodstains left on many pages as if the criminal had hastily hunted for some number in the book. These fingerprints were likewise ignored and never identified.

The explanation for this was that the first person who discovered Sir Harry's body had touched it, and got blood on his fingers; then had run to call for help and searched the telephone book for the right number to call! No use was ever made of these prints!

Whenever Ray entered the death chamber he had to secure permission from the prosecuting attorney, and, since the place was kept locked and under constant guard, his every move was known to the police. In spite of this he obtained enough evidence to overthrow the entire case of the prosecution. But he was absolutely forbidden even to investigate anybody else he might consider suspicious. All he was allowed to do was to try to exculpate de Marigny.

The prosecution's attitude was that, since one man was

already charged with the crime, it would be improper to look elsewhere for a culprit till the first man was found guilty or acquitted!

Still, Ray longs to examine those prints on the telephone book. Even at this late day they might well retain their identity, though the bloody handprints on the wall were erased beyond recovery. From the telephone book enough blood could still be secured to type it. If it were of the same type as Sir Harry's it would probably be his. Otherwise it would be of vital help in running down the killer. Even the prosecution did not pretend that de Marigny had touched the telephone book. They did not even bring it to court.

The handprints by the windows where someone apparently looked out to make sure that the coast was clear, and the bloody marks in the telephone book were not all.

Ray repeatedly studied certain doorknobs, on which there were blood marks. These were the knobs on either side of the door to the porch from the bedroom in which Christy slept. It struck Schindler that, after the killing, someone had visited that bedroom.

But when Christy was questioned he said that he was too confused to remember where he went or what he did. No other person was questioned on that subject, or even searched for.

Since the feud between de Marigny and his father-in-law was by no means the only one that Sir Harry was carrying on, Ray begged—in vain as usual—to be allowed to bring Dr. Keeler and the lie detector into play. He would be glad to go to the island even yet and put through that soul-searching machine a number of Sir Harry's friends and acquaintances; and he believes that he could find out if any of them had made any threats, or had heard of any threats, against Sir Harry; if any of them cherished any mortal grudge, or knew of anyone who did.

The more one studies the prosecution the more bewildering it becomes. It has some of the elements of such an investigation as might have been expected if Nancy Oakes had been Alice in Wonderland.

Sir Harry's papers were left undisturbed. No search was made through them for any reference to the danger he must have foreseen. The revolver found in the bedstand was not held by the police or studied by them. Since Sir Harry was not shot, they said: "Why keep his revolver?" The fact that he had, on two or three occasions, slept in a bedroom other than his usual one as if he were hiding from somebody against whom he kept a revolver within reach—that did not even interest the prosecution. They gave the revolver to the caretaker to "keep it out of the way lest it confuse the issue." The issue was, of course, de Marigny's conviction.

Ray dug up the fact that one of Sir Harry's close associates had a criminal record in the United States. He had the evidence in documentary form signed by Franklin D. Roosevelt as President of the United States. He could not get this evidence cleared by the Nassau censor in time to present it in court. He would be glad to present it now, if anyone away down in Nassau cared enough to look into it.

Indifferent as the prosecution was as to details that Ray Schindler felt to be of infinite importance, there was one subject on which the greatest stress was laid. That was the matter of de Marigny's shirts. Since he was nominated for the killer and there were bloody handprints on the walls and the telephone book and burned surfaces everywhere, it was certain that de Marigny's clothes must bear some signs of his night's work.

They asked him where the shirt was that he had worn that night. Without hesitation he said that he had stuffed it in the soiled clothes basket where he put all his used linen. They were welcome to look over the basket. They did and found nothing with a drop of blood or a smudge of smoke. He presented them with all his shirts. Nevertheless, they accused him of making away with the bloody one.

He said that he owned exactly two dozen shirts and the

total of soiled shirts and unworn shirts made a total of twenty-four, all exactly alike as his wife and servant maintained.

This did not prevent the prosecution from saying that he had lied. But the prosecution continued to insist that de Marigny had disposed of the tell-tale garment. They even quoted him as saying that it had mysteriously disappeared, though he had said exactly the opposite.

When it came to the trial the judge and jury believed de Marigny and ignored the imaginary shirt the prosecution waved.

There were gruesome and uncanny features about the burning of the murdered man. If he had been sleeping under the sheet, the woolen blanket and the coverlet, these would have had to burn before the flames could reach Sir Harry's flesh.

So Ray took pieces of the unburned bedding and the spottily burned carpet, and also bought duplicates of them for experimentation. He and his associates spent weeks in study of the behavior of these materials during combustion. Even with the most inflammable material sprinkled over them it took from thirty to forty-five minutes to consume them. The murderer, then, after having killed Sir Harry, must have spent a long time completing his deed. Why?

More mystifying yet was the fact that, after the covers had been burned off and then the pajamas, after Sir Harry's body had been so fiendishly mutilated with flame, it had been almost covered with feathers.

The prosecution said that these had come from the pillow when it caught fire. But there was an electric fan at the foot of the bed and it was still going when the police arrived.

As Ray pointed out, the feathers from the burned pillow would have been blown away from the bed, and away from the body by the strong current of air. But the feathers had been sprinkled over the body after the burning and they adhered to the seared flesh. Few of them were even singed; so they must have been sifted over the body after the flames had died down.

Why had the murderer, after slaying Sir Harry, lingered the better part of an hour to burn the body and then cover it with feathers?

In the Bahamas as in Haiti there are many natives who practice fanatic rites akin to voodoo.

The questions rose: did Sir Harry have a feud with some vindictive native, or did some enemy of Sir Harry's hire or incite a native to do the deed?

These questions were ignored by the prosecution, but Ray would have liked, and would still like, to send operatives in among the natives with hard cash to loosen tongues. He could find and train natives to practice the art of "roping." They would make friends with the possible murderer and perhaps win a boastful or remorseful confession.

Ray managed to save de Marigny from the net the prosecution cast about him, but he aches to find the evil fiend who was not satisfied even by Sir Harry's death but must revel in the sight and sound and scent of his burning flesh, then scatter triumphant or penitential feathers over it.

Even the weapon actually used in killing Sir Harry was never found or much sought for by the police. The four wounds in the head were triangular and some thought that they might have been made by the pointed end of a wooden picket. That would have been a weapon as fantastic as the rest of the details. But the garage contained a number of wooden pickets and one of them was found leaning against Sir Harry's car in the garage, as if the murderer had picked it up, discarded it for another, and tossed it against the car.

But Ray is sure that no such weapon could have been used. Unless Sir Harry had been drugged before he undressed and put his money and revolver away so carefully, a blow with such a picket would have wakened him. Being a very powerful and hot-tempered man he would surely have put up a fight for his life.

But the bedroom disclosed no signs of the slightest struggle. Ray is not even sure that Sir Harry was slain in his bed.

In any case no X-rays were taken of his skull and the four wounds. In fact the authorities were in such haste to be rid of Sir Harry's body that they put it on a plane for burial in the United States. After the plane had flown from the island, it had to be recalled by radio to permit the police to make even what few records and photographs they felt they needed.

In British legal procedure, there is no Grand Jury indictment as here, but there is a public police court hearing at which is shown such evidence as "The Crown" will submit to a jury. A judge decides if there is evidence enough to hold the accused for trial.

When Ray reached Nassau there had been such a police hearing and de Marigny was kept in prison. Ray was enabled to read the evidence submitted and it did not convince him.

He was especially shocked by the fingerprint that was the most damaging evidence against de Marigny. It was said to have been taken from the screen by the bed. It placed de Marigny on the scene of the murder with a vengeance.

The detective who produced it was an expert from the United States. He had had years of experience and had recently taken a refresher course in the F.B.I. Laboratory at Washington.

He produced and the prosecution accepted as damning proof of de Marigny's guilt a fingerprint which he said he had found on the screen and had lifted from it with a rubber tape. He did not take or show a preliminary photograph of the screen, and he did not claim that anyone saw him lift it.

This procedure astounded Ray as something unheard-of, since a fingerprint should not be removed unless the object is so huge that it cannot be taken into the courtroom. The screen was not too big to carry in and show to the jury. In fact just that was done.

But first, with his inevitable thoroughness, Ray consulted

all the fingerprint cases he could find in many countries and made the most complete survey of the subject he had ever made. This only confirmed his belief in the ethical and legal impropriety of this allegation.

The screen had been carelessly moved out into the hall during the first investigation of the crime and it admittedly contained the fingerprints of the house servants and some of the officers. These prints were studied and eliminated from consideration. They had been lifted on Scotch tape. The detective who claimed to have found, a fortnight later, the fingerprint of de Marigny said he had lifted it on rubber tape because he had run out of Scotch.

This detective had been called in from Florida immediately after the murder and had arrived by plane at Nassau by noon of the same day. De Marigny was locked up the next day and it was not till about ten days later that this detective turned up with the print. His testimony at the police hearing had been sufficient to convince the judge that de Marigny should be held for a murder trial.

When, much later, Ray was permitted to examine the screen and was furnished with an enlarged photograph of the alleged fingerprint, he noted that it was filled with little circles. Then Ray and his assistant, Leonarde Keeler, and Maurice O'Neill, the fingerprint specialist, made experiments with fingerprints on the screen. They touched their fingers everywhere and lifted the prints. Not one of them showed little circles. Every one of them showed little ridges such as would be expected on a wooden surface. They spent days and nights for weeks trying to find a spot that would return a fingerprint with little circles in it.

Furthermore it was easily shown that de Marigny's fingerprint could not be fitted into the space where the detective said he had found it.

As soon as it was learned that Ray and O'Neill and Keeler were making these tests—under police supervision, of course —the prosecution sent for one of America's best experts, one connected with the New York Police Department. He flew to Nassau and, to the chagrin of the prosecution, confirmed the conclusion of Ray, Keeler, and O'Neill.

When it came to the final trial, the detective told the judge that he wished to correct some of his earlier testimony. When he was asked why he had not photographed the print on the screen itself, he said he had not brought his fingerprint camera with him and the one owned by the Nassau police had broken down.

Ray's answer to this was that any good camera would serve and in fact he had made his own photographs with a camera borrowed from a local photographer. Furthermore, the British Army had at its air base the finest camera equipment and a very competent photograph department. One of their cameras had been used to photograph Sir Harry's body and the pictures had been developed at the Army laboratory, where, indeed, Ray had had his own photographs developed.

That fatal fingerprint was fatal to the detective. His testimony and that of the prosecution broke down so badly here that they convinced the jury of de Marigny's innocence.

Ray did not fail to call attention to the peculiar fact that the chief detective of the local force had been sent on a mission that kept him from testifying. The judge in his charge to the jury commented forcefully on this absence, and also on certain strange changes that some of the prosecution's witnesses made in their testimony previously given at the police hearing. In fact, one police officer testified concerning a person he had seen on the morning of the murder in the town though that person had sworn he had not left his bed. The policeman was threatened with a loss of his post if he so testified, but he was brave and honest enough to say what he had seen.

The case against de Marigny had broken down utterly so far as the prosecution's evidence that he was present at the scene of the murder.

There still remained the problem of giving him a good

alibi and showing where he was and what he was doing at the time of the killing.

Now, de Marigny had never denied that he had driven within a block of the scene of the murder and at a late hour. But he said, and there were many witnesses to confirm his statement, that he had given a party at his house that night to eighteen or twenty people, some of whom were strangers to him. The day before he had met two British aviators at a hotel and invited them to the party. They could not get away but their wives were present.

His home was small and in the upper story was an apartment occupied by a friend of his, George de Vivolou. This apartment was reached by an outside stairway only.

The party ended about eleven o'clock and de Marigny offered to take back to their homes the wives of the two aviators. It was testified that he tried to get one or two of the men to go along with him so that he would not have to ride back alone. One of them accepted, but later went with someone else.

These trivial matters, familiar when all parties break up, had a mighty influence on the jury. It did not seem probable that a young man about to murder his father-in-law and spend an hour burning his body with diabolic fanaticism would urge his friends to come along for the ride.

It was a long ride, too, in a furious rain storm—about seven miles each way. There were several servants in de Marigny's little home; for servants are cheap in Nassau. They testified that he was back home within three quarters of an hour after he left.

Ray made that drive himself more than once and timed it both in good weather and bad. He admitted that de Marigny might have stopped off at his father-in-law's house, emptied a revolver into him, and got back without delay. But he could never had made the drive both ways and paused to steal into the house, find the sleeping man and, without waking him or the other man sleeping two doors away, bash in Sir Harry's skull, then spend half an hour or more burning his body and bedding with a blow-torch, scattering feathers over the roasted corpse and leaving bloody marks on the walls, the telephone book, and the other man's doorknobs.

When de Marigny reached his home he parked his car at the far end of the narrow driveway, which was thirty or forty feet long. He was already in bed in the room below when George de Vivolou returned from driving a young lady home, parked his car back of de Marigny's and went up the outside stairway to his room. He took his car keys with him.

Even if, after that, de Marigny had decided to dash over and slaughter and cremate Sir Harry he could not have got his car past de Vivolou's. He would have had to go upstairs and borrow de Vivolou's keys.

When the case came to trial, Ray had a miniature of de Marigny's house ready, with the driveway and two tiny cars all built to scale. When this was exhibited to the jury it left no doubt in their minds that de Marigny could never have left the house after his return, and he had returned too soon for the murder. Seven witnesses confirmed this.

Ray also had ready an exact replica of the top of the screen from which the other detective claimed to have lifted the fingerprint on rubber tape, and lifted it so completely that its previous existence was incredible. But as the trial proceeded, the whole screen itself was brought into the court and it confirmed the detective's confession that he must have been mistaken.

Such little mistakes often cause an innocent person to be found guilty of a heinous crime.

In British justice, Ray says he has "one hundred per cent belief." The judge who gave the charge to the jury was plainly thoroughly disgusted with the conduct of the Nassau prosecution. He demanded that the police department be thoroughly investigated. He also sternly rebuked the American detective whose two testimonies under oath were flatly contradictory.

The jury acquitted de Marigny of every suspicion. And his wife Nancy, whose intervention had saved his life, was present with him the next night at another little party, this time in the home of his lawyer, Sir Godfrey Higgs. Outside the house there was a mob of well-wishers cheering and applauding.

The next morning de Marigny was up betimes. He went back to his cell, shaved, wrote some notes and left his old home after an hour. But there were many who did not regard him or his victim with favor. Their only chance for revenge now was to declare him unworthy of old Nassau.

Fortunately, in proving a man not guilty of a certain murder, it is not necessary to prove him a saint or an angel. He may have been a devil at times, but the prosecution must prove that he was one at exactly the place and time of the crime.

Now, gasoline was more difficult to get in Nassau in those days than it was even in the United States. Most of it was flown to Nassau from the United States in planes so heavily overloaded that many of the pilots were killed in landing on the island.

The rationing permitted only enough petrol for a few miles a week. As was not entirely unknown in our own beloved country, those who had the money to buy it, bought it. A bank president and one of the leading real estate dealers and others were convicted of illegal purchases. They were heavily fined—"scolded but not sent away from home."

De Marigny was fined double the amount and banished. Ray had begged him to depart before he was deported. But he waited to be exiled. And was.

During the trial, Ray himself was threatened with deportation if he spent any time trying to investigate any other suspect than de Marigny. But they could not keep him from longing to return and prove his theory. His appeal to the governor-general, the Duke of Windsor, was icily rebuffed by a letter from the Duke's secretary. There are many men of business and other interests who do not want the case re-opened.

Ray wrote an article on the subject and flatly titled it: "I could crack the Oakes case." In the course of it, he tells how, one night before de Marigny's enforced exodus from the island, a party was given for him and Nancy by the Baron Trolle, in whose house Ray was staying, along with Leonarde Keeler, who had brought his lie-detection apparatus with him but had been refused all opportunity to use it.

He was persuaded to bring out his machinery and test the guests. He would have one of them look at a playing card which was not shown to him. Then he would ask such questions as "Was it a spade, a heart, a club, a diamond? Was it the ace, deuce, etc."

The guest would try in vain to conceal the truth. The needles always gave him or her away. After the polygraph had amused them all for some time, de Marigny suddenly asked for a test concerning the Oakes case.

It threw the guests into a grim mood, though, of course, even if the lie detector convicted him, he could not be tried again. Keeler and Ray were eager for this, to them, infallible proof, but they proposed that the test be made in private. De Marigny insisted on being put through then and there. He stipulated only that he should not be asked about his past.

The blood-pressure cuff was fitted to his upper right arm, the respiratory cable was fastened around his chest. The pulse measure was fixed to his wrist. The questions began:

"Is your name de Marigny? Do you live in Nassau? Have you had something to eat today?"

These answers were a quiet "Yes," but it was no more calm than the quiet "No" that followed the stabbing queries:

"Do you know who killed Sir Harry Oakes? Did you kill Sir Harry yourself? Did you put your hand on that screen?"

Ray and Keeler have seen the needles betray many a criminal, but the responses of de Marigny were final conviction that, when he was acquitted, an innocent man was saved from a cruel and odious injustice.

Ray will never be satisfied till he can go to Nassau and run through that polygraph mill a number of persons who would have to tell the lie detector what they know in spite of themselves. For, in Ray's words:

"Physical clues can rust and crumble with time, but a man's conscience remains fairly constant as long as he lives. The ability of the subject to differentiate between truth and falsehood and a fear of being unmasked are all that the lie detector needs to point an accusing needle."

But it is as certain as anything in this wavering world that the fearsome partnership of the polygraph and Schindler will never be invited back to Nassau.

# 5.

## HIS HARDEST CASE

Some people do not like stories of high life. They cannot
feel any sympathy for anybody who has fine clothes and a lot
of money. And they assume that any mishap to the rich
serves them right.

For such readers, here is a story of very humble people.
There is a banker in it; but he is a small-town banker and he
should be easily forgiven because of the modesty of his pros-
perity and because he spent more than he could afford trying
to save a Negro from going to the electric chair.

The New Jersey villagers had almost unanimously elected
the poor wastrel to it, just as the Bahamans chose the Count
de Marigny as their most popular candidate for the gallows.

The victim of this murder was the lowliest of the lowly, a
little ten-year-old girl seized on her way home from school,
dragged into a thicket and outraged, mutilated and slain.
And this was not far from the very spot where the accused
Negro admitted he was sleeping. It seemed that even so, the
screams of the child and the noise of the murder must have
caught his ear; but he claimed that he was too drunk to know
what was going on.

This appalling business of raping and butchering little
girls has grown to be a frightfully familiar commonplace in
our America of today; but it is always unbelievable and unendurable when it comes close to home. And it brings out
every resource of the mighty engines of justice to avenge it,
and keep the enraged people from wreaking vengeance in
blind wrath.

On the outskirts of that once fervently religious summer

116

resort, Asbury Park, New Jersey, is the Bradley public school. Among the pupils there was a young girl, Marie Smith, whose modest home was about a quarter of a mile straight down the road. On one side was a small forest; on the other, the gardens, the greenhouses and the home of Max Kruska, who kept a flower shop in the center of the town and lived in the house along with his wife, and a Polish servant, and a young German named Frank Heideman, who worked in the greenhouse and slept on the second floor of the house.

The school classes ended at three in the afternoon and little Marie was always home fifteen minutes later. One raw November day she did not come home on time and her mother went out in the road to look for her. The child was not to be seen. Her mother was worried and made inquiries.

Some of Marie's schoolmates said they had parted from her at a crossroad, and waved goodby as she struck out for home. The woods had hidden her from them almost at once. The mother's bewilderment turned to alarm. Soon the neighborhood was aroused. Searching parties ransacked the woods and the whole region in increasing bafflement. Day and night they hunted until on the third day they found what they had feared to find—the shattered and frozen body of the little girl thrust under a pile of brush close to a path through the woods.

The pitiful thing had been dragged into the woods, beaten over the head, and strangled with her own stocking cap, then beaten to death and outraged in hideous fashion with fiendish malice.

The first suspect was Thomas Williams, a Negro, an ex-convict who used that very path through the forest regularly on his way to cut wood for a woman living just beyond it.

On the very afternoon of Marie's disappearance, he had been seen going into the path and carrying a small axe. But he had not appeared at the house where he was expected as a wood-chopper.

He told the police that he had sat down on a log to take

a drink, had emptied a flask of whiskey and fallen asleep. He could not or would not explain what had become of the axe and he guessed that he "must have lost it somewhere." The axe could not be traced but a bloody towel was found in his room. And his mistress, with whom he had quarreled, gave him a reputation worse than his own and even said that he had told her he was "out after a little white girl."

What more evidence could be asked? Who can wonder that the townspeople, even of Asbury Park, were wrought up to a lynching fury? Such crowds collected at the jail that the Negro was slipped out secretly by a back door and hurried off to a prison in another town.

The county prosecutor, John B. Applegate, felt that the traditional speed of "New Jersey justice" was called for as never before and made ready for a swift trial. There was no excuse for delay. The evidence was clear and unmistakable.

But the county sheriff, Clarence Hetrick, had a doubt in his mind. The proof of Williams' guilt was a little too pat. He saw gaps in the evidence. He told his worries to Randolph Miller, vice president of a bank and president of the company that employed the father of little Marie. And just because Williams was worthless and good riddance, it seemed to those two just men that his guilt of murder should not be lightly assumed.

Miller proposed that a private detective be called in to work on the case secretly. He offered to share the expense with Sheriff Hetrick. So Ray Schindler was engaged and three weeks after the murder was committed, he reached Asbury Park with his brother Walter and a few helpers. Nobody but the sheriff and the banker knew of their errand.

They did not dare even to ask for a look at the evidence collected by the prosecutor. They had only what had been given to the public.

And now the Schindler method showed itself. The report of the autopsy stated that the girl had been hit on the head with a blunt instrument. But it did not say what kind of an instrument, of what shape or what weight. It said nothing of the number of blows or the angle from which they came. The wound was described as "from two to four inches long." Where was the all-important accuracy? There was no suggestion of a hunt for fingerprints.

Fortunately, the girl's body had been taken to Brooklyn for burial and it was possible for Ray to secure an exhumation and a careful autopsy without notifying the Asbury Park prosecutor.

Also, he had the little forest gone over by his brother with the utmost minuteness, and a detailed map was made of it.

Next, the process of elimination was begun. It had to be conducted with great care to avoid arousing suspicion. Thirteen people could have seen the little girl after she waved goodby to her playmates. One by one they were ruled out, women as well as men. There was a woman who, Ray suspected, might have heard some useless gossip, since she was a clairvoyant and astrologer by trade. To get her to talk freely, Ray had an advertisement inserted in a local paper calling for just such services as hers, and saw to it that the bait reached her. She bit at it and he sent a woman operator to talk to her.

Nothing came of all this trouble, but it is part of a detective's work to put bushels of chaff through the sieve with often not a grain of wheat to show for the toil.

At least she was eliminated both as a suspect and an aid. So were twelve others who might just possibly have had some knowledge.

With the sheriff's assistance, Ray also put a young Negro operative into the cell next to that where Williams hopelessly awaited his doom. For weeks this detective applied every known method of making him betray himself if he were guilty. All unwittingly Williams merely convinced his cellmate of his innocence.

The home of Max Kruska was the only house the little girl had passed, and all its occupants were studied. But the florist had been at his shop all the fateful afternoon; his wife had been seen shopping. The Polish maid had been busy in the kitchen, and also said she had seen Heideman working at his tasks all afternoon.

Young Heideman had the best of reputations. He had come from Germany and for three years had worked on the place and lived with the family. He never went out nights for dissipation and had saved most of his wages.

On being questioned he said he had known Marie Smith by sight but had never spoken to her and had not seen her on her last afternoon alive. In fact he had joined the searching parties and was one of those who discovered her. The prosecutor had ruled him out of consideration.

But Ray took no chances on appearances or reputations and he cabled to Germany. The answer stated that Heideman had been a rather gloomy boy, and had once been complained about for making indecent advances to a young girl. The magistrate had let him go with a warning; and before long Heideman had left for America.

He withstood all the tests Ray dared put him to, including the surprise confrontation with a bloody axe. Heideman took it calmly.

His employer refused to discharge him so that the detectives could get at him to question him thoroughly and "rope" him. In his desperation Ray remembered Conan Doyle's "Hound of the Baskervilles," the famous story in which the howling of a hound breaks the nerve of a murderer. He was reminded of it by the big and ferocious watchdog kept on the Kruska place. At night his chain was attached to a wire so that he could run the whole length of the yard and warn off possible marauders. Ray decided to try a bit of plagiarism.

That night, as soon as the lights went out in the Kruska home, Jack Stilwell, one of Ray's operatives, hid in the bushes and threw stones at the dog. The beast howled and leapt in fury. The lights went on in the house and Kruska and Heideman hurried out to see what prowler had excited the dog. They walked around the house but there was no trace of a trespasser.

The poor dog got a good scolding and Heideman and Kruska went back into the house. The lights went out. All was still.

Exactly an hour later, Stilwell resumed his bombardment and the dog renewed his uproar. His indignant owner put his head out and indulged in a few comments and warnings. An hour later, the dog went into hysterics again. Any disapproval he may have inspired was kept indoors, but the light went on and off in Heideman's window every time the dog made his hourly outburst. Peace came only with the daybreak.

The next night the dog began again his oratorio exactly at midnight. Kruska lighted up, marched around the house, cursed the dog, and went back in. With a maddening monotony the dog yelped and snarled every midnight for nine nights. Kruska's light did not go on again, but Heideman's did. It stayed on longer and longer. His shadow could be seen on his window shade. It was evident that he was pacing the floor.

Finally it was learned that Heideman had gone to his employer and said that the dog was getting on his nerves. Since he had never taken a vacation in all his three years, he thought he would like a respite of ten days in New York. Kruska said he had certainly earned it and wished him a happy time.

Heideman did not know that guardian angels from the Schindler stable shadowed him to the furnished room he rented in the German quarter near Fourteenth Street.

It is hard for the reader of what followed to realize the countless hours and the expense of time, money, and sleeplessness it cost Ray's staff to watch that young man's every movement. It is easy and brief to tell how it was discovered that he took his meals at the same little German restaurant with a regularity as to hours; but it took dreary days of watchful waiting to learn this.

Next was the business called "roping." It is Ray's principle that the suspect must never be approached by an operative. He must always approach the operative. Ray set one of his staff, Karl Neimeister, to the grim job of forcing Heideman to strike up an acquaintance with him. Ray picked Neimeister because he had been born in the same province as Heideman and knew the region perfectly.

His harrowing task was to reach the German restaurant ten minutes ahead of Heideman thrice daily and pay no attention to him. This went on for days before, at one crowded hour, Heideman chose the empty seat at Neimeister's table. Neimeister paid no attention to him, but went on reading his copy of the German daily paper, the *Staats-Zeitung*. Neimeister left first and took his paper with him. The next day the lonely Heideman sat down with Neimeister and commented on an item in the paper, which he read while it concealed Neimeister's indifferent face.

Even Job might have lost his patience if he had practiced being a private detective, but Neimeister managed to kill time for a week or two until Heideman invited him to a movie, then to a pinochle game. It was soon discovered that they came from the same neighborhood.

Ray had provided Neimeister with a bank credit and a banker to back up his fairy-tale that Neimeister had quarreled with his father and left for America, only to learn that his father had died and left him an estate of $90,000, from which the executor was paying Neimeister $75 a week till the inheritance could be legally cleared. This accounted for Neimeister's means of existence and his leisure. He took Heideman along to the bank one day while he drew the money, and the bank officials played their rôles like good actors.

Ray is forever recruiting the strangest people to play parts he may cast them in when he is producing one of his spectatorless dramas.

Within a week Heideman was so fond of Neimeister and so sick of his lonely existence that he proposed taking a room together to save them both money.

It is not hard to get anybody to tell his life story. It is hard to keep most people from doing just that. Neimeister knew Heideman's past better than it was told to him. For one thing Heideman said nothing about having ever worked in New Jersey. He said he had always worked on Staten Island. This alone proved that he had special reasons for extending his "vacation."

It was Ray Schindler's hope that Neimeister could somehow wheedle Heideman into confessing his crime to his friend. But he showed no such inclination. Slowly as time dragged on, it was running out perilously fast for poor Williams in his cell. The prosecutor was impatient to be rid of him by way of the Chair.

This was before the lie detector had been perfected; but Professor Hugo Muensterberg, then at Harvard, had attracted attention by his "spymograph" which recorded changes in blood pressure under the influence of various emotions.

Ray longed to reenact the crime at Asbury Park and test Heideman's reactions. But there was no way of bringing him to the test without alarming him.

Ray did the next best thing. He persuaded the manager of Heideman's favorite movie theater to run a short Italian horror-film which Ray had found. It cost $80 to persuade the manager. The film showed a young girl fleeing through a forest to escape from a fiend. She ran on until she had to jump off a cliff to escape him.

Ray put four operatives in the seats in front of, at the side of, and behind Heideman, when Neimeister easily persuaded him to drop in and see a show.

During the desperate flight of the little girl Heideman began to pant and squirm. When she leapt over a cliff and her broken little body was shown, Heideman leapt to his feet and told Neimeister that he had a splitting headache and must go for some medicine.

Neimeister let him go, and met him later in their room, where Heideman said his headache was better. He did not mention the film. Neither did Neimeister.

Having recruited a movie manager, Ray went next to his friend the publisher of the *Staats-Zeitung* and induced him to print on the front page of one copy a brief story about a young man named Frank Heideman, who had worked for a florist named Kruska in Asbury Park at the time of the murder of a little girl. The item said that a hammer had been found that might have been the instrument used and the sheriff wanted to show it to Heideman in the hope that he might know whose hammer it was. But according to the article Heideman had long overstayed his vacation and his employer was worried lest he might have met with some accident.

While they were at breakfast, Neimeister glanced at the paper and then shoved it to Heideman, saying in German something to this effect:

"That's funny, Frank. Here's a fellow with your very name in the paper."

It can be imagined how keenly Neimeister kept his eyes on Heideman as he read the story. Startled at first, he regained the self-control that had steeled him so long. He said calmly:

"That's me all right. I did work for Kruska at Asbury Park, but only for three weeks, and I didn't like the job so I came up here. I was there when the murder took place, but they've got the killer in jail now. They don't need me."

Neimeister quietly suggested that it would be a nice thing for Heideman to go down to Asbury Park and help them out. But Heideman did not think it was a nice idea at all. So Neimeister was once more at a dead end.

A good detective earns his money and more, and rarely tastes the sweets of fame. His greatest performances are enacted and improvised with only a small audience or none. There is no applause, and no praise from the critics.

A great actor is paid big money. His picture is put up on billboards and published in the papers. He calls himself an artist and may well be one. But he memorizes lines written for him by somebody else and he gives and takes cues to and from other actors whose lines have also been memorized. If the actor is lucky he plays the same part with the same expressions six nights a week and at two matinées for as long as may be.

The writer of plays considers drama the highest of high arts. He invents or borrows characters and plots and works them out at his leisure, changing his situations and his text till all runs smoothly to the conclusion of a happy or a tragic ending as he prefers. If the public agrees with his opinion of his work, the play runs on and on, perhaps for years, perhaps for centuries. Many troupes may play it at the same time in different languages. Posterity may acclaim the author a Euripides, a Molière, a Shakespeare, a Chekhov, or a Pulitzer Prize winner.

For this play-business which Shakespeare called a "two hours' traffic," the public gives its time, its money, its applause, its homage and its gratitude.

But the poor detective must write his own play as he goes along and act it with whatever actors may make their exits and entrances. He has a rough notion of the plot as he'd like to write it out, but he knows he never will. He has a dream of a last act, but never knows when or where it will be played and with what result. He must take whatever clues may be flung at him and improvise his replies to fit. He may spend long nights and days in watching a door or a window in rain or snow or frying sun, without attracting a bit of that attention which is the regular actor's meat and drink. At any moment he may have to make pursuit afoot or by car or train, and it may lead him through city streets, villages, deserts, forests, or overseas. At any moment he may find himself in an ambush where he will be beaten or slain, or worse yet, recognized.

And for all this, his reward is usually only a living wage and a life of oblivion and anonymity. Once in a while he may gain recognition by some brilliant fluke covering an age of almost unendurable monotony. But the best he is likely to get is to be told that he is another Sherlock Holmes, or a rival of some other imaginary sleuth whose work is carefully cut out for him by an imaginative author.

Once in ages the detective acquires fame and fortune by managing a detective bureau where, like a general, he lays the plans and supervises the strategy while he sends other men into the firing line.

So it was with young Karl Neimeister. For weeks and weeks he sought and endured the society of a stodgy young gardener whom he knew to be capable of mad frenzies and most horrible murder. He slept in the same room with this unpredictable maniac, and spent his waking hours trying to win from him confidence and a confession without once betraying his own identity or his true purpose. When it was safe he reported to his superiors what little he had learned and took his orders over the telephone.

Meanwhile, his employer was busy on a dozen other cases, and growing increasingly afraid that the innocent Negro would be put to death before he could win from the real murderer not only a confession, but a confession that could not be repudiated and could not be broken down in open court.

Convinced beyond a doubt of Heideman's guilt, Ray found it maddening not to seize him and hand him over to the Asbury Park prosecutor. But the prosecutor was just as convinced that Thomas Williams was the murderer, and Ray had no proof at all that could change his mind.

The item Ray had had published in the *Staats-Zeitung* was a desperate resort. It had resulted in Heideman's confession that he had been in Asbury Park, which Ray knew already.

But the knowledge that his presence was wanted in Asbury Park by the sheriff drove Heideman into a panic. He grew so restless in his sleep that he said he wanted to get out into the quiet of the country. Neimeister reported this to the office and Ray jumped at the idea. At his direction Neimeister proposed a quiet place in Yonkers. Heideman enjoyed the change, but was as far as ever from showing any signs of making a confidant of Neimeister.

The time was growing desperately short and Ray was driven to desperate measures. He talked it over with his brother Walter, saying:

"All murderers want to unburden their souls, and Heideman wants to unburden his; but he doesn't really trust Neimeister. He is still afraid that his friend might turn him in to the police. We've made Neimeister too respectable."

As Walter tells it, Ray broke off there and dashed up to Yonkers, whence he returned smiling:

"It's all arranged. Neimeister is going to commit a murder."

"A murder?" Walter gasped.

"A murder," said Ray. "Once he has done that, Heideman will feel that Neimeister is in the same boat with him and would not dare tell on him. Then he'll spill his own story. Just wait and see."

Now Neimeister was given a new and detailed scenario to perform. Suddenly he grew restless, expressed a need of fresh air and proposed that they hire a horse and buggy and go for a ride in the country. Heideman was all for it. They were soon enjoying the snow-white hills and the keen February air.

Eventually, on a lonely road, they overtook a roughly clad Italian workman who stopped them to ask for a light. Neimeister tossed him a box of matches. The man stood between the side wheels while he lighted his cigarette. The horse shied suddenly and the man yelled:

"My foot! You've run over my foot."

To a stream of profanity he added violence. He picked up a stone and hurled it.

In a rage Neimeister handed the reins to Heideman and jumped to the ground. The Italian ran back, then turned with his fists clenched. After a few blows were exchanged, the Italian drew a knife. Neimeister whipped out a pistol and fired twice. The workman toppled over in the snow and as his coat fell back, a big red stain showed on his shirt.

The panic-stricken Neimeister ran back to the buggy, seized the reins, whirled the horse about and drove back to Yonkers at top speed. Frank Heideman expressed his regret and horror, while Neimeister congratulated himself that there had been no witnesses of the scene except his friend.

But that very evening a newsboy was crying an extra of the Yonkers *Herald* in front of their house and, when Neimeister bought it, he showed Heideman the headlines:

## "ATROCIOUS MURDER DISCOVERED ON MIDLAND AVENUE

### Bloody Body of Italian found by Wilfred Smithson—

### Police on Trail

### Good Description of Stranger seen in Immediate Neighborhood has been Secured."

This threw Neimeister into a storm of terror. He cried, "I'm getting out of here this minute." Heideman would not desert him, and they got away to Philadelphia.

Heideman never dreamed that the Italian had risen from the dead as soon as his murderer fled, or that the Yonkers *Herald* had obligingly contributed one single copy of the front page story. But still Heideman could not be lured into any confession despite Neimeister's remorse and terror.

It was now March, and Marie Smith had been unavenged for four months. Furthermore, Ray was warned by Sheriff Hetrick and Banker Miller that their money was running as short as the time. They could grant Ray only three more weeks.

It was plainly necessary to speed up Heideman's unburdening of his soul. Ray's inventive mind sketched out another act. This must have an audience.

Leaving to the imagination the countless details, the planning, and the coordination of scenes, this is the way it worked out.

First, Ray went to Asbury Park with his brother and met by appointment the Banker and the Sheriff, this time in the office of the hostile Prosecutor. When Mr. Applegate learned that for three months all this action had been going on behind his back, he was furious. He was completely convinced that Williams was guilty and he ridiculed the story of the howling dog, the horror movie, the fake murder. He accused Ray of fooling Miller and Hetrick for the sake of the big money he was making out of them. He offered to put Ray under arrest then and there as Schindler the Swindler. When Miller and Hetrick would not prefer charges, he ordered them all out of his office. Worse yet, he absolutely refused to go to Atlantic City, where Ray promised to bring Heideman to the confession point in a hotel room fitted with a dictograph connected with an adjoining room.

But Ray was not whipped yet. He said:

"If Applegate won't come to the confession, we'll bring the confession to Applegate."

In the meanwhile Neimeister was persuading Heideman to go to Atlantic City where, he said, they would not be noticed in the off-season. Ray was now adding the North German Lloyd Steamship Company to his production. On their letter head he had a letter written saying that Neimeister's check had been received and a stateroom reserved for him on the *Kronprinzessin Cecile*. This was conveyed to Neimeister in a gaudy envelope.

By now Heideman's money was low and he was urging Neimeister to collect his inheritance and go to California,

where they could set up a florist's business. Neimeister said
he thought it an excellent idea, and agreed to it. But he left
the hotel room to buy some cigarettes, and left the envelope
conspicuously sticking half out of his coat pocket.

And now the audience and the ensemble were assembled,
wondering if the climax would be a triumph or a fiasco. In
the next room were Walter Schindler, a number of operatives,
and a stenographer.

The dictograph brought them the sound of Heideman's
chair as he pushed it back and rose to see what the envelope
in Neimeister's coat pocket might mean. There was a smoth-
ered curse. Then silence. Neimeister came back. Heideman denounced him for a false friend, pretending to be ready
to go to California even while he had his ticket for Germany
in his pocket.

Neimeister confessed his deception but said he was fleeing
from this country for fear of the discovery of his crime.
Heideman had been a witness but, in spite of his promise of
secrecy, Neimeister said he would not trust even such a
friend as Heideman not to turn him over to the police.

There was a silence almost unbearable in the next room.
It must have been torture to Neimeister, whose histrionic skill
had now reached the breaking-point of his three months'
ordeal.

Suddenly the dam broke in Frank Heideman's soul. He
cried out:

"Karl, I am a murderer, too. I killed that little girl in
Asbury Park. Now you can see why I could never dare give
you up to the police."

Neimeister rose to the heights. He pretended unbelief and
Heideman had to convince him by telling the gory details:

"When the little girl passed me on the road I asked if she
wanted some flowers to take to her mother. I took her into
the greenhouse; but I pretended I could not cut any flowers
for her because I must have dropped my knife while I was
cutting some ferns in the woods. I asked her to help me look

for it. I led her by the hand. In the woods I frightened her and she screamed. I tried to quiet her with her own stocking cap. I couldn't. There was a hatchet in the pocket of my overalls. I had to use it for fear she would tell."

All of this was recorded by the stenographer as the breathless listeners heard it through the tell-tale dictograph.

Walter telephoned the great news to Ray, who came down from New York on the first train.

It had not been hard to persuade Hetrick and Miller to come to Atlantic City and steal into that adjoining room. The problem now was to rope Heideman into repeating his blood-chilling performance.

The almost incredible Neimeister pretended that he was still incredulous, and forced Heideman to insist on his own guilt and prove it by adding further ghastly details.

Still Neimeister had to remain with the terrible Heideman while Ray and Miller and Hetrick hastened to Asbury Park to lay the report before the Prosecutor.

The corroboration by the Banker and the Sheriff swept away Applegate's last doubts and his old beliefs. He took it big. He confessed his complete conviction and offered his complete cooperation.

There was a final exquisite touch; to avoid the complication of arresting Heideman in Atlantic City, Neimeister was told to promise that he would take the wretch with him to Germany. Their train to Hoboken would pass through Monmouth County.

So Heideman went gratefully along on what he supposed to be a return to Germany. As the train stopped at Red Bank, a county detective who knew Heideman took him off the train and Karl Neimeister put on a last show. He waxed so violent in protest that he was taken along and thrown into the same cell.

Even yet there was danger that Heideman would engage a lawyer and be advised to repudiate the confession. Once more Ray had one of those one-copy newspapers of his printed. It carried a story telling of Heideman's confession and giving a number of the details wrong. Neimeister showed it to Heideman and the Prosecutor and the Schindler brothers listened by way of a dictograph in the next cell.

"It says here that you hit the girl on the head with an axe, then choked her," said Neimeister.

"That's wrong," Heideman snapped, "I choked her first with the stocking cap. When she still screamed I hit her with the hatchet."

"It says here you threw away the axe in the woods."

"No, it was a hatchet. I buried it behind the greenhouse. They haven't got anything on me yet. We can still go to Germany, can't we, Karl?"

The next day Ray Schindler entered the cell with the confession all typewritten out. Heideman was stunned, but that magnetic way of Ray's soon had his signature. The hatchet was found where he had said it was buried.

The trial was held promptly and the jury's verdict was inevitable—death. The long-suffering Williams was released and the county paid him far more money for false arrest than he would ever have earned if he had been free. His ex-sweetheart confessed that she had maligned him because she was mad at him.

Sheriff Hetrick was elected Mayor of Asbury Park and kept the office for 22 years.

Monmouth County refunded to Hetrick and Miller the money they had spent for the investigation by the Schindler Bureau.

Heideman was naturally bitter against Karl Neimeister whose magnificent artistry he could hardly be expected to applaud. He would never speak to his old friend again.

But toward Ray Schindler, who had invented and stage-managed the whole drama, Heideman had no bitterness. He said Ray had a job to do and did it. A good detective story seems to be irresistibly fascinating even if you are the victim

of it. And it would be hard to find a better detective story—
almost as hard to find as to tell well.

Shortly before Heideman's last day in the death cell, he
sent for Ray and had a long and friendly talk with him. He
offered to answer any further questions and said he was
not averse to paying the penalty.

That sordid tragedy in low life cost Ray Schindler more
time and toil for less reward than any other in his crowded
career. He says of the young murderer:

"When Heideman sent for me and I visited him in death
row in the Trenton, New Jersey prison, I was very curious to
know what he wanted of me, and was also interested in the
fact that he had sent for the very man who caused his conviction.

"Heideman had been away from his home in Germany for
eight or ten years and had not kept in close touch with his
family. They did not know of his conviction for the murder
of little Marie Smith, and he did not want his sister or his
mother to know of it. He wanted to talk over with me some
plan by which eventually after his death, I could arrange
to have some kind of a letter written as though I were an
acquaintance of his and that he had met with an accidental
death. If by any chance his family should hear that he had
committed a murder, he wanted me to assist in having a
proper letter of explanation written to his mother so that the
true facts would not be so revolting.

"He apparently had no feeling against me. He compli-
mented me on the job that I had done, and said it was all in
my day's work, but he said that he would give anything if
before he died he could get his hands around the neck of Karl
Neimeister, the man I had used in roping him and getting
him to confess the killing of Marie Smith.

"Heideman, like Dr. Waite (and there are few such instances), refused to allow his attorneys to ask for a stay of
electrocution. Practically all persons convicted of murder

are granted a stay and a later date is set for the death penalty. Heideman and Waite wanted to get it over with at the first possible moment. Heideman wished to plead guilty to the charge of murder, but, properly, the State of New Jersey does not accept a plea of guilty in a capital case.

"In actions, looks, manner of speech, he greatly resembled Bruno Hauptman, who kidnapped and killed the child of Charles Lindbergh. Both boys committed similar terrible crimes; both were from Germany, and they were the same age, about twenty-seven years."

# 6.

# THE WOMAN OF
# TOO MANY PASTS

When a young woman has beauty, brains, ambition, and courage but no money and no morals, she is apt to go far—too far for the good of one or more deluded, infatuated, otherwise useful men.

There was the poor little Lithuanian orphan named Martha Skovronsky, whose guardians married her off to a Swedish dragoon. She did not live with him long, but rose steadily in her social career by serial degradation as the mistress of a private soldier, then of a corporal, a sergeant, and so on and on till she was captured by the Russians and presented to a Prince. In his house the young Czar, Peter the Great, met her, gave her a child, then divorced his Czarina, and made his mistress the Empress of Russia under the name of Catherine I.

He loved her so well that, when she was accused of flirting with a young man of the court, Peter the Great simply had the young man's head cut off and put in a bottle of alcohol, which he compelled his wife to keep in her apartment. That did not keep him from continuing to visit her there. He let her nurse him when he was dying. She made a wonderful Empress.

The second and more famous Catherine the Great, was a German girl who was married to the nephew of the Czarina Elizabeth. Elizabeth had a lover but they cut his tongue out lest he should talk too much. Rugged fellows those Russians! When Catherine II's husband became Czar she brushed him aside and finally had him brushed off by a little murder party. She reigned magnificently thereafter.

Then there was Madame de Maintenon. There was Madame du Barry; there was the West Indian adventuress, Josephine, who married Napoleon. But why go on?

This is the story of an American girl, who began humbly as the daughter of a Chicago butcher and made the most of her opportunities with as little scruple as those royal mistresses. She never got a chance at a King, but she did her best with what she could find. She obtained great riches; but she was robbed of her just dues of fame. And I am not going to give even her name.

For her final defeat Ray Schindler was to blame. He was called in to suppress both her and her ambitions. And he snuffed her out like a candle, leaving only a little bad smell not discoverable at any distance.

He never had less trouble finding evidence against anybody. It was dumped upon him till he was knee-deep in it. She had collected it herself and kept it together for her own purposes. Then it was accidentally spilled at the feet of her stupefied husband, whose love and trust were annihilated in one dreadful moment.

Once more we have an elegant story to study. This is no shabby and toilsome account of saving a low Negro convict from being put to death for killing the child victim of a young German gardener.

This is a story that opens in the mansion of a millionaire and runs backward through palaces in Europe and the splendor of titled folk.

Ray's problem was what to do with his evidence. It was an embarrassment of riches. But the finding of it did not stop the lady. She had just begun to fight. Her ways were dark, but she was perfectly willing to face the glare of publicity —which was the one thing her latest victim dreaded.

This story is a kind of duel in the dark. Ray Schindler's principal aim was to keep it dark.

It would be hard for the most reckless melodramatist to concoct a scene of such paralyzing surprise as befell the hero of this tale. Since suppression was of the essence of his appealing to Ray Schindler for salvation from the front pages, all the names in this chapter will be imaginary except Ray's.

John Andrew Belton (so to speak) was a famous plutocrat whose first wife had died leaving him children and grandchildren. He mourned her for fifteen years before he was infatuated by a beautiful American—call her Mrs. Bogus—whom he met in Europe. She was forty, she said; he was sixty, he admitted.

They met again in America after their separate homecomings, and he proposed marriage. She consented and he gave her the title to his great Fifth Avenue home along with a quarter of a million dollars in cash.

In her travels she had accumulated much fine furniture, bric-à-brac, and souvenirs of all sorts. She had kept her precious belongings in storage in Chicago and he gallantly offered them more convenient shelter in one of his warehouses. Forgetting all about a deskful of letters, she agreed and went to New England for a brief visit.

During her absence, her husband was called to the telephone by the warehouse superintendent with a tale of woe. One of Mrs. Belton's desks had been broken in transfer and a mass of personal papers had fallen out. They were so confused that the superintendent sent them to the house for Mr. or Mrs. Belton to rearrange.

If he had had more curiosity Mr. Belton would never have married Mrs. Belton without looking into her past a bit. So he got it all in an avalanche.

As he was toting the cardboard boxes filled with her papers into her room, a passport caught his eye. Even a passport photograph could not disguise his wife beyond his recognition.

But the name under it was not Mrs. Bogus. It was—say, Mrs. Frieda De Seaver. Furthermore, her age, as he rapidly computed it with trembling fingers, would now be fifty-one, not forty-one.

It is a minor sin for a lady to lop a few years off her age, but when she takes off ten and fails even to mention two or three previous husbands, her latest worshipper may be excused for feeling a major disillusionment.

Mr. Belton could be also excused for going through the rest of her papers. From neat bundles of letters, he learned that his trusted spouse had been on most intimate terms with at least a score of men. Mrs. Belton, in her modest way, had collected as many lovers as Catherine the Great.

If he had had a weaker constitution the latest recruit to her regiment would have crawled to the telephone and panted for a doctor. Instead, he dialled a famous lawyer.

The lawyer was a famous one and a wise one. After a brief glance at the memoirs of the polyandrous Pollyanna, the lawyer said that this was not a matter for one who tried cases in courts. It was a case for a keeper-outer of courts. It was a case that only Ray Schindler could handle.

Within an hour the bushels of documents were transferred to Ray's private apartments. He set about sorting and arranging the chaos and he found what he has described as "a library of novels in which the plots were identical and only the names and locations different."

That butcher's daughter must have had more than her share of charm and less than human scruples about pouring it on. One German baron, after squandering a fortune on her, had shot himself because she had said she had no further use for him. A rich American had heard of his son's mad passion for the woman and had dashed to the rescue, only to tumble head over heels in love with the siren himself.

Freida's first important conquest, after she began business in Chicago, was one of America's greatest and most profligate railroad promoters. He made a serious mistake—or had the good luck to take her to a concert, where a Danish pianist stirred Freida's musical emotions—also her ambitions.

She met the pianist and married him up. He took her to Europe and introduced her to the artistic and aristocratic world over there. They entertained in their home the King of Belgium and other high titles. But when he lost his health and with it the use of his gifted hands, he lost his Frieda.

She did not return home to the parental butcher shop. In fact, her mother and father died without knowing what had become of her; and when Ray began ransacking her labyrinthine career he turned up two brothers and a sister, who had not heard from her for thirty-five years. They had supposed her dead long since.

The first thing Ray had to do was to unmarry her from the millionaire. If her Danish pianist had not divorced her by dying, she was still his wife, and "Mrs. Belton" was only a sort of pen-name with no legal force.

So Ray packed up a mass of papers concerning her European adventures, and took ship for Copenhagen. There he learned that the Dane, who had once been a court pianist, had retired to a hamlet in Scotland.

Edinburgh was Ray's next stop. In its outskirts he found the first of Mrs. Belton's husbands. He was nearly eighty years old, and was earning Scottish pittances as a piano teacher.

Ray's arrival was an earthquake in the old man's eventless existence. But he ridiculed Ray's story of Frieda's livelihood, because she had been dead for years and years. He proved it by a newspaper clipping that he still possessed.

Divorces are difficult in Denmark, so Frieda, with fine American impatience of delay, had simply paid to have her own obituary published in an American newspaper. Nothing could be easier. She had seen to it that a clipping reached her husband, and that was that. Whom God had joined, a newspaper notice had put asunder.

Evidently the Dane still believed anything he read in an American newspaper. Distance lends not only enchantment, but conviction. So the pianist decided that he had been divorced by the Great Reaper, and he was now free to marry again. Which he did.

A divorce by way of a fraudulent obituary notice is not legal in America—not even in Nevada—at least not without establishing what is laughingly known as a "residence" and paying a few fees. Even then, for the plaintiff to demand a divorce on the ground that she was dead, would puzzle those demarriers. They would not be sure just where she had established her residence. So Frieda sued the Dane she had deserted and alleged that he had deserted her. A genial judge granted her the divorce.

Ray offered the Danish pianist another pleasant and profitable tour of America without the necessity for beating his livelihood out of the ivories. The Dane refused but Ray persuaded his present wife that he had better go and contradict the slanders Frieda would utter if he didn't. So he went.

Having provided for his transportation to America, Ray went South and East as far as Leipzig where there was an enormously rich manufacturer who had a grudge against Frieda, because she had given him whatever the German is for the double-cross. My *Deutsches Lexikon* gives "*Doppel-Kreuz,*" but refers it to the sign of the double sharp used in music.

In any case, the Leipzig *millionär* was still bitter enough against Frieda to consent to visit America.

Paris was Ray's next station and there he hunted for a French Count whose letters were numerous in Frieda's dossier. But the Count had lost his chance to join the convention in America. He had been dead for many years. The insatiable Schindler, however, traced an old family butler who knew things about Frieda that only a butler can know. He thought it would be rather nice to have a look at *l'Amérique* at Ray's expense.

Then Ray sped back across the Atlantic with three unimpeachable witnesses to prove that Frieda had married wisely but too often.

On his arrival he found a new complication. In addition to his mansion on Fifth Avenue, Belton owned a majestic castle on the Hudson. His lawyer planned to have a quiet annulment of the marriage in a little village near by, where reporters would not break in and break out in headlines. It had been easy to get the unsuspecting Frieda into the castle. But getting her out was something else again. And Belton wanted that ancestral home at any cost. He wanted Frieda out of it as well as out of his life.

Relying on the power of her old thrall, Frieda insisted on talking things over. Belton had to consent. But he took Ray along to the tryst. As soon as Frieda saw her once so compliant slave, in Ray's words, "she flowed toward him. 'John darling!' she sobbed in a rich contralto."

She made what Ray considered an excellent speech. But she suffered the handicap of repeating the fascinating tricks she had already used, not only on Belton, but in the letters that had already made his eyes pop and flare.

He coldly advised her to get a lawyer and get out. Ray served the annulment papers on her, and departed with the husband in name only.

Getting Frieda evicted was like extracting a tick or a chigger. Belton tried everything. There was a vast amount of coal in the cellar and he ordered his servants to burn it all in a week. When he failed to sweat out Frieda, he gave orders that the furnaces were to be shut down, though the weather was now bitter cold. He also took away all the servants.

It was a midwinter before Frieda was frozen out. Then she made a flea-like hop into the Fifth Avenue home.

Meanwhile, the trial was quietly held in obscurity. The Dane, the Leipziger and the butler from Paris testified, and the court "took the case under advisement"—a legal expression for "put it in cold storage."

And now Fate intervened with two swift strokes that no one could have foreseen and no author would be unscrupulous enough to ask a reader to believe.

The long series of shocks and the blows to his pride and his affections had not only broken Belton's heart but worn it out. Suddenly and quietly he died.

The indomitable Frieda claimed to be his widow and put up such a bluff and made such threats of publicity that Belton's children by his first marriage gave her half a million dollars to withdraw her claim to Belton's name and wealth.

She consented. But Frieda, too, had lived under a strain that would have crushed or paralyzed a normal being. She enjoyed her ill-got gains for just two weeks. Then pneumonia got her and this time, when her obituary appeared in the advertisements, it was for keeps. The judge probably still has the case "under advisement."

And now, by what Thomas Hardy would have called one of "life's little ironies"—though this was a pretty big irony—Frieda's two neglected brothers and her forgotten sister suddenly had half a million dollars to divide among them. What evil or good that unearned fortune did to them was none of Ray's business—or ours.

If this story had been imagined and written by a good writer of mystery stories, he would never have dared do to his characters what real life did to them. But since this is a chronicle of fact, it seems a pity not to tell Frieda's real name and give her credit for the resourcefulness and the courage that carried her so far from the shabby butcher shop where her father carved meat while she carved golden destinies for herself.

The famous—or infamous—Betty Jumel—of Jumel's Mansion—started a little lower, went a little farther, and lived a good deal longer and will live forever in the history of America's wily women. But to give Frieda's real name to posterity would not only undo all the benefits of Ray Schindler's skill and toil, but would cause unnecessary harm to the good name of an honorable family. Frieda did enough to them while she lived. Let them—and her—rest in peace.

# 7.

# CINEMA SHAKEDOWN

Successful criminals keep one jump ahead of crime-detection; and unsuccessful ones try to. The motion picture had hardly begun its world-shaking career when swindlers swarmed to it as a new weapon.

This story dates back to the time when New York and New Jersey were the scene of the growing pains of what was to become one of the major industries and recreations of mankind. At that time Hollywood did not envelop the whole motion picture spirit. Hollywood was still a rural suburb of little Los Angeles. The studios, such as they were, were established in upper New York City on Long Island and across the Hudson on the New Jersey Palisades.

Since the beginning of the world, mad moralists have been laying the blame for the eternal wickednesses of the world on the latest novelty in costume, amusement, mechanism or entertainment. At one time it was the sofa; at another the horse and buggy; then the bicycle, the automobile, corsets, short skirts, makeup, cigarettes, newspapers, novels, the theater, the motion picture. Of late television has been attracting the attention of the frenzied blamers. But the most modern sins are the same old primeval sins with a slight change of costume and dialect.

So, in this instance, the then very modern motion picture just happened to be a handy instrument for the extortion of hush-money. And extortion under threat of exposure is as old as man and woman.

There was certainly nothing novel in the fact that a certain wealthy man had an affair with a young woman who was not

143

his wife. He was not the first, nor the millionth, man to squander money and jewelry on his fair companion, and to travel with her. And, rash as he was, he did not invent the silly risk of trying to keep secret from his family what was no secret to innumerable other people.

Well, this man—call him Adamson to indicate the antiquity of his folly—and this young woman—called her Lilith, to indicate the antiquity of her most ancient profession— used to travel about together. Adamson lived in the midwest, but he had occasion to make an annual business trip to Europe. His wife stayed at home to keep house for the family, and Lilith went abroad to keep the husband company.

Some men buy their wives jewelry as an atonement for their outside affairs, and some men buy jewelry as an inducement for those outsiders. This Adamson bought his Lilith gleaming souvenirs of every one of those trips abroad. She smuggled them in without paying any duty. She had a rather light notion of duties.

This went on for years and years till finally even the U. S. Customs Department took notice. When one of its detectives, Bill Nye, by name, was assigned to the case, he unearthed a startling total of loot. So Adamson was arrested and compelled to pay one of the largest fines ever imposed on a smuggler. This exploded in the headlines.

Adamson promptly lost his taste both for headlines and for Lilith, and he was willing to call it quits. His wife and family forgave him on condition that the affair ended there.

But Lilith was not one of those whom cruel men discard and toss overboard into oblivion. She was a capitalist as well as he was, and she was eager to capitalize on the splendor of her jewels twice-paid-for. She had ambitions for a stage career and there were managers who would have been glad to take advantage of all the glowing publicity at her command. She thought also that her life-story would make a very interesting serial and a best seller.

But Adamson was sick enough of having to lick his

wounds; he had no desire to advertise them. So he paid a big firm of lawyers to buy her off. They drew up a really binding agreement by which she agreed to keep his relations with her absolutely quiet in return for an annual fortune. He took a 99-year lease on her silence and paid a high rental for it.

She kept her part of the bargain for several years. But love will find a way. She cast her lot with an enterprising young man who had entered the new field of writing suddenly opened by the infant industry whose father was the kineto-scope and whose nursery was the nickelodeon.

But this young scriptwright who had fallen in with Lilith had dreams of his own. She told him her story, of course, and he saw in it possibilities for fortune far beyond the shabby wages of the scenarists of that day. He said that the big money would come not from expression but suppression.

If that man Adamson would pay Lilith a handsome yearly income for just keeping her lovely mouth shut and her face out of the newspapers, what wouldn't Adamson pay to keep her story—and his—off the screen, which was just dazzling the world by the vast and vaster multitudes being drawn to the vast and vaster movie palaces?

This script-writer was as wise as he was wicked. Call him by the name of an ancient highwayman, Claude Duval. He realized that it would be stupid just to go to Adamson and say:

"I am going to write the story of Lilith and you as a sce-nario, unless you pay me a lot of money."

Adamson would either beg him off at prevailing literary rates, or have him jugged as a blackmailer. So Duval built a structure worthy of the later Hollywood word "colossal."

He wrote a scenario so closely illustrating the romance of Adamson and Lilith and the Customs House and the an-nual retainer that everybody would have recognized Adam-son as the leading character, no matter what name was given him on the screen.

Duval did not stop there. He pretended to have unlimited

backing for the production, and he signed contracts with several of the most prominent actors of the day. No less personages than William S. Hart and Bert Lytell were engaged for the leads, and equally prominent women stars were engaged. The natural stipulation was, of course, that salaries would begin as soon as the shooting began. Duval hoped that the first day of shooting would be never.

But he did not stop there. He went to one of the most glitteringly high-priced directors, Herbert Brenon, and signed him up at his own price.

Motion picture trade-magazines were already springing up, so Duval wrote out a sketch of his plot and had it printed in one of them, along with the names and pictures of the galaxy of stars he had engaged. Since the Adamsons were not likely to read the trade-magazine, Duval placed clippings of the article in a number of envelopes carrying no hint of his name or address or purpose.

He sent these clippings to all the members of the Adamson family and to the firm of lawyers that had drawn up the contract pledging Lilith to silence. A hasty glance at the outlines of the plot was enough to remind them all of those horrible headlines. They realized that Lilith had found a way to increase her income without breaking her vow of silence. Wasn't the story to appear only in the silent pictures? Adamson and his lawyers could see that the whole affair smelled of blackmail to high heaven—or low hell.

So they called in Schindler.

And Ray began to construct a little scenario of his own. Talk of "Hamlet" containing a play within a play! Before Duval got through with the scenario he had written around Adamson, he learned that a cleverer hand had written a scenario around the man who had written a scenario around a man.

First Ray did a bit of reconnaissance. He soon learned that Duval was living with Lilith, and doubtless on the money she extorted from Adamson. For Duval had neither money of his own nor backing enough to finance anything.

Next Ray approached him as an agent of Adamson and flatly offered to buy Duval off if terms could be agreed on.

Duval was almost prophetic, for he named a sum that was appalling in those days, and would but yesterday have kept a mediocre screenwriter comfortable for half a year.

Ray said he would talk it over with his clients. He had already proved that Duval was only a blackmailer.

Next, Ray called on Herbert Brenon, whom he had never met and whom he found directing a Russian picture, "The Fall of the Romanoffs." It was as hot and humid as only New York can be in mid-July, but the poor actors were toiling in an imitation Russian street piled high with imitation snow. The furs they wore were not imitation and their problem was to keep their sweat from cascading over the pelts in which they were buried.

Ray stood mopping his brow and marvelling at the actors martyrized for art's sake. When the shot was ended and the company dismissed for a change to even heavier costumes, Ray asked Herbert Brenon for a few words.

That most amiable and honest of men granted the request with a smile. It did not take Ray long to explain what Duval was up to and what Brenon was signed up to. As soon as he realized his part in Duval's scheme of extortion, Herbert put on a scene that would have made Czar Boris Godunov envious. When he had calmed down a little he cheerfully consented to play a leading rôle in Ray's scenario based on a scenario.

When Ray had fitted Herbert's office up neatly and completely with dictographs, and arranged for overhearing and recording the ensuing parleys, Herbert invited Duval in for a conference. Then he did his stuff as an actor and read lines to this general effect:

"I was reading over your scenario and I've just discovered

that it bears a striking resemblance to the—the—oh, the Adamson case that made so much noise some years ago. Had you noticed it?"

Duval smiled and winked and murmured:

"We planned it that way."

"But," Herbert protested, "they might object to having that old family scandal revived. They might sue us for heavy damages."

While Duval grinned on like a cat about to eat a canary, Herbert forced his innocent Irish features into as much of a crafty smile as he could manage and laughed:

"Perhaps they would pay us a handsome sum not to make the film at all. Had you thought of that? Oh, I see you have."

He tried to substitute a look of greedy admiration, for the loathing he felt and Duval felt his ambitions soaring. Feeling sure that in Brenon he had found a zesty collaborator, he said:

"We planned it that way, me and the little woman, Lilith. But it occurs to me that the bigger investment we can show beside the expectation of profit, the bigger sum we can shake out of that old plutocrat. So I was just thinking—if I tear up your contract and sign a new one with you for double the present figure, it would make a better showing, especially when we add to it the salaries of all the actors and actresses engaged, and the art-directors, set-builders, lightmen, crew-men, costumers and what not. We'll make up a grand total that will make that old capitalistic rake feel sorry he ever treated poor Lilith so mean. Of course, I'll take good care of you for going along with us."

Herbert promised to go along with him and suggested another conference that night to settle all the fine points. He suggested also that it might be well to bring Lilith along since she had really inspired the whole idea and it would be well to keep her satisfied that she was not being double-crossed by her new partners.

The purpose of this was, of course, to get Lilith involved and the whole plot recorded in its ugliest details.

That night Lilith and Duval and Herbert met in Brenon's office. Duval and Lilith were so delighted with their conspiring that they never thought to wonder if they could be conspired against. It never occurred to them to look into the adjoining room, where Ray and a member of the Adamson family and the whole firm of lawyers sat in silence and listened to every word that was said.

Lilith, the pretty bloodsucker, was elated at the golden opportunity to threaten with bankruptcy and shame the fellow-sinner who had already heaped jewels and riches on her. Duval gloated over his skill in both plagiarizing his plot from Adamson and making his victim buy his own story. The vile mistress and the viler man whom she was keeping were so proud of their infamy that they needed little coaching from Herbert to tell the whole story over and over and repeat the foul purpose of their collaboration.

While they were waxing gleeful over the look in old Adamson's eyes and his lawyers' eyes when they saw the full amount of the bill they'd have to pay, the door opened and in walked a little procession. Ray Schindler, one of the Adamsons, and the lawyers.

The only reward Herbert got out of it was when Duval accused him of being a double-crosser. That gave the Hibernian Herbert a good excuse for vaulting over his desk and presenting Duval with a pair of lovely black eyes for imagining that Herbert could have really meant to take part in the business.

The first thing Ray had to do was to rescue Duval from the director and lift him off the floor. The baffled blackmailers were so crushed by the suddenness with which their castle in Spain had fallen over on them, that they waited in meek terror while the lawyers drew up a full confession for them to sign.

Poor Lilith even consented to give up her annual stipend

for silence. Menaced now with a long prison term she was glad to be given her liberty at all.

She and Duval departed into the outer darkness. All they had now was each other. And with their knowledge of each other and all that crooked money vanished before it could be grasped, what a loving couple they must have been! There's quite a story there, a romance of a Gorki sort, if anyone wanted to go underground to get it. That girl's memories must have been quite a treasure of a sort.

As for the actors and actresses and all the others who had signed contracts with the great Duval, it is doubtful that they ever knew what was going on or had gone on. When they received word that the production was called off, they doubtless took it as just another of those things. The Adamson case was probably the most successful silent picture that was never done.

# 8.

# BLACKMAIL AS AN INDUSTRY

Few human beings have lived long without committing some sin or folly that they would almost rather die than have known. There's the story of the man who said: "There isn't anybody on earth who hasn't something in his past that would ruin him if it were published."

"Oh, I can't believe that," said an optimistic friend. "There must be lots of people who have led faultless lives."

"Maybe so, maybe so," said the cynic. "But the best man I ever knew was old Bishop Coldwell of our town. And just for a test of my theory we sent him an anonymous telegram simply saying, 'All is discovered.' "

"Yes? And what did the good Bishop do about it?"

"Nobody knows. He's never been seen since."

On the other hand there is the famous story of the Duke of Wellington.

According to the legend, he wrote some indiscreet letters to a young woman and when he withdrew his financial support she thought she might turn a dishonest penny by giving them to the press. The Iron Duke made the best answer one can make to such a blackmail. He answered her threat with his usual succinctness. He said:

"Publish and be damned!"

But then not everybody is as unmarried as the old hero of Waterloo was. Not everybody is as used as he was to losing battles and winning unpopularity. He had been hooted in the street and forced to put iron shutters on his windows. It is not everybody who can face odium with a Wellingtonian indifference.

Blackmail is a terrible weapon to aim at people who have yielded to temptation or have been lured into ambushes where they have committed what are mildly called "indiscretions."

Some people commit suicide to escape exposure. Some commit murder. Others bankrupt themselves. Once the first blackmail is paid, the road to ruin has been entered; for a blackmailer's promises are worthless and there is no end to the extortion. If the exposure is for the public good or for the destruction of a good reputation that is undeserved, the person in possession of the knowledge should go to the police with it, or to the press. But the victim of blackmail rarely dares to visit the police with the news of the threat because it then becomes the duty of the police to act upon the information publicly.

This is where the private detective comes in. One of his chief tasks is keeping private affairs private.

Sometimes the blackmailer preys upon the father or mother, husband or wife of the guilty one. Sometimes there has been no real guilt but only a situation that can be made to look ugly in the public prints. Sometimes a man or woman is entangled in an innocent affair that can be made to look atrocious by a description easier to misunderstand than to explain.

One day I had a luncheon engagement with Ray. I received word that he would have to change it to dinner. He had had a sudden call. He was unable to keep the dinner engagement either. I learned the reason two days later.

There was a certain wealthy man who had found an old friend of his without a job and in great need of help. The millionaire gave him a confidential position at a big salary. One day the millionaire received a cablegram saying that a woman in Italy was dying of a slow obscure disease that could be cured only by a certain new drug made only in America. Her doctor implored the millionaire to send some of the drug by airmail at once. The millionaire learned that the drug had been recently put on the list of forbidden narcotics and a heavy penalty placed on the sale of it. The manufacturer, hearing the story, offered to give, not sell, the millionaire a sufficient quantity of the drug. The millionaire told a friend in the State Department, and he consented to put the drug in the diplomatic pouch for England. This was done. The medicine was there placed in another diplomatic pouch and flown to Italy. There another State official gave it to the doctor. He gave it to the patient.

The millionaire felt as glad and proud as a Boy Scout who has done his good deed for the day. He had saved a life without breaking a law.

But the young man he had lifted out of poverty saw a chance to get rich quick. He told the millionaire who had befriended him that he would tell his own version of the whole story to the Narcotic Squad unless the millionaire paid him the tidy sum of $150,000.

The millionaire saw ahead of him a public trial with a blaze of the most unpleasant notoriety. Even if he went to the police himself, there might be very serious difficulties about clearing, not only himself but everybody else involved in the transaction.

So he telephoned to Ray Schindler. Just how Ray silenced the blackmailer is one of the numberless secrets of his busy career. The laws against narcotics were meant to prevent criminals from getting rich by selling forbidden drugs to addicts. The business is a gigantic and a loathsome one, and extracts a frightful revenue from human misery and crime. But the law was not intended to prevent a manufacturer from delivering a narcotic to a physician through an intermediary, especially when nobody makes any profit out of the transfer except the patient.

This was an unusual case; a man blackmailed because of a noble deed for which he asked no recompense. That is one of the most criminal things about criminals: they are so unkind, so ungrateful, so ungracious! They make the life of the virtuous and the industrious so difficult! They ask such high wages for so little work!

The annual amount of hush-money paid to blackmailers is as staggering as it is hard to compute. But it is known that the total runs high into the millions annually.

And catching a blackmailer is like picking up a viper. The captive is more dangerous than ever.

Ray Schindler has called blackmail "one of the major industries of the United States and Europe." He lists among the easiest victims famous stars of the stage, the screen, and the radio. Bad publicity may bring ruin not only upon them but also upon their backers. A wave of disgrace or obloquy sometimes closes most of the theaters to some unfortunate star. This may mean a loss of millions to the producers and theater owners. It opens a Golconda of wealth to blackmailers and awakens their ingenuity.

The industrious blackmailer does not wait for the mistake to be made. He lures his intended victim into traps and nets stealthily spread. A kind gentleman may befriend a strange girl weeping in distress. A diplomat may be drawn into a conversation for a cocktail, an intimate chat. A hidden camera does the rest. The dictograph is a handy tool for the criminal as well as for his pursuers. A weak and temptable man may be decoyed into an apartment for a farewell drink, and there surprised by an alleged husband with a gun and a blank check book. The pretended wife may weep and implore forgiveness, beg the come-on to save her from disgrace, perhaps from death. Even if he realizes that the woman is in on the game, he thinks of the headlines and buys himself out.

The Mann Act was passed as a blow to the "White Slave" business, an ugly business, indeed; but never as large as advertised. The purpose of the Mann Act was to prevent the transportation of girls across State borders for immoral purposes.

But the Mann Act was welcomed with hushed shrieks of

joy by the blackmailers. It opened a new world to them. They watched the trains; they kept lookouts in hotel lobbies; they studied hotel registers with a suspicious eye for instances where "Mr. and Mrs." really meant "Mr. and Mistress." They would telegraph to the home town of the man and receive promptly a description of his wife, then compare it with the appearance of his companion. With such ammunition in hand one of the blackmailers may approach the man and call him by name, claim to be a cousin of his wife's and ask to see her, denounce the imposture and threaten to notify the real wife. The victim buys himself off the hook as cheaply as he can. And the blackmailers usually know how much he can afford.

Ray Schindler has estimated that in New York City alone blackmail amounts to millions a year. He has known of rich men being nicked for ten thousand dollars for one evening's simplicity.

One case that came to his office concerned a wealthy youth of the highest social position. He loved his fiancée and was true to her after his fashion. When he would leave her he would drop into a nightclub for a nightcap. One night he fell into conversation with a pretty girl there. She was there the next night, and the next. They had a few friendly drinks together; then he gallantly dropped her off at her apartment. He never went beyond the entrance door of her apartment house.

One day as he set out for his office, a menacing male of large bulk accosted him by name and accused him of having alienated the affections of his girl, and threatened suit. To prove that he had grounds for action, he produced a detailed report of the young man's goings and comings for three months. Emphasis was placed on the fact that the young man always went from his own fiancée to the nightclub where he met the other man's alleged fiancée.

It was particularly sickening to have the young man's trusting sweetheart dragged into such a nasty business. And who would believe that he had never made an advance to the nightclub siren? A public scandal would not only wreck his marriage to the girl he sincerely loved, but it would probably kill his invalid mother.

So the young man bought the blackmailer off with a check for ten thousand dollars. Only a week later the fellow demanded fifteen thousand more.

Then, with belated wisdom, the victim appealed to Ray Schindler. Very discreetly Ray studied the nightclub girl. He was convinced that she was ignorant of the way she was being used. Her lover, by the way, was a confederate of the notorious Arnold Rothstein, whose own buddies finally bumped him off.

It is part of Ray's business to deal with the most murderous criminals. He has to make them afraid of him by weapons more awe-inspiring than the guns they probably have in a shoulder-holster or elsewhere, or the possibilities of a fatal ambush. On this occasion Ray went to Rothstein's pal and said words of this general tenor:

"Listen, big boy. So and so is my client and I realize you've got him over a barrel. It's only fair to you to say that the minute you file your alienation of affections papers, I'm dropping in at Headquarters to whisper what I know about a certain little bond robbery last February. Here's my card. When you decide what you're going to do, call me up!"

Within an hour the man had Ray on the telephone and was saying that he thought that both of them had better call the whole thing off. Ray confesses that he took a chance. He had no legal proof of the blackmailer's share in that bond robbery. Ray calls it "cheating cheaters" and admits that now and then he is wicked enough to deceive deceivers.

According to him, the noblest of all the achievements of blackmailers was the complex game by which a Hindu prince was scared into paying no less than $750,000 to persuade an indignant husband not to sue his wife for divorce because he had broken into a Paris hotel room and found the

Prince there with the Englishman's wife. The neatest thing about it was that it was not the husband who broke in but a pretender. The real husband did not learn of it till five years later.

Ray never had a $750,000 blackmail case to deal with, but he had one in which the very wealthy victim had paid out $40,000 and was being dunned for more before he turned to Ray for salvation from progressive poverty. This case was made the more picturesque by the fact that the blackmailers soon discovered Ray's interest in the matter and with a rare sense of humor began playing jokes on him and his staff. It was very annoying; but Ray all the more grimly resolved to have the last laugh.

The case was not laid on Ray's doorstep until his client had suffered humiliation and terror for three months, and forty thousand dollars had been frightened out of him. When thirty thousand more was demanded, to be paid within an hour, he promised to dig it up, and went to his office. There his partner noticed his desperate mood and dug the story out of him.

The partner called the firm's lawyer and the lawyer called Ray Schindler. He listened to the story while the blackmailers waited. They had said that they would stand in the doorway opposite till their victim fetched the thirty thousand; but, by the time Ray could take a look out of the window, the doorway was empty. The blackmailers had grown footsore or alarmed. This, of course, did not mean that they had withdrawn the threats that had already netted them forty thousand and promised them a life income.

In Ray's version of the case he gives the young unmarried millionaire the pseudonym of Harrington Harker. It will serve as well as any other. The victim's story was almost unbelievably innocent. He had met a charming young woman in a nightclub. They met often. He always took her home to the Waldorf-Astoria; but had never gone farther than the lobby or an elevator. She told him she was married—Ray calls her Mrs. Elaine Adams. To Ray, young Harker confessed that he had never asked nor received more than an occasional kiss. He did not want to kiss and tell; but Ray guessed that the woman was willing to kiss and sell.

Ray had an intuition that the fair Elaine did not live at the Waldorf, but simply used one or another of its countless entrances and exits as a runway to her own hiding place.

Harker said he never suspected that his innocent philandering was being taken seriously by the girl's invisible and unreasonable husband. Then, one morning when he went to Central Park for his regular canter along the bridle paths, he was overtaken by two mounted men, who closed in on him and stopped his horse short. One of them said:

"I've got a warrant for your arrest."

"For what, in God's name?"

"Playing around with the wife of another man. Mrs. Adams' husband has squawked to the District Attorney. Get off that goat and we'll all ride down to Headquarters in a taxi."

Harker turned his horse over to his groom. By the time the other horses were disposed of, Harker was in a state of panic. His family was famous for its wealth. He was afraid that his mother would die of shock if she read her son's name in the papers as a home-wrecker.

Even the deputies seemed to take pity on the desperate young man, for one of them said to the other:

"Let's give the lad a break."

The other slowly allowed mercy to overrule his high sense of duty. But he put a high price on his honor. He thought he might save Harker from prosecution and exposure, but it would cost twenty thousand dollars to buy off the other men in the way.

To Harker twenty thousand dollars was a cheap price to pay for golden silence. He went to his bank, drew out the amount in cash, paid it over and breathed easily again.

He told himself that if he never saw Mrs. Adams again it would be too soon.

He had two months' reprieve, and then, one morning as he set out to walk to his office, the two horsemen, now on foot, closed in on him again. They told him that they had not found it easy to buy him off for that twenty thousand; and now the lady's revengeful husband had sworn out a second warrant.

The two men showed Harker an alleged copy of a front page with headlines to the effect that a "Park Avenue Playboy's Love Nest" had provoked an "injured husband" to court action. When Harker's bulging eyes saw this, he nearly fainted. The two men had to hold him up physically as well as financially. They consoled him with the kind word that they could stop the publication; but it would cost thirty thousand dollars.

Poor Harker was a bit short financially and could raise only twenty thousand. The two men graciously accepted it on account.

A month later Harker's morning walk to his office was again interrupted. His tormentors forced him into a cab and demanded, not only the ten thousand he had cheated them out of, but twenty thousand more. Harker pleaded that he did not have that much cash in the bank, and he would have to put up securities and borrow it. They consented to wait in the doorway opposite.

It was then that Ray Schindler was called in and took over. He had nothing to go on except Harker's vague descriptions of the two men and the girl. He said he had met Mrs. Adams at an expensive and reputable nightclub. But Ray knew that the proprietor, "Mike Mura," had a bad name and associated secretly with gangsters.

He had to move cautiously, for the premature arrest of the wrong men would only precipitate the beautiful publicity which Harker had already paid so much to escape. Ray subjected Harker to a study of hundreds of pictures in the Rogues' Gallery. But they gave no clue to his tormentors, and he had no photograph of Mrs. Adams. She did not re-appear at the nightclub and it took several nights' work there for Ray's operatives to learn from another girl where Elaine lived.

The manager of the small hotel was a friend of Ray's—as who is not?—and he collaborated. He let Ray's men inspect all the telephone calls from Elaine's room. The reward of many hours of turning over these records was absolutely nil.

The next source might be the hotel maid who took care of Elaine's room. She was a friendly soul and Elaine loved to chatter with her and show off her clothes. She received many presents but not from her husband, if she had one at all. She called herself "Miss Adams." Once Elaine had shown the maid a platinum wristwatch sprinkled with diamonds, and with Elaine's initials engraved on it. Only, the last letter was B. Which was odd. There was a middle initial, too, but the maid could not recall it. She had noticed, however, from the wrapper that the watch had been sent from a California town named Santa Something.

Since the watch was not available, Ray sent his men to jeweller after jeweller till he found a watch like Elaine's. He had it photographed and many prints made of it. The next thing was the town the watch came from. There are dozens of Santa Cities in California. But that did not stop Ray. He telephoned his Los Angeles office that he was mailing photographs of the watch and the operatives there were told to begin with the nearest town whose name began with Santa, then spread outward in circles from there.

It was not till Santa Clara was reached that an operative ran down a jeweller who remembered both the sale of the watch and the engraving of the initials. He looked up the name of the man who bought it and it was "Edward L. Jonnas." He came to Santa Clara every year to buy citrus fruits for a New York commission merchant.

The operative trudged from the jewellers to the hotels and the fruit growers and, by asking skillful questions, secured a good description of Jonnas, and learned the name of the New York house he dealt with; also that the middle initial on the watch was "A." There still remained the problem of where to find Jonnas.

All this had taken a month of toil and travel, telephoning, photography and the running down of endless clues that ran up a dark alley and vanished. It must have been a long and busy month for the blackmailers, too. They had done some sleuthing on their own and had finally detected the detective.

So Harker came to Ray to say that a familiar voice had called him on the telephone to say that it would do him no good to put his case in the hands of detectives. That was all.

The next morning the same voice called him and told him to find a man of a certain description and send him to wait on the third of the front steps of the Hotel Astor with a certain newspaper in his hand. Between 4:30 and 5 that man would be accosted by a representative of the voice. He would show letters, telegrams, and photographs, which could be purchased for a price to be agreed on. The minute description of the messenger whom Harker was warned to send made a stir in Ray's office, because it was an exact portrait of one of his own operatives. But Harker declared that there had been no telegrams, letters or photographs involved in his little affair with Elaine.

Ray sent to the rendezvous the operative the blackmailers had asked for, and had two other operatives watching at a distance. Nobody appeared.

The next day, however, the mysterious voice upbraided Harker for not "playing fair"—a sweet phrase from such a source! The voice described Ray's two other operatives who had been sent to tail the blackmailers. It was a case of the tailer tailed and it proved that Ray's office was under close observation, especially as the voice gave Harker another minute description of another of Ray's operatives and told Harker to have him and no other on the Hotel Astor steps that afternoon.

Meekly Ray obeyed the orders of the criminals he was trying to identify. He sent the operative the crooks had demanded but had him watched by two more men. These operatives, however, had been lent to Ray by a former manager of his bureau who had opened his own office.

Ray's second operative completed his vigil without being approached and the borrowed watchers did not see any suspicious person in the neighborhood. The next day a third telephone call to Harker said that the man he had sent was all right, but that any meetings with him must be held outside the city at a place to be named the next day. Furthermore Harker's representative must have ten thousand dollars with him when he reached the spot to be designated later.

Ray advised Harker to tell the man when he called up next to go to hell. But Harker was afraid the blackmailers might go to his poor mother and wreck her health. The next morning Harker tried to be a little cold to the voice; but he broke when it threatened to go to his mother. He was told to send the second man to Buffalo on a certain train. This man was to go to a certain hotel, taking ten thousand dollars in an envelope. He was to register under a certain name and hand the envelope to the cashier to put in the hotel safe. He was then to go to his room and wait for further word.

Instead of ten thousand dollars Ray put two fifty dollar bills on top of a bundle of stage money, and sent his operative to Buffalo. He also telephoned to an associated agency in Buffalo to keep Ray's operative under secret observation without letting the operative know.

Reading a condensed record like this gives hardly a hint of the long, long hours of delay, the long journeys, the agonies of suspense, the endless repetitions of failure and deferment. It was Ray's belief that Buffalo had been chosen as the meeting-place because, once the money was seized, the blackmailers could could dash over to Canada.

Arrived in Buffalo, the operative tried in vain to do a bit of scouting. All day and all night he waited in his room and nothing happened. The next morning he was told by telephone to take the 10:15 train to Niagara Falls, sit on the left side of the last car near the end and have the money with him. He was also told that if nobody spoke to him, he was to take the 3:21 train back to Buffalo, return to his room, and wait. Wait!

The moment the voice ended, the operative called the operator and asked her if she could trace the call. She said she could not; but she had heard two other voices speaking as if the man who had been talking to Ray's operative had spoken from a telephone booth with two other men at his elbow. She had heard one of them say, "I've got a nice corner-room with a shower at three-fifty a day."

This is a striking example of the way real detectives work and what use they make of little things. Ray's operative telephoned to him in New York and reported all this. Then Ray telephoned his Buffalo associate and asked that a swarm of operatives visit every Buffalo hotel that might have shower-baths and find if anybody had taken a room at about the hour and moment of the telephone call.

In two hours Ray was told that three men had registered at three hotels at just that hour. Two of them were plainly innocent of connection with the blackmailing game, and they were innocent of the fact that they were closely shadowed for the next twenty-four hours. The third man was Ray's man —at least one of them.

The operative went to Niagara Falls as directed and gained nothing from his visit but a view of some well-known scenery. He did not even know that he was being shadowed at Ray's instructions. But the blackmailers were aware of it and when he returned to Buffalo, the voice on the telephone reproached him for having two "flatfeet" following him.

The operative in his ignorance denied this so violently and convincingly that the voice was convinced, and told him to go to Niagara again on the same train the next day. The weary detective made the dreary trip, spent the dismal hours alone, and took the dismal train back. While he was sitting in the rear car near the end on the left side, a voice poured down across his shoulder:

"Tell Schindler he's wasting his time. We're getting sick of all this gumshoe business. But give a look!"

He held out a photograph of Harker naked from the waist up and embracing a naked girl. The voice went on:

"We've got the negative of this and a bundle of hot letters. You can have 'em all for that ten grand you got in the hotel safe. Go get it and we'll make a new date in Canada. Make sure the money isn't marked."

Even a hasty glance at the photograph showed the operative that it was a crudely doctored picture, with Harker's head cut out of another photograph, pasted on, then rephotographed. Also the operative took a long look at the man with the voice and decided that he was the man who had bought fruit in Santa Clara. But the man got off at a way station. He did not notice that two Buffalo operatives got off with him.

They did not seize him because Ray wanted to reach the big boy higher up and put an end to the endless demands.

After another night and half a day of solitary confinement in his hotel room Ray's operative was instructed by telephone to take the same train next morning but go on across the river into Canada, and be at the railroad station at one.

On the same train with him was the blackmailer who had talked to him the day before. This time he told Ray's man to take a room in a certain hotel and wait there with the money in his pocket, till the blackmailer called on him. He would come directly to the room and knock once. He promised to deliver the photograph and the letters and take the ten grand.

This plan was communicated to the Buffalo shadows and Ray's operative was instructed to flash his telephone the moment he heard a knock on his door, and flash it again when the visitor left.

To make brief what took hours, the blackmailer knocked, and looked carefully everywhere, not neglecting the shower curtain in the bathroom. Then he handed over the pretended photograph of Harker with the letters and accepted in exchange the pretended ten thousand dollars.

As he left the elevator on the first floor, the Buffalo operatives in ambush grabbed him, and searched him thoroughly. But they could not find the envelope full of stage money. He had dropped it down the mail chute, addressed to his partners, who must have been pained when they got it.

When the news was telephoned to Ray, he told them to turn the man loose. Ray was not collecting small fry.

Meanwhile the man who had taken a room with a shower for $3.50 a day had been traced, and his room so carefully ransacked that a blotter was discovered on which had been left a backward print of the letters "P -ksk- l. N.Y." and the name "Jephson."

It was "elementary, my dear Watson" to look up a Peekskill directory and learn that there was only one Jephson in Peekskill. Ray sent an operative there. Ingeniously he secured from the telegraph office a transcript of the telegram sent to Jephson. It was from "Joe" and reported that he was "in luck and would put over the deal the next day."

To the Peekskill operative was assigned the wearisome job of keeping watch on the big Jephson estate. He called in his wife, who was a landscape painter, to help him, by pretending to paint, while he watched. The operative followed Jephson's car wherever it went. One day it sped all the way to New York. There it stopped at the very nightclub where Harker had met Elaine. A man and a woman got out and entered the club. They were strangers to the operative. He telephoned Ray.

This was a chance for Ray to try out his latest invention— a camera hidden in the spotlight of his car and worked from the inside. Ray drove to the nightclub and secured a parking place next to the entrance by tipping a taxidriver to drive on. The Peekskill operative joined Ray and they sat there for a whole hour before the operative said, "There they are!"

Ray snapped the picture. The woman was Elaine Adams. He guessed that the man was the Santa Clara fruit buyer who had bought the watch for Elaine Adams and put on it the initials E.A.B.

The photograph was airmailed to Santa Clara and many people thoroughly identified the man as the fruit buyer Jonnas. Furthermore, Harker identified him as the man who threatened him on that far-off ride in Central Park. He was also identified as the man who had handled the Buffalo meeting.

Now the nightclub was put under observation and it was learned that Jonnas and Elaine often held long talks there with the owner, "Mike Mura."

After all these maddening delays and false starts and dud finishes Ray was at last drawing near the higher-ups.

And now he found that the much advertised and highly necessary "camera-eye" and elephant memory of the detective were getting to work. The picture of Jonnas reminded him of a number of photographs shown to him once by a Federal agent. All of the subjects were, of course, criminals wanted by the government for one crime or another. On investigation Ray found that his memory was good. "Jonnas" was indeed wanted by the Federal police, but not under that name.

Still the search went on. Elaine had moved to a new hotel and registered as Elaine Bartz. And that explained the E.A.B.—Elaine Adams Bartz.

And now entered a new mind. Ray's father was then above seventy-five but keen for research. The name "Bartz" was rare and he went to the Public Library to find what there was to be found in genealogical and other books. He learned that a number of Bartzes had settled in central Wisconsin. A study of directories and telephone books showed just where.

So Father Schindler took an airplane to Wisconsin. There he hired a car and a young driver who knew everybody. At last Father Schindler found Elaine's own uncle. He identified her photograph and said he had not heard from Elaine for some months; but she had asked that her mail be sent in care of C. K. Vining, whose address was Baltimore.

By this time the average person would have been ready to throw Mr. Harker and his fortune to the wolves. But Ray was still as eager on the scent as an eager bloodhound who has nothing else to do but pursue. He decided to take an active part when he saw how pretty Elaine was and he waited for her in the lobby of her hotel till she came out, then invited himself to join her for a stroll.

He introduced himself as a friend of Hamilton Harker's. This chilled her. He gave her messages from her uncle and aunt in Wisconsin. This uncanny news alarmed her. She asked what they knew about her. Ray said that they didn't know about the blackmailers she was working for. Neither did Mr. Vining.

This almost flattened her. Ray took her to the Waldorf for a talk. There he told her that he had plenty of information "on" her but nothing "against" her. He said he doubted that she realized how, through her aid, her friends had scared forty thousand dollars out of Hamilton Harker because of his illicit relations with her.

This horrified her. It was easy for Ray to learn the name of the unknown third man: Joe Bell known as "Ding Dong." Ray told her that he was going to telephone C. J. Vining, but not to harm her. In fact Ray promised to protect her and set her right with Vining.

He called Vining, told him that Elaine was in trouble and needed him. Vining reached Ray's office by the first train and began the conversation by saying that he had a permit to carry a revolver, and carried one. He was there to protect Elaine.

"I've never carried a revolver in my life," said Ray, "and I never lost a man for lack of one. Tonight I'm giving a party and I want you there—but not with a gun."

So Vining turned over his pearl-handled .22 to Ray.

Before the party, Ray had a caller, a Federal agent, Sam Pelling. Ray was glad to see him and Pelling joined the party at Mike Mura's nightclub. Mike was seated at a table with two of the blackmailers, Jonnas and Ding Dong Bell. Ray went over to the table with Harker and asked him to tell Mura how much blackmail he had paid. Harker said, "Forty thousand dollars." Mura said that that was a lie—a divinely condemned lie.

Ray showed him the withdrawal slips from Harker's bank account. Mura invited them all into his private office. The first thing he did there was to slug Bell on the jaw and snarl: "You so and so, you gave me only five thousand."

It was not the blow so much as Bell's weak heart that toppled him over on a couch. Then the Federal agent Pelling took over. In a few crisp words he reminded Bell of a series of gross real estate swindles for which the government had long been hunting him. Also, Jonnas bore a striking resemblance to a man "Jennings" whom the government was pining for. He handcuffed the twain and led them away. Elaine hurled after Jonnas the initialled watch he had given to her. It missed him.

What thousands of miles of travel it had cost Ray and his people! What numberless hours of searching and enduring the most maddening boredoms, waiting for someone who never arrived, or telephoned to say tomorrow—and tomorrow —and tomorrow!

I have not tried to dress this history up as a mystery story. It has seemed more important as a comprehensive example of the art—the multifold arts of the detective hunting through the dark for men whose ways are dark.

And the end of the long, long trail was that Ray chased his men into the arms of the Government, which gave them five to ten years each in Federal prison on charges that did not mention Hamilton Harker.

And that was just what Harker wanted—silence and oblivion for his harmless but costly philandering with the fair Elaine.

This history is also a proof of the need for private detectives. Harker was innocent, of course; yet three criminals had terrorized him out of the sizable fortune of forty thousand dollars and were on their way to wreck his life. It took dozens of private detectives and months of hard work to save him from ruin.

Imagine what would have happened if he had gone to the police. They could not and would not have given him any protection at all. Ray Schindler has said of his own art:

"Right at this moment there are countless blackmail plots in the making throughout the world. And blackmail will continue to be one of the safest and most lucrative 'professions' of the vultures who prey on the rich, because just so long as men and women become wealthy and prominent, they will be the unwilling but submissive victims to this vicious racket."

Incidentally, the story is not entirely devoid of love-interest. One result of the affair was to drive Elaine and her Lancelot, Mr. Vining, into each other's arms, where they lived happily ever after. Or did they? Anyway, they have not called on Ray Schindler. At least, not yet.

# 9.

## A FEW HORS D'OEUVRE

As a tribute to French culinary skill, our bills of fare are full of French words. Instead of crudely speaking of "side-dishes" we make them sound smart and taste better—and cost more—by calling them *hors d'oeuvre*. Few of us can pronounce the term so that a Frenchman would know what we meant; but, in this case, it is permissible to point.

Literally, the term means "out of work." It is applicable to this chapter because it will serve as a much-needed relief from the heavy dishes of murder, blackmail, and other crimes that make up the bulk of this book.

For a few pages let us trifle with some of the lighter phases of Ray Schindler's manifold tasks. They concern people who make a business of being out of work. They like it; but their leisure keeps the insurance companies working overtime and causes Ray's operatives to lose a lot of sleep.

As far back as the old Roman days, and doubtless farther back, it was well realized that when you put a guard over somebody or something, your troubles are only half over. The next problem is,

"Who will guard the guards?"

So it is with insurance. You can buy insurance against almost anything nowadays. The next problem is:

"Who will insure the insurers?"

A great part of the liabilities and expenses of insurance companies consists of the attempt, often vain, to keep swindlers from looting the funds so that there will be nothing left to pay the honest claimants. Thieves take out policies against theft. Firebugs take out policies on buildings, then set them on fire. Swindlers take out accident policies, then manufacture accidents. Even people of honest intent and careless performance take out huge policies to protect their jewels from theft, then mislay them, take affidavits that they could not have been mislaid, and demand the full value of the gems, or even more.

The story has already been told of how Ray Schindler, acting for an insurance company, followed a woman's pet monkey and disclosed that he had been stealing her diamonds one by one and hiding them in a big jar.

A large part of Ray's business, and that of other private detectives, is the business of keeping people from swindling insurance companies, and their policyholders, for whose follies and misfortunes the insurance companies are pledged to pay whatever amount the policy may stipulate.

Once a fraud or a crime is successfully committed, the perpetrator is apt to take it up as a business. Bilking insurance companies has long been a thriving industry, and the protective work of the private detective is a vitally important form of crime-prevention. Life insurance is one form of bequeathing money, and the beneficiary is often left in the dark as to his or her expectations. Often the insurance companies are instructed not to let the beneficiaries know what is waiting them until they learn it after the funeral of their benefactor.

On many occasions there are beneficiaries whom the insurance companies cannot trace at first. A letter to the latest address may be returned to the company. Certain insurance company employees have access to the lists of such people and are instructed to make every effort to find them and inform them of their unsuspected fortunes.

Realizing the large sums thus awaiting distribution, a certain crooked lawyer conceived a scheme for digging his fingers into all that idle money. He took into partnership two bribable accountants who gave him lists of such names. The lawyer bestirred himself to trace the ignorant beneficiaries until he found them. Needless to say he did not tell them of the money awaiting their mere demand.

He slyly visited them and, with a know-it-all air excited them with vague and mysterious references to large sums which he could secure for them by certain devices that only a clever lawyer could manipulate. He did not ask for any advance payment. No money, no fee. All he wanted was a little contract to pay him half of whatever was received.

Almost anybody would agree to divide the profits with a man who knew the way to the end of the rainbow, so this lawyer piled up contracts with beneficiaries and collected large sums where the policyholders had died and the beneficiaries were unaware of the money waiting the discovery of their correct address.

One insurance company that engaged Ray was paying hundreds of death-claims a day, and the number of pleasantly surprised people was not small. When a certain beneficiary suddenly found himself far richer than he had ever dreamed of being, it hurt him to turn over half of the inheritance to the funny little man who had foreseen the gift and signed him up. This beneficiary made inquiries; whereupon the insurance company made further inquiries. Then they turned to Ray Schindler to look into the puzzling matter.

By the time Ray got through with the case the lawyer found himself disbarred and many future beneficiaries received all that had been bequeathed to them.

In one of Ray's cases he used the motion picture to advantage. It concerned one of those almost innumerable instances in which an accident insurance company has to pay a stipulated fee during a time of disability. This form of insurance is so popular, and properly so, that the big companies carry policies totalling hundreds of millions of dollars. The disability clause has cost them so much money through fraudulent abuse that extra premiums are now required—and also extra vigilance.

One business man in Brooklyn took out so big a policy that,

when his heart grew weak, he drew $1,200 a month. He spent all his public life in a wheel chair. But when he announced that his monthly checks were to be sent henceforth to Florida the company asked Ray Schindler to look into his case.

Ray's operatives saw the man wheeled to his automobile and wheeled from that to the train. In Miami more Schindler seraphs saw him wheeled from the train to a beach hotel. For two days their man was toted from his room to the veranda, where he spent hours.

Then came a miracle. On the beach, the cripple rose up and walked! He threw off his invalid robes and squirmed into a bathing suit! He promenaded up and down the healing sands on his gay bare feet. He ran and dived into the surf.

Ray's motion picture camera recorded this miracle for those who would never believe human testimony. The camera portrayed him chasing a bathing girl down the beach as if he had found that long-lost fountain of youth which Ponce de Léon reported in Florida.

The print was sent to New York and Ray gave a showing of it in a dark projection room to just one spectator. He was the lawyer of the Brooklyn man. When the lawyer saw it he wrote to his client: "Come on home and go back to work." The cruel corporation not only stopped payment of the $40 a day pension, but insisted on the repayment of all the back-pensions.

There was another man who had similar ideas of earning a living. He had the foresight to take out disability insurance with three different companies for a total of $2,000 a month. Then he proceeded to acquire a painless disability so acute that, though he owned several dress-shops in New York, he could visit none of them. He had to sit at home and transact his business by telephone.

But he tired of solitude and could not even wait till his first two thousand was due. Three weeks after his collapse he was rolling the rhumba in the Stork Club.

At the Stork, as at many other nightclubs, pretty girls go about taking flash light pictures of couples and others at their tables. So this gentleman was not at all disturbed in his rhumba-routine by the occasional flare of a flashlight. He was horribly disturbed, however, when he learned later that one of Ray Schindler's operatives had flashed a camera on him several times and perpetuated the capers of the dress-shop man. The sight of the photographs cured his disability. He gave up his bedroom office and returned to his regular routes from shop to shop.

A somewhat humbler victim of Ray's Argus-eyed bureau lived in the Bronx, where he drew disability insurance as a "house-bound" patient. He was barely able at night to limp out to his front porch in the evening for a last breath of fresh air before returning to his wearisome bed.

This performance was for the benefit of any suspicious neighbors and more especially for any spies that might be lurking about in the pay of the insurance company.

But one morning a lingering operative caught a glimpse of the cruelly crippled wretch bounding over his back fence, and making his way to the subway. He skipped down the steps, boarded a train, left it in the heart of Manhattan, skipped up the steps and pranced to a doughnut factory on Sixth Avenue. He was so agile and deft that his machine did its business in the front window. He presented a perfect target for a motion picture machine that one of Ray's men operated from inside a truck, which paused unnoticed for a few minutes in front of that show window.

The resulting film saved the man from having to limp out to his porch every night and gasp for a little air. It saved him from making his exit by the back fence of mornings.

Another man whom Ray turned up was drawing complete disability pay for a complete nervous collapse. It did not prevent him from digging graves in a Brooklyn cemetery.

Then there were the men whose doctors injected a little digitalis and gave them a pulse-flutter that deceived even insurance doctors into a diagnosis of heart disease. There are the—oh, there are thousands of tricks that conscienceless malingerers have played and are playing to defraud insurance companies out of millions of dollars a year.

Not all these thieves on the installment plan are men. Women do their share of the swindling; and in case of trial by jury, their chances of acquittal are even better than those of the men.

Perhaps here is one of the reasons for the general feeling that homely women are more virtuous than pretty women. A homely woman knows that she is about the only kind of woman that a jury might convict of something—unless, of course, she can somehow steal enough money to hire an expert criminal lawyer. Without crooked lawyers, the demand for good detectives to outwit them would be cut in half.

Here is a case, one of the innumerable and often undiscovered cases, where the criminal lawyer was more criminal than the criminal he "defended."

A great five-and-ten-cent chain was sued for $100,000 damages by a woman who said that she had bought at one of their shops some cheap celluloid combs. She had kept them in her hair while she was drying it under an electric lamp. Suddenly the combs exploded and set her hair on fire. Before the blaze could be extinguished she was in a sorry state, and any jury would have been happy to make her rich for life as a stinging rebuke to malicious millionaires.

The company immediately withdrew from sale all of its inflammable combs; but, before making ready to pay the hundred thousand to the woman, along with the heavy court costs, the officials told their woes to Ray Schindler.

He threw the usual human network about the woman and the neighborhood, just to see what he might drag up. All the neighbors confirmed the poor woman's story, except one woman who did not like her. A woman operative found her, and casually talked with her about this and that till she picked up a good deal of the backbiting chatter that makes up neighborhood news. There were whispers that made an important difference in the hairless lady's claim.

The operative learned, and confirmed the fact, that the explosive combs had not been bought at any of the stores of the huge corporation, but at a small shop on a side-street.

While his wife was suffering in the hospital, the enraged husband had called in a lawyer to sue that petty shopkeeper. The lawyer was energetic and ambitious and showed a most commendable desire to do the best he could for his clients. In any case, he said to the husband unrecorded words of this general tenor:

"If you sue that little hole-in-the-wall feller for damages, you win the suit, maybe—especially with me in there orating about what a beauty your wife had and ain't got, and how woman's crowning glory is her hair, and now she's lost her crown—and stuff like that.

"Well, so you win the suit, and the jury votes you for damages all that feller's got. What has he got? Debts! You'll have to pay the costs of the suit yourself prob'ly—not to mention paying me the lease possible fee I could charge you.

"But for your sake and your wife's sake—not to mention for my sake—if we could just shift that case to one of the big chain-stores, why, it could make us all rich. Rememmer that song: 'I found a million-dollar baby in a five-and-ten-cent store.' Well, we might not make maybe a million, but say, a hunnert grand. That wouldn't be so bad, would it?"

And so an ardently criminal criminal lawyer seduced a most unfortunate woman and her devoted husband and a pair of tender-hearted neighbors into a little perjury. He was ready also to seduce a jury of twelve good men and women and true into serving as accessories after the crime by overlooking evidence and fairplay and fining a corporation a fortune for what it had not done.

It always gives a jury a touch of the mania of grandeur to

issue a verdict for a huge amount, especially when it comes from a corporation, which has no rights anyway.

But this wicked corporation called in a wicked private detective, and one of his wicked operatives proved that the unfortunate woman had been doubly unfortunate in not buying her combs of a wicked chain-store. So the suit was withdrawn. The clever lawyer got no fee at all, and the small shopkeeper was not even sued.

In a certain expensive Connecticut hotel, there dwelt a lovely white-haired lady and her even lovelier daughter. For more than half a year they were well-paying, well-liked guests with a host of friends.

Suddenly, one Sunday night, the crowded dining room was horrified by a shriek of terror and pain. That exquisite girl leaped to her feet in terror. The napkin at her lacerated lip was red with blood. She held up a sliver of glass that she had snatched from her tongue. But she gasped that she had swallowed a bigger, sharper piece in the dessert she had just been eating.

She was helped to her room, and all the other guests wondered uneasily if there had been glass in their own food. The management was aghast, and the kitchen was a scene of turmoil. The least profitable form of advertisement a restaurant can get is to acquire a reputation for mixing glass in its menu.

A doctor was hastily summoned and did all that art and science can do about a jagged dagger of glass in the alimentary canal. The girl tried to be brave, but her helpless gasps indicated that the glass was leaving its scars as it slipped. Since the average alimentary tract is about thirty-four feet long, the glass had a long, long way to go to Tipperary. And nothing could be more difficult than making repairs on that highway.

For weeks the girl agonized. By that time she and her mother had sued the hotel for a staggering sum. The hotel referred the matter to the insurance company that had, for a modest premium, guaranteed it against any possible damage to its customers.

The lawyer for the insurance company found that he knew surprisingly little about the dear old lady and the dear young daughter who had spent their money so generously for so long, and now suddenly made such a generous demand for ruinous damages.

So he called in Ray Schindler. How incessantly I keep using those words!

Ray's first task was to find just who the women were and where they came from—and why? Nobody has less curiosity about anybody than a hotel keeper has about paying-guests who pay. It is enough that they register from some place and their checks show no resilience. All that the proprietor knew of this couple was that they had written themselves down on the register as coming from Palm Beach. But when Ray made inquiries in that city, the name meant nothing there. So Ray sent an operative to the hotel as a guest and she managed to get acquainted with the mother and daughter, who still remained in the hotel, still paying their bills.

Ray's operative grew friendly enough to play cards with the mother and daughter, and take long walks with them. But, though she talked and talked about her own travels, they never spoke of theirs. Weeks passed and all the operative had elicited was a casual reference to Seattle, and another to Denver.

By this time Ray had had many pictures taken of the two women. He sent copies to Seattle and to Denver. Their names were equally unknown in either place. But their attractive faces were instantly recognized in both those cities by the managements of two luxurious hotels. In both those hotels, that beautiful girl had petrified a crowded dining room with a shriek of pain and terror, had pressed a bloody napkin to a bleeding lip, had held up a splinter of glass and announced that she had swallowed another.

A suit for whopping damages had followed: in both cases the hotel had lost the suit.

The third hotel was not eager for the wide publicity of winning the suit and all that Ray had to do was to call on the mother and daughter, mention the Seattle and Denver hotels and the two lawsuits and watch them drop the new suit, pack up and depart for points unknown.

They have never been heard of again, but if, some night in a crowded dining room you should see a beautiful girl with a bleeding mouth leap to her feet, scream she has been glassed, and hold up a sliver as a proof of it, it would probably be safe to say:

"If you need a doctor, call in Ray Schindler."

Sympathy is a noble thing to feel, but a bit of suspicion is a good thing to take along with you wherever you go.

# 10.

## EVEN HIS INITIALS
## WERE R O B

"The gamest of all big game is Man." So Ray was told by Frank Buck, his friend, and his former rival as one who "brings 'em back alive."

Ray has never killed any of the bad men he has been pursuing. He doesn't seem to be able even to dislike the criminals who give him so much time and trouble, legwork and brain-fag. The nearest I know of his coming to hating a man was his statement that Robert Owen Bain caused him "more vexation of spirit than any other man he ever trailed." One reason for this was that, after detectives had been looking for the fellow for more than four years, he came willingly and cheerfully into Ray's office and spent a whole afternoon with him, then strolled out into a blizzardy New York night and kept Ray's shivering and snow-caked operatives suffering for hours before he slipped easily away into the invisible.

This story concerns the period when Ray was managing the New York office of the William J. Burns bureau, which handled the enormous business of the American Bankers Association. From time to time Ray looked over the files of "Men Wanted" to keep his memory fresh. Among the oldest of them was the dossier of a man named Robert Owen Bain. He had embezzled $10,000 from a midwestern bank, of which he was a trusted employee.

According to the files, Bain had come of a good family and had worked for three years in the bank before he excited suspicion. He suddenly turned up missing one afternoon, and so did $10,000.

Most banks have large or small deposits whose owners do not draw on them for a long period; so they are set aside as "inactive." Such an account was that of $40,000 credited to an elderly woman who had left it stagnant for many years. At his lunch hour one day, Bain wrote out a check for $10,000 of this woman's money, forged her signature and made it payable to an imaginary "Ralph O. Bosworth." This check he carried to another bank in the same city. There he introduced himself as "Bosworth" and said that he had gone into the contracting business, and would carry quite a large payroll.

Bankers do not insult people whose letter of introduction is a $10,000 check for deposit with promises of large business to come. This bank accepted "Bosworth" with cordiality and put the check into the hopper for clearance. When the check reached his own bank, Bain was right there to clear it himself. Then he destroyed it, after charging it off against the old woman's account.

The next lunch hour found him again at the other bank, where he explained that his payroll had to be made up, and he supposed it would be all right if he left $50 in his account to hold it. Bankers do not love such rapid transit money, but they must pay on demand and the $10,000 check had been cleared. So Bosworth wrote himself a check for $9,950 and departed with promises to make another large deposit very soon.

That bank and that city never saw him again. When he did not reappear at his own bank, the anxiety for his safety soon changed to anxiety for the bank's safety. His dealings were hastily gone over and it was found that the inactive account of the old lady had suddenly grown active. The case was promptly turned over to the American Bankers Association, which turned it over promptly to the Burns Agency, which sent copies of all it could find out to its branch offices, along with as good a description as could be pieced together of Bain. He was a young man 5 feet 8 inches tall. He wore glasses but no mustache. He had a slight stammer, and weighed 130 pounds.

Two years passed with no trace of Mr. Bain-Bosworth. Then one day Ray received a routine warning to look out for a certain Ralph O. Boswell, who had been an assistant cashier of a steel company in Chicago.

One day he had gone to the bank with a company check for $18,000 to make up the payrolls. He had no bodyguard, but he brought back the money without an incident. So, a week later, he was sent to the bank with another check for $18,000. He got the money, but the steel company never saw him again.

This, too, fell into the hands of the American Bankers Association. Along with the growls of the big steel company went the agonized shrieks of two women. Mr. "Boswell," before moving in on the steel company, had won success as a floorwalker in a large Chicago department store. There his lordly manner and genial charm had won the heart of a pretty bookkeeper. She had married him and taken him to live with her mother, whose husband had recently died, leaving an estate consisting of an insurance policy for $10,000 to be divided equally between mother and daughter. As a nice gesture, the bride put her $5,000 in her new husband's bank account. As another nice gesture her mother lent him $1,500 to tide him over a business deal.

When Boswell skipped with the steel company's $18,000, he took along his wife's $5,000, his mother-in-law's $1,500, and the proceeds of a forged check for $5,000 more. He also took along some of the steel company's blank checks.

It was learned long afterward that, in both cases, he had gone to Canada and settled in an obscure place near Quebec, where he spent most of his time in the wild woods, passing himself off as a gentleman of wealth, a lover of fishing, hunting, and forestry.

The thefts from the steel company and from the two women were duly filed in Ray's cabinets, and the initials ROB were stored in the back of his brain.

Another two years passed and then the Chicago branch of the Bankers Association reported to the Burns office, which relayed it to the New York branch, that a forged check for $200 had come in. It was written on one of the forms of that same steel company, and signed by one "J. Arthur Watrous," who was unknown to the company. But the check had been made out to "Roger O. Billings," who had endorsed it over to the Calvert Hotel of New York, and received the hotel's cash.

By a series of coincidences in those pre-airmail days the check had sped through the New York clearing house in time to catch the Twentieth Century train that same afternoon, and to arrive in Chicago the next morning. When the Chicago office of the Burns agency learned of this, it flashed word to Ray Schindler by private wire.

Those initials ROB rang a bell in a back room of Ray's brain. He thought that R. O. Bain and R. O. Boswell might be related. Also it was the second time that steel company's check had appeared before him. Ray sent an operative to the Calvert Hotel to see if Boswell had fled. Also he telephoned the New York office of the American Bankers Association for a photograph of Bain. None was in its files, but the Chicago office had one and promised to put it on the eastbound Twentieth Century due the next morning.

That was considered as breath-takingly swift in those days before the telephoto and the airplane as our ways will undoubtedly look old fashioned and snail-slow to the next generation of speedsters. But by that time the criminals will also have inventors at work in their behalf.

The operative who called at the Calvert Hotel informed the manager that the check he had cashed had bounced with record-breaking velocity and that he might have been entertaining the long lost R. O. Bain unawares. Both were pleasantly surprised to learn that Mr. Billings had not yet checked out.

Knowing what he did about the banking business and clearing houses, the man had counted on a little longer leisure. When the hotel manager knocked at his door he was welcomed with smiles. Even the news that the stranger was a detective did not chill Mr. "Billings." But he was deeply hurt when he learned that the check was not good. It just showed how untrustworthy certain people were. It almost destroyed his faith in human honor.

He explained that the check was in a sense a debt of honor—that is the nicer name for a gambling debt. He had come from San Francisco to New York. On the train he had fallen in with some nice chaps who finally made up a friendly game of poker. It looked like a straight game; for he had been the biggest winner. A charming chap named J. Arthur Watrous had been the heaviest loser; but he complained that if he paid everybody off, he would have no cash left when he got off at Buffalo, where he must spend a day or two before he came on to New York to continue his pleasant acquaintance with R. O. Billings.

Watrous had lost to Billings $80; and, if Billings would cash a check for $200, Watrous would pay off the other men and have enough left to get him to his bank in Buffalo. Since he said he was an official of that same old steel company and showed one of their checks to prove it, "Billings" said he had not hesitated to give him the $200. Billings announced that he would, of course, reimburse the Calvert Hotel in full for the full amount and charge it off to experience.

He was so plausible and so shocked by the duplicity of this J. Arthur Watrous that, when the operative asked him if he would mind stepping over to Ray Schindler's office to clear the whole matter up, Mr. Billings made no demur.

The operative telephoned Ray that they would soon be there, and Ray jubilantly prepared to gather in this elusive ROB, who had been at liberty now for four years. Ray studied such descriptions as he had and instructed his staff to drop into his office from time to time and ask questions about office details. This would give them a chance to memorize the man's features; for Ray was determined to keep him under observation somehow till that photograph arrived the next morning.

When R. O. Billings arrived, he brought with him bitter disappointment. He told his story again and it was a good story. Crooks have to be good story-tellers or go out of business. What upset Ray was that Billings did not fit the written description of Bain. Bain wore glasses. Billings wore none and had no crease on the nose to hint that he had ever worn any. Bain had a slight stammer; Billings was glib. Bain weighed about 130; Billings must be about 145. Bain was five foot eight; Billings was taller than that.

The only points that agreed were that both men had hazel eyes and dark brown hair. But you can't arrest a man for having hazel eyes and dark brown hair.

But Ray was determined not to let the fellow go till he saw the photograph. He made talk and Billings seemed to be in no hurry. Ray asked catch questions to trip Billings; but B. knew all the right answers.

He did not object even to Ray's searching him. Nothing incriminating was found on him, except $260. Ray figured that if B. repaid the hotel, he would have only $60 left and, if he were a crook, he would have to get more money in a hurry.

Billings did not even object to taking lunch with Ray in the office.

Ray was wearing out rapidly but the triumphant Billings grew fresher and fresher. Finally Ray said in desperation:

"You're as anxious as we are to catch this man who robbed you, and you say he said he would come to New York right away. Everybody who comes to New York crosses Broadway at Forty-second street sooner or later. How would you like to go along with one of my men and keep watch there so you can point him out? It will show you how we detectives work, and my man will be glad to pay for the occasional drinks you'll both need to keep warm on a nasty night like this."

Billings said he'd be delighted. He'd like nothing better than to lay hands on that fellow "Watrous."

It was dark and snowy by this time and Billings set out with one of Ray's unfortunate operatives, while another was assigned to the windblown task of tailing them. "Billings" and his companion kept up a patrol punctuated by nips at this bar or that. They studied the crowds going into the theaters, and kept on going till they could study the crowds coming out of the theaters. Then they had a midnight snack.

Finally they parted at the door of the Calvert Hotel. Billings said he was going to bed, but the operatives stayed to watch the hotel's one door. The manager promised to signal if Billings gave any sign of departure.

By three in the morning a blizzard was blowing away nearly everything but those two icy-eyed and miserable operatives. At half-past six in the morning a taxicab dashed up to the hotel door and a heavily bundled-up man darted into it. And away it went before the operatives could even decipher its number in the snow-laden gale.

One of them rushed to the night clerk and asked if it were Billings who had just left. The night clerk yawned a Yes. As usual, the signal-giver had forgotten to give the signal. All the clerk remembered was the telephone number of the taxicab company.

At that dull hour, the company was actually able to furnish the number of the cab that had been called to the Calvert. Later, the driver was found. He reported that he had taken his fare to the Grand Central Terminal.

When Ray called on the manager of the hotel to protest, he learned that Billings had paid back the $200 and also his bill. That had ended the hotel's interest in him. When Ray reminded the man that if it had not been for his intervention, the hotel would not have got back its $200, the manager haughtily answered:

"You mind your business and I'll mind mine."

The bitterest pill for Ray to swallow came in the morning mail. It was the photograph of Bain. It was an early photograph of "Billings." He had grown taller and fatter and outgrown his glasses and his stammer, but he had spent eight hours in Ray's office, eaten a hearty lunch, and kept two operatives on ice all night. They had also paid for many drinks and the midnight supper.

The pursuit of Bain was no longer a matter of pure justice. An element of revenge for many humiliations had entered into it. But all that Ray could do now was to make and distribute many copies of the photograph with a description pointing out the recent changes in Bain's aspect. A photograph of the check was made and included in a leaflet, of which thousands of copies were made. Burns men, in all cities where there were branches, were sent to all first and second class hotels, to leave leaflets. Every police department in the nation received one or more. Steamships were watched. Everything was done to make it difficult for Bain to show his face with impunity.

But so unobservant and unremembering are most people that neither criminals nor detectives have need of disguises except in rare instances. People just don't observe or remember.

The reward for five days of publishing Bain's picture and his story all over the United States was a telephone call from Chicago: another of that steel company's checks had bounced! This one was for $500 and the Hotel Astor had cashed it. It was signed by "R. O. Brewster."

When Ray reached the Astor, "Brewster" was gone. He had already learned that checks on Chicago rebounded fast. Ray's men found the taxicab driver who remembered taking "Brewster" to the Pennsylvania Station.

Thinking things over with fierce concentration, Ray decided that, though the man was a far traveller and a fast, he had gone from the Calvert to the Astor via the Grand Central. He might have gone to some other hotel in town via the Pennsylvania Station.

So Ray sent his men with several pamphlets and a picture to every New York and Newark hotel. One pamphlet went to each room clerk, one to the cashier, and one to the house detective. Also, the operative asked at each hotel "Is this man here now?" Negative answers were received everywhere.

At the Waldorf-Astoria the head-detective was a warm friend of Ray's and he personally took the circulars and showed them to every hotel employee. He pasted one picture right over the cashier's window.

Ten days later that very cashier, with Bain's picture smiling down on him, cashed one of those steel company's checks for $400. It was signed "R. O. Brigham."

"Brigham" had left almost immediately, of course. But Ray made a check of the laundry, the valet, everything. At that time all telephone calls from a room were simply noted as "Local" or "Long Distance," though the operators noted down for the hotel's information each number as it was called.

To trace a number to a room was then almost unthinkable. But appalling problems of research do not deter Ray Schindler. He also yields to hunches. Here was a swindler who could not seem to get away from New York. What could be holding him?

The answer was, of course: A woman!

So Ray assumed that Mr. B. was still in town somewhere and still making up to some woman for one reason or another. And there are more reasons than one by which a woman holds a man.

So Ray approached the head-detective, Joe Smith, with a job that almost anybody else would have laughed at. This man, "R. O. Brigham," had been in the hotel from January 6th to the 15th. If all the thousands on thousands of telephone calls sent out from that enormous caravanserai were sifted through, it might be found that a certain number appeared during those days and did not appear a week before the 6th or a week after the 15th.

Even an astronomer counting stars might have flunked that one. But Joe Smith liked the idea and assigned a girl to go over the tower of slips. Eventually she turned up the information that "Watkins 9999" was not called before January 6th or after January 15th but had appeared daily, sometimes three or four times a day, between those dates. The supervisor of the hotel telephones had a friend in the Watkins exchange and was able to learn that the subscriber to that particular telephone was a Mrs. Evelyn Saunders in a certain apartment house on West 57th street.

This did not prove, of course, that she had received those calls from ROB, because many other people had checked in on January 6th and checked out on the 15th. But it was worth looking into after all that toil.

So Ray took one of his men with him and went at once to the apartment house, reaching it at 8:30 on another of those bitterly cold and blizzardy nights that ROB seemed to choose for the particular torment of the Schindler establishment. The elevator boy, when asked if Mrs. Saunders were in, said that she had gone out half an hour before with a gentleman. Ray showed him a picture of Bain. The boy's eyes bugged.

"Dat's him! on'y he all dress up tonight."

So Ray departed. But he came back with two more men in two taxicabs. They took posts, one headed East and one headed West; so that if Bain dashed out again there would be no delay in circling round to pursue him.

The reader might as well know now what these four freezing men did not know till the next day. Even before Ray reached the apartment house the man they were hunting had told Mrs. Saunders that the night was too wild for any fun and proposed that they return to her apartment and have a wild time there. While they debated, the elevator boy had gone on up. Since Mrs. Saunders' apartment was on the second floor they had taken to the stairway; and the elevator boy, not having seen them return, had innocently misinformed Ray as to the departure they had not taken.

So, while Bain was cozy and warm, those four men kept their eyes on that doorway all night long. At five o'clock A.M., Ray dismissed one of the cabs and had the other deliver him to his apartment. He left, of course, one poor sentinel on watch.

After two hours' vain effort at sleep, Ray went to his office. As he let himself in, he heard the telephone. The operative he had left on guard told him that at 7:34 their man had suddenly dashed out of the apartment house (where, so far as they knew, he had not yet entered). He had run like hell toward Seventh Avenue and caught a passing cab. Unable to follow the cab or reach Ray at his apartment, which he had just left, the operative had called Ray's assistant manager, Walter Russell. And Russell had just arrived outside the apartment house.

Ray instructed Russell to go at once to Mrs. Saunders' apartment and learn what he could. Russell walked up the stairs and rang the bell. A maid answered that Mrs. Saunders was asleep and could not be disturbed before noon.

While Russell kept his foot in the door and groped for a good reason to waken the sleeper, he heard a piercing shriek. The maid turned and ran, and Russell followed her.

And so he confronted Mrs. Saunders. She was in pink pajamas, but her eyes were bloodshot and her mouth was puffing out cries:

"My jewels! My jewels!"

She was too hysterical to note that Russell was using her telephone to call Ray. By the time Ray reached the apartment Mrs. Saunders had shrieked herself calm. When she heard what Ray had to say of her boy-friend, "R. O. Brigham," she was in a vengeful mood.

She told her story quite frankly. She was a widow with an eight-year-old boy at a private school. She went about a bit and one night at a nightclub a very attractive man had made eyes at her, and so fascinated her that she stole away from her escort long enough to slip her telephone number, her name and address to the handsome stranger.

He did not remain a stranger long—or so she thought. He confided in her that he was the son of a big boy in a certain steel company—a name that made Ray's ears ache. "R. O. Brigham" told Mrs. Saunders that he was in New York as a representative of his father's firm, but he was going to ask for a vacation of two months so that he could marry her and honeymoon in Europe.

He begged her not to telephone him at his hotel, since he did not answer calls because the daughter of one of Chicago's richest families was infatuated with him, and kept pestering him till he had had to change hotels from time to time.

Mrs. Saunders had a good deal of gorgeous jewelry but "Brigham" begged her not to wear so much of it in public. It was ostentatious he said; and it was tempting to thieves. He was such a home-body that, only the night before, when they faced the storm, he had told her how much he'd love to be just alone with her.

For dinner they had had a mere Welsh rabbit prepared by the maid. Then they had settled down for some earnest drinking. Love and liquor had finished Mrs. Saunders by daybreak and "Brigham" poured her into her bed.

Just before Russell had rung her bell, she had wakened enough to note that her future bridegroom had stolen away. Something led her heavy eyes to note the absence of the jewels she had left on her dressing table. She looked farther and found that all her jewels were gone.

It was not quite a miraculous coincidence that one of the Schindler staff should have been on hand at just that moment, seeing that various operatives and the chief himself had spent an arctic night watching for her to come back from where she had never gone.

As Ray cross-examined her he learned that "Brigham" had a habit of telephoning her every day at exactly half-past twelve. She said she could have set her clock by him.

It occurred to Ray that he might set a trap for him. The fellow might telephone his victim once more at 12:30 as had been his habit for months—so that he might learn if she had discovered her loss and reported it to the police. It was a long shot but Ray played it. He arranged that in case the man called, he was to be kept on the telephone as long as possible so that the number might be traced and his whereabouts discovered.

So Ray instructed the maid to pretend that her mistress was asleep and would take a bit of waking. When Mrs. S. finally reached the telephone, she was to pretend that she had not yet discovered the loss of her jewels. She was to be her old sweet self and honey the man along for half an hour if possible. Meanwhile, Walter Russell was to be exhausting all the devices for finding out from a reluctant telephone company who was calling whom from where.

At twelve-thirty the telephone rang. It was "Brigham." The maid answered. Russell heard her say, "Yes, Mr. Brigham, she still asleep; but she sho want to see you soon's she git her eyes open."

Then Russell departed and Ray sat and heard Mrs. Saunders put on a wonderful bit of acting about what a head she had after what a night. She asked, "Is this Thursday or February?" and poured out an endless stream of honey.

For twenty minutes she improvised admiration for a man she wanted to choke, while Walter Russell implored some narrow-minded telephone supervisor to disclose the number —and implored in vain. He appealed to the American Bankers Association and they appealed to the company to help them catch the man they'd been chasing for more than four years. In vain! Russell telephoned the Waldorf supervisor who had helped them before. It was her time off.

When Russell returned, despondent, Mrs. S. was still chattering away, but running down a little. Ray wrote a note and put it under her eyes: "When he's through, don't hang up." As she prolonged her last "G'by-ee-ee!" Ray took the telephone from her hand and heard the click of "Brigham's" telephone. Ray jiggled his telephone and told the operator that he had been cut off and he didn't know where the important call had come from. Would she please—?

That persuasive voice of Ray's, combined with the familiar appeal, did more than all of Russell's prayers. In a few moments the operator said that the number was Bryant 7777. But that was the big Rogers Peet store at 6th Avenue and 34th street.

Ray called that number but could not learn who had called from what one of the numerous telephones in that huge emporium. So he and Russell dashed down the stairs and finally secured a cab. It buffeted the blizzard and the traffic jams with ghastly deliberation.

They finally reached their destination with no hope of finding their man still there. But fate loves to deny prayers; then, when hope is dead, spring a surprise.

Ray and Russell questioned everybody who might have seen "a man" among all the men milling about the store. The photograph meant nothing, and Ray went up to a mezzanine cubbyhole where the switchboard operators sit. One of them vaguely remembered putting through a call to Watkins 9999. But she remembered no more.

In the last dregs of that vexation of spirit which ROB had caused him Ray went to the mezzanine railing and glanced dolefully down. Up from the basement came the top of a hat. Under it was a face—the one face of all the faces in the world that Ray was pining to see.

It was Bain, himself, in person, not a motion picture.

Ray stood not on the order of his going, but swung over the rail and dropped. He was unnoticed by Bain, who had stopped at a counter to look at the latest thing in collars. He got it.

With a leap that would have knocked a football out of the clutch of an All-American runner nearing the goal-posts, Ray flung himself on Bain's back and collared him, Bain went flat on his face to the floor. Ray brought the captive's two hands up behind his back in a way that neither Nature nor Bain wanted them to go.

Seeing such impolite goings-on in a haberdashery, somebody went to the door and howled "Police." Two plainclothesmen happened to be passing and came in; but did not arrive until Ray and Russell had robbed ROB of $900 in cash, and nearly $50,000 worth of jewelry, as well as two pistols.

The plainclothesmen believed Ray and took Bain to the destination he had been trying so hard to reach for four years and more.

Later in the day, Ray paid a bread-and-butter call on Bain in his cell and once more discussed the detective business. Bain sheepishly admitted his final mistake.

The blizzard had reminded him that he needed a heavier overcoat; but, instead of buying it first and telephoning tauntingly afterward, he had telephoned first, after pausing at a pawnshop to pawn one of Mrs. Saunder's rings for a thousand dollars. He had enjoyed his long love-talk with her but had not heard her say what he had expected her to say, which was that she had been robbed.

He took his capture calmly and cheerfully admitted his mistake in giving the telephone priority to the overcoat. But then nobody is perfect, not even a criminal. As Bain confessed, "You can't think of everything."

Mrs. Saunders really paid for that coat since she got her jewels back and all of the thousand except the cost of the overcoat. But she learned the unwisdom of giving your telephone number, your trust, and your affections to strange men of whom you know only what they tell you. And you can't really be sure of that.

The bank did not get its $10,000; the steel company did not get back its $18,000; the wife and mother-in-law in Chicago did not get back their $6,500. Certain hotels did not get their advances back. If the Burns company got something for its time and trouble, it certainly earned whatever it charged. And the world was a little safer when one of its most leisurely and effective swindlers was put out of commission for several years in the Sing Sing Storage Warehouse.

The American Bankers Association put a "detainer" on Bain so that when he had finished his term as a jewel-thief, he might be held and tried as an embezzler. But his family managed to raise enough money to buy him out of this second ordeal.

During Bain's rustication his wife divorced him. She had about all the grounds there are.

But Bain was of so cheerful a nature that he held no grudge against the world or even Ray Schindler.

About twelve years after Ray had first begun to look for ROB, he ran into the man again when he called one day on a big executive. His secretary came out. It was Bain! He looked more like his first pictures; for he had gone back to glasses. But not to his original stammer. He greeted Ray almost with affection, and boasted of his fine wife and two fine children. He really owed them to Ray. And Ray, who cannot keep a grudge overnight, had long since recovered from his vexation of spirit.

The last time Ray visited that office Bain was still there, and his wife still did not know that he had ever worn the initials ROB till he nearly wore them out and RCS with them.

If you see her, don't tell her what you know.

# 11.

# THE DICTOGRAPH
# AS A PUBLIC DEFENDER

The bulk of a detective's business concerns the crimes of individuals against individuals or corporations. Ray Schindler has done vast execution in that field; but he has also done spectacular things with groups of malefactors.

He was invited to put a whole city government into the penitentiary and he landed seven of the chief malefactors there. In the course of his attack he had to put into their greedy hands in one night no less than $100,000 in cash—probably the largest bait any detective agency ever fastened on a hook at once. His clients had to risk that amount to put an end to an unending extortion.

Guests at summer or winter resorts look on hotel keepers as ruthless robbers. They do not realize that the hotel keepers are often the victims of robbers higher-up. One reason, of course, for the high prices charged by resort hotels is that the guests demand the best of everything yet visit the hotel only during a few months of the year. The short season must pay for the entire annual upkeep.

That is one of the reasons, too, for the greed of their political parasites. They never know how long they might be allowed to stay in office. The public is fickle. They may throw out the party in office and put in reformers for a while. Soon it tires of the reformers, but the political grafter has to work hard and fast as well as secretly.

This is the story of a gang of grafters bleeding a whole

196

city for years till the hotel men revolted against the blood-letting and sought relief. In this amazing instance of detective work on the wholesale, Ray was rescuing a whole city from political bloodsuckers and tapeworms. The individual taxpayers were powerless to do anything but pay the taxes.

As a young man, Ray Schindler had entered the detective business by way of the San Francisco political earthquake that threw Abe Ruef and Mayor Schmitz out of office and into prison. Many years later, he engineered a similar political cataclysm to shake off the rogues who had bound and gagged Atlantic City. This was one of the first cases ever known in which the dictograph demonstrated its witch-like ability to overhear unseen and to record unheard. In this affair, Ray showed his genius for operating on an enormous scale with complicated strategy.

The hotel keepers there made big money when the season was good; but their overhead was huge. And over the overhead was the blanketing, insatiable graft of a city government that seemed to have neither mercy nor honor. It taxed the hotels at many times the rate imposed on other property-holders.

The crooks kept themselves in power by bringing whole trainloads of repeaters from the slums of Philadelphia to vote early and often in every election. The city stepfathers encouraged and protected gambling and prostitution and taxed them for all the traffics would bear. To every contract for municipal improvement a heavy percentage was added for graft.

The owners of ten of the bigger hotels finally took their problem to the owner of the Atlantic City *Review*. The managing editor said that a vast amount of money would be needed to overthrow such an establishment. The money was subscribed and the Burns Agency was engaged to release and redeem the hogtied city.

As the New York manager of the agency, Ray studied

the grafters and their habits before making any attack on them. Since they were interested only in graft, Ray decided to feed them enough to choke them to death.

What was Atlantic City most famous for? Why, the Board Walk, of course. What could be done about the Board Walk to interest the old insatiables? Turn it to concrete. Where would the graft come in? That was easy. Under the concrete, where it would not show, must be a mattress of crushed rock. It ought to be at least four inches deep. If the city fathers voted money enough to lay such a four-inch foundation, they could arrange with the contractor to put in only three inches of crushed rock. The saving on that inch would run into big money for the thievish supervisors.

First, Ray arranged to have plans drawn up for a real concrete walk. J. W. Howard, the leading municipal engineer in America, was engaged to make the plans and the estimates. Mr. Howard did not know that his plans had any ulterior purpose.

To engage his interest it was necessary to have a plutocratic contractor as a front. For this difficult office, Ray selected one of his own staff, Edward G. Reed, whom Ray described as "one of the greatest experts in 'roping' and finesse that I have ever met."

First, Reed had built himself up as a big money man, a contractor of unquestioned means even for such a job as turning the Board Walk into miles of concrete splendor. Before he finished with Reed, Ray had provided him with a high commercial rating so that any suspicious grafter who asked for a secret report on him would be satisfied.

When he was ready and Reed had engaged Engineer Howard to lay out the plans and draw up the costs, Reed descended on Atlantic City. He set up offices in one of the most sumptuous hotels. The city fathers promptly made the free-spender welcome. They blushed when he complained that the famous Board Walk offended him. He said that it made Atlantic City look cheap compared to any number of seaside resorts and spas in Europe. He showed photographs he had collected during his many jaunts about the old world.

The proud fathers regretted that they could not bring their dear city up to European standards, because the people could not afford it. But Reed pointed out that, in ten years or so, the walk would pay for itself by the lesser cost of upkeep; and soon after that it would earn for the city several hundred thousand dollars a year. This made the city fathers' mouths water, but twenty years was a long while to wait.

Reed dropped into their ears the sweet thought that if the people could be persuaded of the big savings to come, they would not balk at the heavy initial expense. They would doubtless welcome a big bond issue.

Reed had hundreds of thousands of postcards printed showing his engineer's plans and the beautiful improvement that such a face-lifting would make in the city's looks. These cards, exhibited everywhere in Atlantic City, aroused the public interest to such an extent that by-and-by one of the more slithy fathers began to feel out Reed to see if he were inclined to do the right thing by the supervisors in case they advocated the project. Reed made it evident that he expected this as a matter of course. He said that he was not born yesterday, and this was not the first contract he had ever made with a city government.

But before such a contract could even be considered, the city charter would have to be amended. He knew that, too, and he knew that it would take a lot of time and trouble, for which busy men should be reimbursed. He made it plain that he was not in the contracting business for art's sake. His estimates included a handsome profit for himself, and also an appropriate sum for those friendly cooperative spirits who might make it possible for him to put over the job.

The crookedest supervisors could not help liking Reed. His hospitality was overwhelming. Though Atlantic City is a vacation spot for New Yorkers and others, it was a workshop for the city fathers. Such of them as were open to bribery were delighted when dear old Reed invited one or two of them at a time up to New York for a change. He bedded them down in the princely suite he kept all the year round at the old Waldorf-Astoria, and he liquored them up and fed them up till they loved him.

When dear old Reed asked them to change the city charter, and volunteered to slip them a little something apiece for their cooperation, they could deny him nothing—especially when he whispered in their private ears that he would pay them anything they thought fair. The more important crooks loved him enough to confide in him that some of them could be had dirt cheap. One man was so poor though dishonest that they said he could be bought for a few thousand dollars. Another, however, held his honor so dear that he considered ten thousand cash a cheap price for it. The rest auctioned themselves off for varying amounts.

As one visualizes those long, recurrent scenes in which each slimy scoundrel haggled his soul into Reed's clutches, one's sympathy goes out to Reed. He had to spend days and nights in double-crossing double-crossers, in riding with them, talking with them, dining with them, swapping barroom stories with them, holding them up while they unbosomed their boozy souls, and belched their treacheries in his face.

One does not envy Reed that long pilgrimage he made among the denizens of the underworld of municipal politics. But it was a noble and a necessary work, and there seems to be no other way to keep the sewers clean except to go down and trap the rats where they work.

The better half of the task assigned to Reed was to elicit and record and compile the confessions these criminals could not otherwise be persuaded to make, the confessions of their past misdeeds.

So Reed played coy. When a city father would express his willingness to sell out himself and his city, Reed would coquet with him, and express a doubt as to the man's sincerity, or his ability to put over such a deal. This show of timidity and doubt always set the rapacious supervisors to boasting of all the other similar jobs they had put across.

They told how, in making the contracts for paving the streets with the required four inches of concrete and cracked rock, they had made deals with some favorite contractor, whereby he would put in a bid a little lower than any of his rivals. Then they would slip over a new regulation requiring only three inches of rock. This would save the crooked contractor sometimes half a million dollars, which he would split with the friendly majority on the board of supervisors.

They told Reed how much they made out of the gambling concessions. They told him what income tax they levied on the prostitutes, and who was the collector of that vile revenue.

They vied with one another in proving how faithless they could be, and were. They were especially confidential after a day or two in the velvety privacy of Reed's hotel suite, where they poured down liquor and coughed up confessions.

They felt free to divulge their sins because they were alone in great rooms where they could see that no eavesdroppers were near. They did not know of a certain new device called the "dictograph." It never occurred to those innocents to look about the room, behind pictures, under the tables and chairs, for microphones. That is the first thing an up-to-date crook does now. The purchasable supervisors were unaware that dictographs were installed throughout both Reed's hotel suite in New York and his offices in Atlantic City. These dictographs gathered up reams and reams of the history of villainy, ancient, modern and future among Atlantic City's city fathers.

After weeks and weeks of approach and huckstering, the deal was all drawn up. Agreement was reached as to the total price for changing the city charter as a preliminary to the bigger Board Walk swindle.

The charge for the new city charter was to be the tidy sum of $100,000—in hand paid, a certain amount to each man according to his private agreement.

Since it might excite suspicion to have the payments made in Atlantic City, it was arranged that they were to be made in a hotel in the nearby city of Trenton. So Ray arranged a suite of rooms for Reed with dictographs and recorders in the adjoining rooms. There were also placed in Reed's hands $100,000 in marked bills whose numbers had also been recorded.

Then when every arrangement was perfected, the applecart was suddenly upset. At the last moment the political boss grew suspicious—not of dear-old-Reed—oh, dear, no! He grew suspicious of the newspapers and his political enemies. He said they would think it strange that so large a portion of the Board of Atlantic City supervisors should convene in Trenton all at once. Questions might be asked.

He decided, and so telephoned Reed, that he had changed his mind, and the pay-off should be made in a certain hotel in Atlantic City, a hotel which was owned by the boss himself.

This devastating message came just a few hours before the time agreed on for the Trenton rendezvous. Any delay in Reed's arrival might wreck the whole work of so many months at so much expense.

An audacious idea occurred to one of Ray's staff. It was the only thing left to try. One of Ray's men telephoned the boss's hotel and asked exactly how many vacant rooms there were. When he was told, he said that the available empty rooms would just take care of the employees of a big bakery company in a small town. Their boss, he said, had given them a two-day vacation in Atlantic City and they all wanted to be together. The room-clerk promised them every consideration, and was glad there were not more of them.

What other incident could more dramatically reveal how important it is for a detective to have a large and elastic bureau of detectives. In such a crisis Ray could almost "summon spirits from the vasty deep" to fill any dangerous and sudden vacuum.

Now he had not only to provide roomers for every empty room, but his technicians and his shadow men as well. He managed the feat with such speed and thoroughness that when the political boss swung into his own hotel, the manager greeted him with the joyous news of the big batch of bakery men that had just rolled in and filled every vacancy.

"Hell!" said the boss, "I'm giving a party myself for some friends. I've got to have a room."

But there was no room for the boss in his hotel! Strangely, at this critical turn, three men who had been loitering about pushed up to the desk to say that they had been called away on an emergency. Now the room-clerk could offer the boss his choice of the three rooms providentially vacated.

The clerk did not tell his boss what he did not know: that the detectives had installed dictographs not only in all three of those rooms but had saved the adjoining rooms for their recorders; so that it would not matter which one of the rooms the Boss selected.

A fiction writer would hardly dare to throw in such obstacles even if he could think of them. A detective has to think of them all the time. Or stop detecting.

By pre-arrangement, Reed was late in arriving. He was lavish in apologies. Fortunately there was room for him in one of the three rooms so luckily vacated. From here on the play went on just as it had been rehearsed, only in an Atlantic City theater instead of one in Trenton.

The dialogue had been written down for the benefit of the dictograph and any judge or jury who might later be trying the case.

As each supervisor stole into Reed's room, he would look about to make sure that there were no spectators to witness his degradation. Reed would welcome him by name, assure him that he was unwatched and that only he and Reed were together. Then Reed would say how happy he was to pay So-and-So so much—$5,000 or whatever it was—for his services in amending the charter to permit the Board Walk Deal. He would ask the man to repeat his words to make sure there was no misunderstanding.

Then he would count out the bills aloud, and ask his visitor to count them aloud to make sure.

Finally Reed would express a hope that he could make many more such deals with his dear friend So-and-So. And So-and-So, of course, would say that he hoped so, too.

Then a cordial good night was spoken; and the next reptile would enter and go through the same dialogue.

Ray, of course, dared not trust those crooks out of sight with all that money. Each of them was tailed to his first stopping-place and where else he went. This individual surveillance was kept up until the last man was paid off. Then the operatives seized each man with the guilty money still on him. The marked money and the dictograph testimony would do the rest in court.

There were only two slip-ups. One man went straight home; and, by the time the arresters had arrived, had so completely hidden the money that it never was recaptured.

One cheap supervisor, whose selling price was only $2,000, had a momentary aberration into honesty or something like it. The operative tailing him was increasingly horrified by the fact that the fellow would not even sit down for a moment. He stopped at the first store he came to; and, while his shadow watched outside, paid a debt there. He moved on to another store, where he peeled more off his roll. The shadowman could not hear what story the supervisor told as to his sudden wealth, but he must have looked like Santa Claus to his creditors. And he must have owed at least $2,000; for he went up one side of the street, then down the other, stopping at every few doors and shedding folding money in each of the shops till he was stripped and strapped.

He went home empty of pocket but doubtless full of pride in his re-established credit, while it lasted.

On that busy night, the detectives recovered 70 per cent of the money doled out. In due time the trials were held. Of the eleven men arrested, seven were convicted—an almost unheard-of percentage in the game of justice as practiced in our dear country.

The boss himself was one of the seven and he served almost three years in the penitentiary before he was pardoned. But his loving constituents, just to show that they had a sense of humor if not of political honor, later elected him to a higher office.

There was one telling result of this wholesale assault on grafters. There was a somewhat similar netting of a number of Ohio legislators who had accepted bribes within earshot of a dictograph. The fruit of these devastations by dictograph was that many state legislatures hastily passed laws making such use of the dictograph illegal! Later laws made its use illegal by anybody but District Attorneys and public officers.

But this was not till after Ray had used the little tattle-tale on no less a personage than the Governor of one of the Southern states. This Governor made a little side-money by selling pardons to criminals. He had a go-between who acted as salesman for his clemency. This drummer, never dreaming that he was being dictographed, quite frankly and flatly offered one of the Governor's pardons for sale to the highest bidder.

The exposure created a great stir, and the Governor lost prestige for a while. But the public memory is short-lived and public resentment brief when clever politicians manipulate the atmosphere. So the Governor's malfeasance was forgiven and he was soon kicked upstairs into the U. S. Senate, where he remained a long, long time.

Gradually the successes of the dictograph added to its difficulties. In Los Angeles there was a candidate for office whose public record was better than his private conduct. He complained to Ray that he was being blackmailed because of a little affair with a little blonde. At Ray's suggestion, he arranged a conversation with the blackmailer in a hotel room, which Ray had wired for sound. To Ray's dismay the blackmailer looked the room over before coming down to business. Inside the folds of a steam radiator he found a dictograph, and uprooted and destroyed it while shouting his opinion of the vile villains who had installed it. But the undiscourageable Schindler worked on him otherwise, and the blackmailer finally reduced his silence-price from $10,000 to $10.

In Westchester County there was a political crook who was wise to the wiles of dictographers and telephone-tappers. Painful experiences had taught him that it was perilous to talk turkey inside any four walls lest four other walls should gather him in.

When the District Attorney of the County, Lee Parsons Davis, later a Justice of the State Supreme Court, put his problem before Ray, and told of the allergy of that boss to any enclosure, Ray managed to get around the man's claustrophobia.

One of Ray's "ropers" opened a deal with the boss to permit the operation of roulette wheels for a fair price. Since the boss would not discuss the matter in a room, he proposed a little automobile ride. Ray had learned that the boss liked a certain obscure spot on a little frequented road where he could observe any approach. The roper agreed and rode out to the spot with the boss after dark.

In the meanwhile, Ray had managed to install a microphone in the boss's own car. But at that time a ground wire connection was necessary, so Ray found a deserted farmhouse half a mile away and ran that length of wire to a pile of dead leaves right close to the spot where the boss always parked his car.

When the boss stopped there, and said to the supposed gambler:

"Now we can talk business." The roper said:

"First, you'll have to excuse me for a moment."

He gave a familiar reason for leaving automobiles at night and stepped out into the dark. There he hastily connected a wire from the dictograph in the boss's car to the wire waiting for him in the clump of dead leaves. Then he returned to the car and told the boss that he was ready to talk business.

They talked business and after much debate, a price was settled upon for which the boss agreed to let the forbidden roulette wheels whirl and protect them from the law.

When the boss went to trial he was dazed to hear his very words as he uttered them in the supposed seclusion of his car. As he was led away to jail, he growled:

"Next time I talk business with a guy, we'll go up in a balloon."

Today the dictograph is marvellously advanced in its techniques, thanks to electronic developments. But even in its crudest days it served as a noble weapon against the sly and secret conspiracies of those enemies of the people whom somehow the people are always boosting into positions of power.

# THE DICTOGRAPH AS A
# PRIVATE EAVESDROPPER

For many years Ray Schindler had the exclusive distribution rights to the dictograph. But that was in the early period of its evolution. Still, it did good work in catching public servants engaged in private betrayal of the public interests. It also served as a long-distance ear listening in on extremely personal misdoings, often of a most intimate nature, when the presence of a third person would have been a crowd indeed. Like other devices in which electricity is involved, the dictograph has been growing smaller and smaller as it has grown more and more powerful and more and more far-hearing.

On one occasion when Ray had to hear through a wall and could find no way to install a dictaphone, he had recourse to the simple but novel method of hiring the adjoining room and shaving the plaster so thin that it was hardly thicker than wall-paper.

But nowadays, thanks to radionics, it is possible to install a dictograph without preliminary access. One of Ray's intended victims insisted on holding an interview in his own office because he was microphone-shy. Ray's operative entered carrying a brief-case and set it on the floor. How could the victim have suspected that the brief-case contained a transmitter so ingenious and so stealthy that everything the man said was tuned in by wireless to an automobile in the street below? Inside that parked car were other operatives who heard every word as plainly as if they had sat in the man's office at his very elbow.

On another occasion, the apparently insoluble problem was to record the conversations of two men who met in a private house where there was no chance to install a dictograph, and no operative could gain access, even with a brief-case. Even this did not stop Ray.

One day after the two men had gone out, leaving only a servant, an expressman brought to the door a box that had suffered such rough handling as to half-obliterate the name and address. The name of the sender was quite indecipherable. The servant, of course, accepted the package.

When his two employers returned, they opened the box, and found inside a lamp with a lamp shade so beautiful that they set it up in the drawing-room and plugged it in the socket. It gave a charming light and they were content to await the letter of explanation that would undoubtedly come along soon.

There is something about the gentle radiance of a prettily shaded lamp that is conducive to conversation, and the two men went on with their plotting and their exchange of secrets. It never occurred to them to examine the lamp's insides.

Had they done that they might have learned that it contained a dictograph potent enough to repeat everything it overheard in an ethereal whisper that a short wave receiving instrument two blocks away amplified loudly enough for a recording machine to take it down.

The distant operatives in the car could see the distant house, and when the victims of this uncanny magic went out, the power was simply shut off till they returned. In two weeks this lamp accomplished its purpose and secured the desired testimony. Without human intervention it transmitted every word uttered by two men who were absolutely alone and seemingly remote from the human ear. In this case, the automobile was two hundred yards away. If there are no distracting noises such dictography can work at the distance of a mile.

What effect the various forms of dictography may have on the morals of the future, when people realize that they can never be absolutely sure that they are really alone, and are aware that the very lamps they put out may be putting out reports of their whispers to far-away detectives—that would take a bit of prophesying.

But the detectives and other instruments of law-enforcement are not in the business of keeping people virtuous in advance. Their job is to overtake the wicked after they have been wicked, or to prevent them from carrying out their conspiracies against others before it is too late.

Some of Ray's experiences with the dictograph as a weapon against dishonest public servants have already been sketched. It has also been of exquisite and most intimate assistance in the strictly domestic field. Two picturesque examples will have to stand for a long list of such interventions. In both these cases, women were involved as the dictograph's objects of inquiry, and in the second of them one of Ray's women operatives was subjected to a long and wearing test of her nerves, her endurance and her ingenuity.

The first one concerned a man of very high standing in Washington. He was high up in the aircraft industry and he was higher up in the air over what used to be called a "light o' love." This light burned so fiercely that he could not put her out. She threatened to burn him up publicly even more completely than she had privately.

Sorrowful men have found that while it may be hard to get rid of a devoted wife, it is nothing to the torments and difficulties of shaking off a tenacious mistress.

This aerial tycoon had fallen very hard, temporarily, for a Spanish girl. Separation from her soon became a matter of self-preservation, the preservation of a home and family from the devastating consequences of a public scandal.

The air-official took his trouble to a friend, who promised to extricate him from the toils of the Spanish ex-charmer. As sometimes happens when one tries to remove fly-paper from another he finds himself stuck with it. This air-official told his friend of his gradual interest in the pretty Spanish girl. She was a fascinating companion when he came to New York on business for a few days or a week-end. She was only a little siren to him, but to her he was a great mind and a great soul whom she could not bear to lose.

When he brutally confessed his fatigue, her pride and her misprized love burst into fire. She would not be tossed aside like a withered flower. She threatened to expose him publicly. She had no reputation to lose. But he had. A scandal would bring him down like a flaming airplane.

The little Spaniard began to make long-distance calls to the high official's office. They must have made delicious conversation when the stenographers and file-clerks met at the water cooler or tucked in their knees at the drug store and exchanged giggles of horrified delight over their nutritious ice-cream sodas. Mr. Big was as comfortable and helpless as Samson after his long hair had been Delilated.

Finally, the little Spaniard put a price on her favors and offered to accept $5,000 as liquidated damages. Her victim said that was Too, Too Much.

In his anguish and shame he turned to his friend to save him and confessed all. Let us call the friend "Ronald." Ronald told the airman that the Spanish girl had finally resorted to pure blackmail—if "pure" is the word. His advice was to "call in Schindler."

When Ray heard the story—a not entirely new instance of how unsmoothly the course of untrue love runs—he said that the first requisite was a record of the blackmail threat. This was a job for the dictograph.

So Ray rented a hotel-suite of parlor, two bedrooms and bath. He locked off one of the bedrooms, and there was nothing to excite suspicion in the fact that he made a recording office of that bedroom, or that in the other bedroom he hung a microphone on a tack in the back of the headboard, and in the living room fastened a microphone to the back of the couch.

Ronald moved into the suite and made it his own. Then he telephoned the Spanish girl and said he would like to talk the matter over with her. Thinking that it was a mere matter of auctioning off her silence for the best price obtainable, the girl consented to come down and discuss the subject in his suite, where they could be alone—with only two dictographs, a recording machine and two or three operatives in the offing.

The cocktails had arrived by the time she got there, and she was in a most hospitable mood. Her heart had a big empty room in it just vacated by a tenant who was going to pay up his arrears of rent. She liked the looks of Ronald as a new lodger, and wasted no time in offering him the affection that had accumulated during the airman's absence.

There followed a scene of the sort that French farces used to revel in, When Ronald said:

"Let's talk business. My friend is—"

"Let's forget your friend," said Carmencita. "He can wait. You're pretty nice yourself."

Then she plopped herself on his lap and kissed him so hard that she almost threw the recording needle off the disc in the other room. Ronald might have weathered the storm if he had not realized that his own every word was being taken down for posterity by a recording machine.

But Ronald was there to save his friend, and he could not dash for the fire-escape. The best he could think of was to say, "Excuse me, dear, but I've got to make a telephone call."

He went into the next room, took up the telephone, and sat down on the bed while he dialled the first number he could think of. Carmencita sat right down beside him. She playfully wrestled with him as she took away his protective telephone.

At that moment the dictograph mysteriously went dead

The little Spanish dancer had jiggled the microphone off the tack. Ray had to think fast, both to save his client and to rescue his microphones from extinction.

He rushed to the telephone in his room and called Ronald on the living room telephone. Ronald broke away long enough to answer it. When he heard Ronald's voice, Ray murmured:

"The microphone's off the hook and I can't hear you."

That must have given Ronald some relief, but he had the presence of mind to answer:

"Yes, I know, but I can't see you now. I'm busy."

Ray said: "You've got to get out of the room long enough for me to fix the machine."

"All right, call me later," said Ronald, and hung up.

It took Ronald twenty minutes to persuade his captress to join him in a brief trip to the hotel dining room. As soon as they left, Ray and his men restored the dictograph to its place.

Ronald had a harder time getting the Spaniard back to his suite than he had getting her out. It took him two hours and she had not been idle with the cocktails.

But at last she returned and the dictograph began to chatter and scratch in the next room while the jumping needle wrote her down for a better blackmailer than Ray had hoped.

She had been rebuffed by both the airman and his friend Ronald. So she said she was going to insist on double indemnity—$10,000 and not a cent less. Furthermore, she would telephone the airman to that effect the first thing in the morning, and furthermost she would also call his mother and father and tell them what a canine their son was.

At this point, Ronald was in a state of complete collapse. As a result of his kind intervention his friend was going to have to pay twice as much as he would have paid without Ronald's help, and was not even to buy secrecy with it.

Suddenly Ray Schindler descended upon the impossible scene. Ronald was as surprised as Carmencita when Ray un-

locked the door to the extra bedroom, walked in and told
Ronald to go on home and let someone else take over from
there.

When Ronald had gone, Ray sat down and told Carmencita that he knew her employer very well. He told her his
name. Then he told her who her people were, from just where
in Spain they had moved to just where in Cuba before they
came to just where in New York. He said they were fine people and called them by their first names and said that it
would break their hearts to learn just what their beloved and
trusted daughter had been doing and was trying to do.

As if that were not enough, he led her into the next room
and played over the record he had made of her recent conversation. One can imagine how her scenes of amorous folly
and drunken threats must have sounded to that poor little
thwarted girl. She had threatened to expose her ex-lover to
the world. Now she was exposed to herself.

"I can take up this telephone and call the District Attorney. He is a close friend of mine and won't object to my calling him at his house, especially when I say, 'I'd like to call
on you and present to you a pretty little blackmailer and let
you hear a fine recording of how she works. I also have three
witnesses to confirm the discs!' If you prefer the publicity,
you can go to the District Attorney yourself, and he will give
you all the publicity you want."

When she recoiled from this offer, he said:

"The man you wanted to ruin was generous with you for a
long while. Then he got over his infatuation, and tried to
forget it. If you want to call the whole affair just one of those
things that happen, and forget it, why, we're willing to forget
it, too."

At this point, the word "forget" sounded like about the
prettiest word she had ever heard in English. She had tried
to sell her silence for much gold. And now she could get Ray
Schindler's silence and the silence of those terrible records
for nothing. Silence is a sweet word, too.

She looked on Ray Schindler now as if he were her rescuer. She gave him her promise and kept it. And he kept the records.

There was another much less familiar family complication in which the dictograph was called in to do its uncanny work. It involved as unusual a situation as ever came into the Schindler office.

There was a brilliant young lawyer who had a beautiful young wife, the daughter of wealthy parents. Their honeymoon was followed by an occasional tiff. After one bitter quarrel, he was stricken by a very bad cold, for which he took a certain medicine every day. One day the usual tablespoonful of it tasted so peculiar that he declared he had been poisoned.

He not only fled from his home, but he notified his wife's parents that their daughter was a Medea or a Borgia, or both. The wife went back to her home in such a state of natural excitement that her mother took her to Florida for her nerves.

The excited husband called in Schindler and asked him to find out the truth about the wife. Manifestly, Ray could not go to her and say simply: "You tried to poison your husband. True or false?"

To get the answer to such a question was not a matter for a man detective. By the time he got to know her well enough to extract such a secret from her, a love-affair would probably be on the fire. And, while Ray sends his operatives to solitary confinement in penitentiaries if necessary, or leaves them standing outside hotels all night in blizzards up to their knees, he does not like to subject them to love affairs especially with ladies suspected of looking on the bottle when it has a skull and crossbones on it.

So he chose a woman operative, a pretty and cultivated young woman who could hold her own in the opulent atmosphere of a Florida hotel. For convenience' sake we might call the wife Helen and the detective Sybil.

Following Ray's principle that the suspected criminal must make the first approach to the detective and not the other way, Sybil went to Florida and threw herself with careful carelessness across the path of Helen for a long while before Helen took the bait and spoke the first word.

Sybil was magnetic, witty, sympathetic, and a good talker. Once begun, the acquaintanceship soon ripened into a warm friendship. Helen grew so fond of Sybil that she and her mother grew jealous enough to eat at a different table in the hotel dining room. Cocktails and meals together became a ritual with the two young women. There were long confidential talks in Helen's own room. Sybil was doing the work of a roper, or a roperess, and finally Helen said to her:

"I'm really down here because I am going to have a baby. My mother is staying with me till it's born."

Sybil commented pleasantly: "I suppose your husband is too busy to join you until the last few weeks. Or will you go back home?"

"I don't dare to," said Helen. "He insists that I tried to poison him."

Naturally Sybil did not exclaim:

"Did you?"

She expressed a proper horror of the ways of jealous men, and the friendship went on. One of the chief difficulties of Sybil's job, beside the endless task of listening to Helen's chatter, was that Helen took to drinking more and more heavily and Sybil had to drink with her.

Finally Ray sent down a handsome operative to pass himself off as Sybil's suitor. As soon as Helen laid eyes on him she went for him. He had almost as hard a time keeping out of her clutches as Ronald had had with that Spanish girl.

Sybil had both to protect him and to avoid quarrelling with Helen over him. But Helen's bibulosity loosened her tongue so that she began to babble more and more about that husband of hers and his terrible accusations against her.

When this was reported to Ray he flew down to join his

two operatives, not as a chaperon but as a dictographer. It was not difficult to plant a microphone in the operative's room, but it was a wearisome business listening to Helen's incoherent and unending prattle. And the recording machine had to be kept going because her mind kept shifting from subject to subject, and there was no telling when she would blurt out some incriminating word.

Ray had brought with him no less than fifty discs—enough to record several sessions of the United Nations, but they used forty of them without more than a tantalizing hint or two.

The three members of the Schindler force were about ready to resign, but the husband had engaged them and Ray hates to give up anything till he reaches the goal.

Helen's husband still loved her but still suspected her. He was afraid either to return to her or to give her up without positive proof one way or the other. Ray himself could not make up his own mind on the evidence thus far turned up at such cost of time and trouble.

When he had only ten discs left he instructed Sybil to worm the truth out of Helen by any means possible. So he and the male operative sat in their room and watched the last discs whirl while they recorded warily Sybil's leading questions and Helen's evasive answers and her rattlepate chatter. For four hours that curious conversation reeled on, Sybil bringing Helen back and back and back to the poison topic without success.

When the last of the records was filled with prattle, and the question still unsolved, Ray and the operative took to their pencils and notebooks and tried to record the talk. The long hurricane of language came to an end with Helen still vague and the three detectives exhausted. They went back to New York to recuperate from Florida.

When they played their records back to their client, he complained that he had paid big money to get records of the chatter of one of Ray's girls. But suddenly Helen decided to brave her husband's wrath and return to New York. Her husband took her back; she made him a proud father, and up to yet there has been no further report of poison in that family.

As for Ray, he can give only a Scotch verdict: "Not guilty, but don't do it again." He has a feeling that the wife's real intention was to give her husband a sedative that would calm his too-amorous nature—a sort of love-potion in reverse. The husband detected the strange taste and jumped to the conclusion that his wife wanted to kill him, when she merely wished to restrain him from loving her not wisely but too well.

Lest any woman who may be reading this intensely domestic story might grow envious of the girl called Sybil because she led the exciting life of a female detective, it may be well to append here another of Sybil's jobs. For a long and suspenseful while she was held prisoner in a sanitarium on a diet consisting largely of milk, orange juice and cod liver oil. This also was a love story of a most unhackneyed sort.

The Schindler office has close association with many other firms of detectives for mutual assistance. In New Orleans is Forrest Pendleton who was once the F.B.I. Special Agent in Charge there. One day he telephoned the Schindler bureau and dumped a task into its lap.

The famous play "Camille" concerns a young man who fell in love with a girl who was in the last stages of consumption. In this instance it was a girl who was in love with a young man in a tuberculosis sanitarium.

Her parents were Mexicans of wealth and had sent their nineteen-year-old daughter to New York for treatment. She had been placed in a hospital in the northern part of the State. Before long her letters home began to refer to a young man undergoing the same treatment. Her letters grew more and more fervent with her consuming passion for the young man and her dreams of marriage with him. The family grew alarmed and asked Pendleton to find out all he could about the affair and put an end to it. Pendleton passed the buck to Ray.

The operative Sybil was assigned to the pleasant task of pretending to be a tuberculous patient. Ray had a doctor who was friendly enough to arrange the formalities for having Sybil admitted for treatment. Sybil is a beautiful young woman of slender form but she looked as pale and wan as she could when she arrived on the train and was met by the hospital bus. At the sanitarium she was hurried to a room, and put to bed.

One of the cardinal principles of the place was to give the patients as much rest as possible. Sybil was nearly rested to death. It was almost impossible to get out of her room, and when she was caught outside she was marched back and restored to bed. Every few hours she was heavily dosed with medicines, mainly cod liver oil.

The nurses paid no attention to Sybil's abounding health; they took the word of the doctor who had sent her there that she was in a desperate plight.

Sybil was kept in the sunlight all day long and the medicine was forced down her throat. Only twice a day was she allowed to leave the cell of her room. Then she was assisted to a porch-chair and allowed to look at the sunlight.

From enforced inanition and helpless rage she began to lose weight so rapidly that the doctors looked forward to her hopefully as ripe meat for a complex and expensive operation. Every time she lifted her head it was pushed back on the pillow or filled with cod liver oil. If perchance she escaped from her cell in her bathrobe she was gently but firmly re-incarcerated by the watchful nurses. Even when she was permitted to sit in a rocking chair for half an hour, the other inmates were warned not to talk to her much because she was too weak to be bothered. The worst of it was that Sybil was not permitted to get to a telephone where she could send in either her resignation or a call for help.

Yet in spite of all the vigilance of the guards, Sybil managed somehow to have a few words with the Mexican girl she had been sent to study and to save. She also succeeded in having an occasional brief conversation with the young man. Here were surprises indeed; the sorts of things that can only be learned at first hand.

The youth whom the girl had written home about as if he were Galahad and Lochinvar and Valentino packed into one handsome frame, was the son of very poor people who had been able to give him very little education. He was in an apparently hopeless condition and actually hardly able to lift his head. Sybil felt that he was too weak even to feel any real love for the Mexican girl and was helpless to resist her almost violent sympathy.

The girl had either mistaken her pity for the love that is akin to it, or had been amusing herself by dressing it up as a wild romance in the letters she wrote home to excite and torment her family.

Meanwhile Sybil might have been hauled off for investigation by way of the scalpel had not the Schindler office begun to worry and made an investigation through the doctor who had kindly furnished the commitment papers. Ray learned in time to remove the "patient" from the baleful clutches of the surgeons, and Sybil came forth like a convict saved from execution by a last-minute reprieve.

She made a report of the facts about the Mexican girl's love affair. It was relayed to Forrest Pendleton, who relayed it to the parents in Mexico. They yanked their daughter out of that sanitarium and put her in another, where, they hoped, her sympathy and her imagination would be less exposed to overwork. The young man doubtless heaved a sigh of relief at her departure. It could not have been much fun for any young man to lie still in a state of almost complete weakness while a young woman hovers over him and belabors him with a devotion he can neither respond to nor escape. Sybil saved him as well as the girl. But at what cost to herself! One thing is certain; the operative's lot is not a happy one.

Our next case tells of a male operative's experience that makes even Sybil's seem easy and brief.

# 13.

## CRIME AGAINST CRIME

I have tried to keep emphasizing the fact that the real detective's life is not all beer and skittles; not all a matter of microscoping a few fingerprints and tracing a few footprints through fascinating scenes of mystery and red horror to a triumphant conclusion. I have tried to neglect none of the elements of drudgery, monotony, blind alleys, icy nights of doing nothing but try to keep awake standing up, futile pursuits and maddening delays.

And yet, in spite of me, enough of the romance and excitement of the chase and the high art and imagination of Ray's achievements may have got past me, to tempt the reader to go and do likewise. There is abundant need of good detectives, heaven knows, and more than enough work for them to do; but people should go into this business with their eyes open to its hardships.

Ray assigned one woman to a long confinement in a madhouse for several months. One of his male operatives had to endure solitary confinement in a jail cell for thirty days and nights. Even Ray could not save him from it. No wonder he sued Ray for damages. The wonder is that he did not collect any.

This case dates back many years; but crime repeats itself so unceasingly that the same thing might happen tomorrow. Just such conditions are being fought today.

The scene is a penitentiary, one of those big cages where the crowded inmates are supposed to be denied all liberty; but they invariably manage to find freedom enough for a vast amount of mischievous industry.

The time is just before Woodrow Wilson became president. It is in the days when he was Governor Wilson of New Jersey. While he was using the gubernatorial office as a prep school for the presidency, he had an Attorney General who was also named Wilson—George H. Wilson. This Wilson was honest and ambitious enough to try to do something about the ancient scandal of the sale of special privileges to well-heeled convicts.

One of the supposed penalties of punishment for crime is a denial of the joys of wine, women, and drugs. A few energetic souls manage to secure all three by the connivance of criminal outsiders or inside officers and guards who like to turn a dishonest dollar.

The situation in a certain New Jersey State Prison had grown intolerable. Attorney General Wilson mentioned it to Justice William P. Voorhees of the State Supreme Court. Judge Voorhees was one among the multitude who know Ray; and he fell back on the bromide: "Call in Schindler."

When Ray was told of the problem, his solution was simple: to plant two of his men in the prison. How to get them in? Let them stage a crime, be caught and condemned to a long sentence.

Judge Voorhees consented to connive and, since he was sitting in Camden at the time, Ray proposed to have the crime committed in that county. The Attorney General felt that he had better get the approval of the Governor first.

So Wilson took Schindler to Wilson. Ray was profoundly impressed by the man with such a future. But all that he remembers of the Governor's office is that he saw there the largest, most ornate and commodious spittoon he ever saw anywhere. It was of pink-flowered white porcelain, and confirmed the tradition that, while Woodrow Wilson never smoked, he was not unlike little Georgie Reed in that he chewed the nasty weed. But he gave Ray's plan his prompt and complete approval.

Ray gathered eight or nine of his available men in his

office, outlined his scheme and called for volunteers. He offered the consolation of triple pay with a bonus of $500 in case of success. The response was so enthusiastic that Ray explained:

"We're not going to take the place by storm, you know. And I can use only two of you."

He noted before him a man so small that he might almost have walked between the legs of the others to reach the first line. He was an Englishman, and Ray asked him why he was so keen to go to jail. Burchard replied:

"I'm getting married as soon as I can raise the price, and I'd spend a month in a swimming pool of ice-water for that triple pay."

The other man Ray selected was another Englishman, Holworthy. He was Englishly tall. Burchard asked only one concession: that his proud fiancée should not know that he had gone to jail for gold, but should be led to believe that he was carrying out a secret assignment in some remote place like San Francisco. This meant that the couple would have to send and receive all their mail through Ray's office.

Since both her letters and his would have to be smuggled into and out of the prison, where he would naturally wear an alias and a number, he asked Ray not to share this intimate correspondence with the whole staff but let no eyes save his own fall on it.

Ray agreed, without realizing that the prison allowed only one letter a week either way, and that Burchard's envelopes would have to bear a San Francisco postmark. There was no airmail then, and the bride-to-be was so prolific a letter-writer that even special delivery stamps and an occasional forged signature hardly managed to keep up the deception. In fact, it was necessary to overwork a woman operative, who pretended to be Burchard's sister, called on him at the penitentiary on visiting days, and received his instructions. She had to memorize them, since taking notes was forbidden, and the listening guard must not have his suspicions aroused. They had to use a code.

Ray made a virtue even of this necessity; and if Burchard or Holworthy wanted to tip him off to the fact that a certain guard was going to New York to pick up some heroin, he told the operative to "be sure to get Mary a birthday gift for next Thursday." Then Ray's men would tail that guard and turn over to the Federal men what they learned.

Having secured two reliable volunteers, and arranged for their indefinite disappearance from all knowledge of their friends, families and fiancées, all that Ray had to do now was to see to it that the two men should be arrested for committing a penitentiary crime in such a manner that they should be arrested by an officer who thought that it was a genuine crime committed by sincere criminals. This took a bit of doing.

Ray chose one of his operatives, Charles Severance, as the victim of the grand larceny and laid the scene in a little summer resort near Camden. He cast the Sheriff as the arresting officer, without the Sheriff's knowledge. He engaged Mrs. Severance to be at her husband's side when he was robbed, and to provide lusty screams while her husband seized his assailant, who was to be little Burchard. Holworthy was to let himself be nabbed by the Sheriff, and the long-legged Englishman was warned that he must run slow or the plump and wheezy Sheriff would lose him.

Everything worked out perfectly. Severance and his wife sauntered along the amusement park followed by Burchard and Holworthy. When they finally located the Sheriff he was arresting a hot dog at a hot dog emporium.

Burchard picked Severance's pocket and took away his wallet. Severance howled "Stop thief!" His wife shrieked. Severance clutched Burchard by the coat collar and held him fast. Burchard slipped the wallet to Holworthy right before the Sheriff's popping eyes. Then Holworthy struck out for the horizon, keeping one eye over his shoulder for the Sheriff.

Finally Holworthy had to fall over his own feet and lie still till he was overtaken and overpowered after an amateurish pretence of a struggle.

So far so good. But the day was Saturday and the two thieves had to spend the Sabbath in the Camden jail. Monday morning they were arraigned before Judge Voorhees. When Severance and his wife and the Sheriff and his son testified against them, they pleaded guilty. And Judge Voorhees, masking his sympathy for the poor detectives as horror at their wanton lawlessness, sentenced them to two years in the penitentiary.

They were now exposed to inspection in a line-up, and several Philadelphia detectives "recognized" them as various hardened criminals wanted for various crimes. Then the two criminals were deposited in the penitentiary. All the baggage they carried was inside their heads; for they had memorized the names and descriptions of the head keeper, several guards, and certain prisoners who were already under suspicion.

The first days went smoothly enough, while Burchard and Holworthy learned the rules and regulations and adapted themselves to prison life.

Then Burchard's memory played a mean trick on him. He mistook a new, and honest, guard for one of the suspects. He called the man to him, passed a five-dollar bill through the bars and asked for a "pill." The new guard summoned the head-keeper.

Naturally the head-keeper was not betraying his narcotic business to the green guard, so he put on a show of virtuous wrath and dragged Burchard before the Warden. The Warden was honestly eager to check the narcotic industry and he gave the helpless Burchard a double penalty for trying to bribe a guard and for trying to buy drugs. The penalty was thirty days in solitary confinement.

This was a triple catastrophe. Burchard could do none of the work he was there for; the operative who posed as his sister was told that she could not see him for thirty days; and the fiancée who was pining away for him while he was "in San Francisco" turned out to be a new problem.

Ray was doing the best he could to keep up the pretence of correspondence between Burchard and his betrothed. But the complication of the solitary confinement led him to skip one letter. This brought the fiancée promptly into the office. She pooh-poohed all of Ray's efforts to explain that probably Burchard was busy, or in some situation where he dared not mail a letter. Ray even suggested the possibility that the U. S. Post Office might have sent the letter to some wrong address.

She dismissed all these theories and flounced out, only to meet one of the operatives who blurted out the truth that Burchard was not in San Francisco on a mission, but in jail. Before he could also let slip the truth that Burchard was on a mission, the fiancée grimly announced that she would never marry a jailbird, and stormed away.

Solitary confinement is no fun, and is not meant to be. It is meant to break the stoutest spirit. When the great prison reformer, Thomas Mott Osbourne, became warden of Auburn prison he thought he would try a taste of solitary confinement, just to learn what it is really like. He instructed his subordinates not to pay any attention to anything he said till his twenty-four hours was up. He later stated that, although he knew he was in the dark only for an experiment and was warden of the prison, there was something so hideous in the suffocating black loneliness of the cell that he beat on the bars and screamed for release. He did not wonder that many convicts went insane as a result of such torture. When he came out, he put an end to solitary confinement wherever he had authority.

Osbourne had had one night of it. Poor Burchard had thirty. He had broken no law and defied nobody. But even if he had been willing to expose his whole purpose in being there, nobody would have listened to him or carried a message. He was buried alive for one endless month.

Perhaps Burchard's presence in the Hole made things more convincing for his buddy, Holworthy, for he was soon as busy as Burchard was idle. Holworthy made no mistake about the first guard he tried to bribe. He bought all the dope he wanted and passed the word in code to the operative, who visited him as his sweetheart.

He finally bribed one of the listening guards not to listen while he talked to his girl in a private room. Now he did not have to use code and the girl could take notes as fast as he dictated them. She came away with a bushel of evidence.

Six weeks after the two men had gone to prison, Ray had enough material for a complete clean-up. He turned it over to the Attorney General, who thought it better not to make a public scandal. He quietly removed six or seven members of the staff, and replaced them with honest men. The guilty inmates were disciplined; and the liquor and drug traffic was ended, at least for the time being.

Now that their business in jail was finished, Burchard and Holworthy naturally "wanted out." According to the laws of New Jersey, a Supreme Court justice has the power to change the sentence of any prisoner whom he himself has sentenced, when new information is laid before him that there has been a miscarriage of justice.

But now it looked as if Burchard and Holworthy would have to finish their two years' servitude, for Judge Voorhees, the one who could release them, had suddenly fallen so ill that his life was despaired of. Even his own family was not allowed to enter his presence—much less a Ray Schindler with an elaborate story to tell and the judge's autograph to collect on a legal document.

So Burchard and Holworthy must languish in durance vile for a whole month. One day the Attorney General telephoned Ray that Judge Voorhees had taken a turn for the better. Ray hastened to his home and the Judge scrawled his signature with a shaking hand on the necessary court-order. The Judge died not long afterward.

Burchard and Holworthy came out into the daylight at last. Burchard's prison pallor went whiter yet when his fiancée refused even to see him, to say nothing of renewing the betrothal.

He sued Ray for damages, which included the loss of one wife. But he had signed a paper stating that he was fully aware of the risks he was running when he took the assignment for the extra remuneration. He had also absolved Ray from all liability. So he was thrown out of court as quickly as he had been thrown into solitary.

He was so fed up with the detective business that he seized the first opportunity to take up something comparatively easy. World War I came along just then and he "went for a soldier."

And Holworthy sailed with him. They went home to fight for their dear England.

For a while both of them sent postcards from "somewhere in France" back to their former colleagues. By-and-by the cards came no more. And to this day Ray does not know what became of them. They may have died for their country as they had suffered for justice in this country.

These are only two of the six operatives whom Ray sent to prison. One of his women operatives was sentenced to a Reformatory for a year to learn what was really going on.

But he has also saved from prison many unfortunate and misguided men. One of them was a very young and very promising composer who had written a number of successes, but fell on evil days. His mother was ill and he could not afford a doctor; he was about to be put out of his home for lack of rent money. In his hungry despair he could not resist the lure of some jewelry left on a dressing table at a Hollywood party. It was insured and Ray's insurance company set him on the trail. He found the man and the Judge sentenced him to prison for a year. But Ray was touched, and he persuaded the Judge to parole the young composer in Ray's custody.

In another instance, a young genius in the employ of one of the great electrical companies needed some platinum wire and simply purloined it. He was sentenced to three years in the penitentiary. "Good behavior" shortened this to two years, but his future looked dark until Ray, who saw how many fine qualities he had, took him into his organization, where he remained for a number of years. Then he started a business of his own and has won big success.

The New York Parole Board, seeking a job for a well-behaved convict who seemed ripe for parole, recommended him to Ray. Ray made a thorough check of his character and was convinced of his honest intentions. For three years he was a valuable man and then his old appetites came back upon him. He looted Ray's country home of cameras, typewriters, golf clubs and such things. Then he began to bounce checks and he bounced himself back into prison.

He was only another among multitudinous proofs of the tragic fact that climbing the straight and narrow path is a matter of endurance as well as good intention. Many an athlete is a wonder at a hundred-yard dash, but can never make a mile-run.

This one man was the only one who violated Ray's trust in him. And there are even now men whom he has put in prison but to whom he has promised help and employment as soon as they are released.

# 14.

## THE KOREAN
## MIND AND FACE

If by any chance or mischance you should suddenly find yourself in jail, be wary of your cell mate.

It is well, of course, to walk warily in all kinds of society, to be careful about making friendships anywhere or imparting confidences to anybody. In prisons of every sort it is especially advisable to be cautious, because even jailbirds may not always tell the truth. Even when they boast of their reasons for being under sentence, they are apt to handle the facts freely. Instead of pretending innocence, these men often brag of crimes they never dared to commit.

Sometimes this is merely the work of an inferiority complex, the pathetic effort of a petty crook to pass himself off as a big shot. But sometimes he may be only pretending to have committed any crime at all. He may be an otherwise virtuous man who is in jail to find out the very things you are trying to conceal.

Suppose, now, that you have committed a murder. It may be what De Quincey spoke of as "one of those little murders that you thought nothing of at the time." It may be a killing that you are proud of, an act of what you felt to be divine retribution. But you run afoul of human "justice" and they put you in a safe deposit box while they try to find evidence enough to prejudice even a jury against you.

By and by some total stranger is thrust into your cell and you have to share it with him. The housing situation is almost as bad inside prisons as it is outside.

Well, your roommate at first shows no interest in you and is very secretive about what brought him there. This may be only a lure, cheese in a rat-trap. Gradually he begins to slip it to you in strict confidence that he has done a lot of things the law has never suspected. It is human nature to repay confidence with confidence.

Even in the narrow confines of a cell, your fellow-criminal may be a detective in disguise, a human suction-pump put there to extract the very truths you are most anxious to conceal. The technique is to swap pretended secrets for your real ones.

So, if you find yourself in jail, awaiting trial for a crime, don't mention it to your cell mate, however long you may have dwelt with him. He may be one of Ray Schindler's temporary jailbirds though the device is an ancient one used long before his time. But, so far as I know, he is the first man who ever put on amateur theatricals in a cell. This was probably the littlest of all Little Theaters.

Ray was driven to this desperate expedient by one of the hardest nuts he ever had to crack. Ray calls this case "one of the strangest I ever handled. I found myself matching wits with an Oriental."

This fellow was born in Korea and his strength of purpose showed itself when he was only thirteen years old. He was so determined to get to the United States that he walked four hundred miles to reach an America-bound ship. He studied at a Presbyterian school in the midwest, then took up chemistry. He went through courses in spiritualism and Christian Science, then practiced as a tailor, a cook, and a valet. He ended his long journey as a houseboy for an elderly, wealthy couple in White Plains, New York.

Lawrence Churchill and his wife, Ida, came to rely on Chang Soo Lee for nearly everything. He was a whole troop of servants, from cook to gardener, valet to chauffeur.

One evening at their winter home in Florida, Lawrence Churchill was suddenly stricken at his dinner table with what the doctor called a cerebral hemorrhage. In three days he was dead. His widow returned disconsolately to her home in White Plains. The faithful Chang went with her, of course.

In her loneliness she invited her niece, Louise Reeves and her husband George to live with her. They were well-to-do but, out of sympathy, they accepted the invitation. Chang met them at the train as chauffeur, unpacked their things as valet; made their dinner ready as cook, and served it as waiter. He arranged everything, foresaw everything like a mind-reader. But nobody could read his mind. He ran the house and made it impossible or inadvisable to interfere. He made the purchases and kept his own accounts in an illegible language that may have been Korean.

Mrs. Churchill was more than eighty years old and so deaf that everything had to be shouted at her. Like most deaf people she was suspicious of any conversations she could not share; like most deaf people she assumed that everybody else was as hard of hearing as she was, and she shouted her most intimate confidences.

One evening, in the voice of an auctioneer, she announced that she had seen her lawyer and made a new will, leaving practically all of her six hundred thousand dollar properties to Louise and George Reeves, with George as executor.

This was very pleasant and the only thing George Reeves could find to complain of was that his sleep of nights was broken by an all-night racket overhead. It was literally a case of squirrels in the attic. They rifled the garden where sweet corn was grown and soon had it stripped down to nine ears.

Chang, overhearing the complaint, went out in the rain to shoot the squirrels with an air-rifle but the rifle was not his weapon. He turned to poison, and soon there were no more squirrels in the attic or in the garden.

But soon George Reeves was being kept awake by gnawing pains in his stomach. He had been sent to bed with two broken ribs suffered when he fell from a ladder. Before long, his wife began to have pains in her stomach, too. The doctor put her to bed, also. He gave them morphine and other medicines for their pain; but finally had to install a nurse.

One day the nurse overheard Mrs. Churchill murmuring in a loud voice to Chang that the niece and nephew she had imported to care for her had become a burden instead. Chang said he didn't mind. He not only prepared the special foods the doctor ordered, but decorated the sick rooms with flowers.

Finally George Reeves howled to Mrs. Churchill his belief that he and his wife were being slowly poisoned to death. He asked for another doctor. A specialist was called in who ordered the couple to a hospital at once. Experts examined them and found distinct evidences of both lead and arsenic poisoning, probably given them in the form of powders.

The District Attorney was notified and, when Mrs. Churchill, after one visit to the hospital, drove away to visit a relation in Pennsylvania with Chang as chauffeur, the police seized the opportunity to ransack the house.

They found arsenic as well as cyanide of potassium in the cupboard; in the cellar a supply of acetate of lead. They searched Chang's room and found a veritable card index of poisons as well as a diary in Korean script.

Chang was seized for questioning and made no denial of the fact that he had gone in heavily for toxicology; but he explained that he used his poisons on squirrels exclusively. The skeptical District Attorney felt justified in accusing him of attempted murder, and he was thrown into the county jail to await the action of the grand jury.

Questioning Chang had so little result that, after six days of defeat, the District Attorney "called in Schindler." His assistant, Elbert Gallagher, laid the case before him as far as the investigation had gone.

Mrs. Churchill insisted that Chang was innocent, though she did suggest that he might have overheard her tell the Reeveses that practically all of her money would go to them.

She had failed to mention Chang as one of her heirs and he might have decided to get rid of the Reeves couple, who stood between him and the wealth he had hoped for.

He might have. But "might have" is not enough to satisfy the demands of the law. A possible motive was evident, and the supply of poisons was there; but there was a gap between "He might have" and "He must have."

The District Attorney's office had found out that Chang had bought poison once under an assumed name, but nobody had ever seen him administer any, and he could always claim accident. The District Attorney's office had found out also that the acetate of lead discovered in the cellar had been previously kept in a mayonnaise jar in the cupboard alongside a mayonnaise jar full of baking soda. In the same cupboard Chang kept the arsenic and the cyanide of potassium. Mrs. Churchill kept one key to that cupboard, and Chang another.

The other members of the household, the maid, the gardener, the doctor, and the nurse were easily eliminated from suspicion.

Ray Schindler promptly arranged for George Harned, one of his operatives, to be arrested for "first degree murder while attempting a robbery." Under the name of George Adams he was thrown into the cell next to Chang. George put up a hard fight before he could be forced into his cell.

Learning how Mrs. Churchill's husband had died years before in Florida, Ray sent another of his operatives down to St. Petersburg to see what he might turn up there. He learned also that, when Lawrence Churchill's personal effects were shipped North from Florida, most of his clothing was missed from one of the trunks. It had been insured and Mrs. Churchill had put in a claim for $475. The company's investigator decided that there had been no burglary; but some plumbers who had been working in the house might have carried off the clothes. The company settled the claim for $375. The District Attorney's detectives had found in

Chang's papers when they searched his room a receipt for three cases of personal effects shipped to a man in Korea.

This interested Ray, and he cabled agents in Japan to look into the matter and see if the man in Korea had received any of Lawrence Churchill's clothes. In due course of time he had a cablegram saying that the Chinese-Japanese war made it impossible to undertake any investigations in Korea.

Investigation nearer home disclosed that the Korean house-boy had accounts in seven different banks, in Florida, New York City and in the vicinity of White Plains. The deposits totalled more than $5,000.

From the Florida operative came word that Chang was notorious for extorting commissions from tradespeople under threats of not giving them the family trade. A detective in St. Petersburg was reminded of a Greek who had poisoned a Chinese rival and he was sure that Chang had got his idea from the Greek, who also kept a box of arsenic alongside a box of soda on his shelf. Furthermore, the Greek had been acquitted.

But the St. Petersburg doctor who had attended Churchill furiously denied that he could have been poisoned. Still, doctors have made mistakes. The graveyards are full of them.

In the meanwhile, George Reeves and his wife were recovering in the hospital; and the charge of murder dwindled to one of attempted murder. Also, Mrs. Churchill came back from Pennsylvania breathing fire. She was sure that Chang was innocent and that the doctor was responsible. The doctor admitted that he had been administering a drug containing some arsenic, and the District Attorney's office was beginning to doubt that Chang was guilty at all.

Ray was not sure himself and asked about the two wills Mrs. Churchill had made. In the first one she had left all her money to old family friends and servants, with $2,000 for Chang. In the second will, practically all her money went to the Reeves couple. Chang was cut down to $200. But there was no evidence that Chang knew the details of either of the two wills.

There were many other developments that led Ray and his men along thorny paths ending nowhere. All he had proved thus far was that Chang had broken the law against poisoning squirrels.

One day, George Harned came to his office, having been led from his cell under the pretext that he was to have a long conference with his lawyer. He told Ray of his difficulties in even scraping acquaintance with Chang. After a long delay Chang had protested that his secrecy with the poisons was due entirely to his fear of being arrested for poisoning squirrels. Later, he admitted that he kept the acetate of lead and the baking soda in marmalade jars alongside each other with only a little pencil mark on the poison jar to distinguish it in his own eyes from the harmless soda jar.

Somehow this convinced Ray that Chang was a deliberate poisoner. He tried to figure out how an Oriental mind would work. In Florida Chang had learned of a Greek who got rid of a Chinaman by letting him take poison "by mistake." He had not been punished. Ergo, a Korean might poison two Americans "by mistake" and get off. That was why Chang had fixed his pantry cabinet so that mistakes would be easy to make and easy to explain.

Ray had Chang's diary translated by a retired missionary to Korea, but it gave no hint of murdering anything but squirrels. Ray had a dictograph installed in a ventilator in Chang's cell. Then Ray went to Chang's cell in person. Harned introduced him as his lawyer and advised Chang to consult him while Harned went out into the prison yard.

Chang was cordial to Ray and bewailed the hard lot of a foreigner in this country. In answer to Ray's questioning about the poisons, Chang still insisted that they were for the squirrels only. When Ray tried to get him to admit some hatred for George Reeves, and his wife, the Korean evaded every snare. But he did ask Ray how long a sentence he might receive if he were convicted.

Ray was soon convinced of Chang's guilt; but baffled as to the way of proving it. When he climbed the stairs to see how the records ran, he learned that there had been practically none made. A crowd of women prisoners on the third floor had kept up a continuous hullaballoo that made it inaudible.

In desperation Ray decided to put on an elaborate trap in the form of a mock trial. He has said that he never took an idea from fiction except in the case of "The Hound of the Baskervilles"; but he may have unconsciously cribbed an idea from that well known Whodunit in blank verse called "Hamlet," wherein that Danish detective put on a play within a play to trap the king into admitting that he had murdered his brother.

Ray had taken his inspiration from the fact that the Korean had said he was worried about how to behave in a courtroom. So Ray, the playwright and impresario, made up a little troupe composed of Harned and three prisoners who were in for minor offenses and who had taken a dislike to Chang.

In Ray's scenario, Harned was to suggest that they rehearse Chang on how to behave in an American courtroom. One of the fellow-prisoners would be judge, another would be the defense counsel, the third would be the District Attorney; and he promised to make it as hard as possible for Chang, so that the Korean would meet no surprises when he faced the real D.A.

Under ordinary jail conditions such a mock trial would have met with difficulties. But in this case the sheriff cooperated, and the guards were kept busy elsewhere. The obstreperous women overhead were kept in their cells.

After much delay below, the dictograph brought up to Ray the word that the trial had started. Chang was in the witness box and "District Attorney" Harned began a fierce cross-examination.

"State to the jury why, when, and where you bought poisons and what excuses you gave the druggists."

Chang's answer was familiar:

"I don't remember."

But as Harned kept probing him he confessed that he had used the name "Charley Ching" when he bought the lead, and "Dan Song" when he bought the cyanide.

Harned went after him about putting poisons in marmalade jars and keeping them next to bicarbonate of soda: "Suppose someone with an upset stomach had gone to get some bicarbonate of soda and had taken poison by mistake while you were out of the house."

"That would be too bad," said Chang, and tittered when he said it.

Harned thundered: "You find it funny, eh. Two people are in the hospital near death from poison and you are in jail for poisoning them. How do you think the jury is going to like that joke?"

This sobered Chang and he grew confused as to the time of the purchases. He admitted that he prepared the food for Reeves and his wife as well as for Mrs. Churchill.

Badly rattled, Chang said that he served Mrs. Churchill's food on a plate with a little chip on the edge. And he admitted that he had taken the lead poison down to the cellar only after the serious illness of George Reeves and his wife. Harned shot at him:

"Then you could have been using that lead poison on the food you prepared for Mr. and Mrs. Reeves for weeks before you took it to the cellar."

To this Chang made no reply and Harned said:

"You'll have to do better than that when you come before the real District Attorney."

Later Chang admitted that the nurse called in to attend Reeves and his wife had taken the poison upstairs instead of the soda, and he had not mentioned it for fear of getting into trouble. It was then that he put the lead downstairs. When Harned snapped:

"Did Mrs. Reeves seem sicker after the nurse gave her the lead?"

"Yes, she very sick," Chang confessed. Then he broke off, "You just trying to make me say what I not going say. I don't feel so good. I go to bed."

This ended the trial. It had shown at least that Chang had been careful to distinguish between the food he served his mistress and that he served to Mr. and Mrs. Reeves. He had confessed that on at least one occasion he had handed the nurse the lead poison when she asked for soda.

Chang could never be persuaded to take part in another mock trial. At last the real trial came on. Mr. and Mrs. Reeves had to appear in court in wheel chairs. The trial was long and slow. At the end of five weeks, the jury stayed out for twenty hours before it compromised on two verdicts of guilty for "Second-degree assault!" But this was enough for the judge to sentence Chang to a five to ten year imprisonment and a $2,000 fine to be worked out at $1 a day. At the end of his sentence, Chang was to be deported.

Soon after he entered Sing Sing prison, Mrs. Churchill died. George Reeves and his wife, inheriting everything, sold the White Plains house and moved back to their old home.

The indefatigable defense lawyer now attempted to get Chang out of prison on a writ of *habeas corpus*. This necessitated a journey from Sing Sing to Yonkers. The judge's room was on the fifth story. Papers were placed before Chang to sign, and his handcuffs were removed for a moment.

The moment was long enough for him to brush his lawyer aside and plunge from the fifth story window to his instant death. The press reported his suicide as proof of his guilt.

Ray Schindler thinks that Chang certainly tried to kill the Reeves couple, and possibly had poisoned Churchill in Florida, his motive being in each case to remove an obstacle to the wealth he felt he would inherit from Mrs. Churchill.

In Ray's opinion, however, Chang's suicide was due to no remorse or sense of guilt, but to the ghastly failure of his prolonged efforts at great riches. He had suffered the one intolerable humiliation for an Oriental. He had lost face.

Chang had walked four hundred miles and crossed the ocean to reach America, where everybody is a millionaire. After all sorts of toil and prospecting he had worked his way into the home of a near-millionaire. The man had died —probably by request—leaving only the widow between Chang and two-thirds of his million. Then a niece and her husband had come between Chang and his goal. He had them on the way out when a specialist carted them off to the hospital and the police carted Chang, the near-millionaire, off to the jail. It will never be known how long he would have let Mrs. Churchill live, once he had her alone.

In court Chang learned for the first time that his cell mate Harned was really one of Schindler's detectives who had made a fool of him in a mockery of a mock trial. Chang suffered five weeks of the agonizing suspense of the court room, then twenty hours of pendulating between hope and despair while the jury debated.

The jury had found him guilty of a second-degree assault. His long, long dreams of wealth, and his most earnest efforts to attain it scientifically had ended in the dismal gray walls of Sing Sing. He was to toil there for years and then be thrown back to Korea where he started from, as penniless as when he left.

So Chang no longer had a name. He had no "face." He was just a number. It is not easy to kill oneself in Sing Sing; but when he reached that high window in Yonkers it looked out on the sky. He dived into it.

What little remorse tormented him must have been mainly for being duped into that mock trial by that mock cell mate.

The Moral in this case would seem to be; whether you are an Oriental or an Occidental, if you find yourself in a cell, don't trust a cell mate.

# 15.

## THE TYPEWRITTEN
## KIDNAPPER

The only blow ever struck at Ray Schindler caught him in the face and was delivered by a young woman. He calls it his "only wound-stripe" and he got it, not from a criminal he was pursuing, but from the pretty girl in whose behalf he was working.

It was a kidnapping case and when Ray was called in he feared that the police would never succeed in running down the villain who had been foiled once but boasted that he always accomplished his purposes.

The highway between New York City and Atlantic City resembles a racetrack in the speed of its motorists. In one small town through which these four-wheeled rockets are always zooming, the passage of one big car was marked by the scream of a young woman. She was found lying in the doorway of a large building. Hysterically she told how the driver of the big car had tried to drag her into it. When she had resisted and screamed, he had sped away, leaving her with a torn frock and a scratched arm.

The police secured a confused story from her, then began to scour the state for the car. It was something like looking for a piece of flying timber in a Kansas cyclone. So the Judge called in Schindler. He found the girl at the office of the District Attorney. She was being interviewed by the Chief of Police and two of his staff. She was saying that the man who had molested her looked so like a Spaniard that she was sure he was one. Also, he had a uniformed chauffeur who might have been another Spaniard.

The police took their departure, leaving the girl to the Judge, the District Attorney, and Ray. The Judge introduced Ray, and his preliminary inspection revealed that the young woman, about twenty-four years old, might well prove irresistible even to a Spaniard. In response to his soothing queries she explained that, though she had never seen her assailant before, she had had four or five letters from him.

She had kept all but the first of them. In that one he had stated that he was "a young Spanish duke, or prince, or something." She didn't believe it, of course; but that was what he had said. He told her that he had seen her as his car passed and she had appealed to his Latin ideals; furthermore, that when the Latins took a great liking for anything or anyone, they never rested till they had "accomplished their purposes."

In his second letter he had announced an intention to come after her and carry her off to his castle in Spain.

When Ray asked if anyone else had seen these letters, she said that she had shown two of them to Harry—the young man she was engaged to. He was the proprietor of a music store.

Some of the letters she had not let him see because they were so passionate that they might have driven him to doing something desperate. She confessed, however, that, instead of being excited by the ones she did show him, Harry had said that somebody was playing a joke on her.

It was the least tactful thing a man could say to his betrothed, but she said that she was tempted to agree with Harry till she received the last letter from the Spaniard in which he said that he was coming for her, and that he always accomplished his purposes. Even that dark threat had not impressed her young man.

Then it happened. As she was walking to the postoffice to

mail a letter, a big car stopped short, the door opened, a dark stranger stepped out, and said,

"Don't be alarmed. I haven't come for you yet; but I want you to take a little ride with me and talk things over."

She was evidently a girl whose mother had properly warned her not to step into the cars of strange gentlemen, especially swarthy gentlemen; for she pulled away from his clutch. He seized her again so violently that he tore her dress and her arm, but, when she screamed, he fled in his big car driven by the swarthy chauffeur. She was so agitated that Ray told her to go home and get a good night's rest.

The next morning Ray called on her and asked if he might have a look at the letters. The girl's parents were in a state of nerves and her eighteen-year-old brother had seized a rifle and gone forth to hunt down the villain. The letters were typewritten and the girl consented to lend them to Ray for further study.

He hurried them away to his New York office with instructions to find out what make of typewriter had been used.

While awaiting this report, Ray called on the girl's young man at his music store. The young man was almost excessively placid and was still not quite convinced that such letters were possible in this day and age. Under Ray's deft questioning he also confessed that the girl was impatient to get married at once; while he wanted to wait till he had saved up enough money to support his wife in the style that she was accustomed to dreaming of. He seemed to be in no hurry for that blissful day.

The next morning Ray had word from his office that the letters were written on a typewriter that was at that time too new to be widely distributed. Indeed, Ray was lucky enough to learn from the manufacturers the name of everyone in that town who owned one. Meanwhile Ray had interviewed numbers of the citizens, and found nobody that had ever seen a car of the kind the girl described, driven by a swarthy chauffeur with a passionate Spaniard in the back seat.

So Ray sent word to the girl asking her to meet him at the District Attorney's office. There he had her describe the man again. He asked if the man were strikingly handsome. He was. Did he have a scar on his face as many Spaniards do? He did. Was it on his cheek? Yes, it was. On his left cheek? That was right. Did he have a mole? Yes, he did. Then Ray stopped asking her and told her.

"You're just a little faker."

This stung her to the quick, and before Ray could put up his guard she slapped him in the face. Ray told her that he could have her arrested for assault, but that the county authorities could do still worse by her. For three days the taxpayers' money had been squandered on sending fifty or more cars all over the State in wild-goose chases after an imaginary Spaniard while her brother was on the loose with a rifle and apt to snap it at any Spanish-looking man he met.

The next day, one of Ray's men brought in the guilty typewriter. It belonged to a schoolteacher, who had let the girl use it when she wanted to.

Confronted with the instrument itself, the girl looked at it in consternation. As she faltered for words, her father and brother stormed into the District Attorney's office and demanded that Ray be driven out of town for bringing his "New York third-degree methods" to that peaceful town for the persecution of an innocent girl.

But the innocent girl told her father not to make a fool of himself and ordered him and her brother out of the office. She wanted to have a word with Ray alone.

In a moment Ray was alone with her. She told him her pathetic little story. Her boy friend, Harry, was in no hurry to marry. He loved her and all that; but he was afraid of poverty and he was not exactly romantic. So she had invented somebody who was.

To American girls all Spanish men are romantic. The Spanish girls think the same thing about American men. The girl had composed the letters and sent them to a girl friend in

New York to mail to her so that they would have a New York postmark. The girl friend worked for the telephone company.

The first two letters from the Spanish duke did not impress Harry, and the impatient girl had been driven to writing more and more passionate avowals till finally she had been pushed to the climax of the imaginary kidnapping.

When she had made this confession of her pitiful little stab at authorship, the police were called in from the highways and it would have been possible for a dark Spaniard in a big car to drive through that town without being lynched.

So Ray bowed out quietly and made no further report. It would be pleasant to say that Harry was so flattered by the girl's eagerness that he married her at once. But, in a way, it is pleasanter to report that she escaped from that human adding-machine.

He is still selling some people's love-songs to other people. But the girl left town and her girl friend got her a job with the telephone company. Now she can listen all day to other people's woes and love-chatter.

She wrote Ray a beautiful letter thanking him for giving her a right start in life. She was the only one who ever struck him, but not the only one who expressed deep gratitude for what he had done.

# 16.

## PAINTINGS VANISH,
## JEWELS REAPPEAR

Unlike many private detectives, especially in fiction, Ray Schindler has great respect for the police, and works in complete harmony with them. But, as many of the stories told here have already shown, there constantly arise desperate situations where the police are too busy with other cases, or too few in number, or too limited in time and expense-money to follow through investigations that require the cooperation of large numbers of experts, long periods of time, vast distances of travel, and often the almost endless study of innumerable records.

There are other reasons which Ray has outlined in his story of one of his most baffling cases. He writes:

"I have frequently been asked: 'Why does a private investigating agency often succeed where the police fail?' The answer is simple, and in no way compromises the worth, integrity or ability of the average policeman. A cop doesn't *have* to produce results. All he has to do is to avoid mistakes. He can go on for years, rise from pounding a beat to detective sergeant and higher. So long as he doesn't trip over something, or stick his neck out, or talk back when strategy counsels a tight pair of lips, he eventually retires honorably and settles down to his little garden patch in the suburbs. A private detective *must* get results. They are his stock in trade, the goods on his shelves, the dressing in his window. Let him stop getting results and he stops getting cases. It doesn't mean that the private investigator is necessarily any more alert or intelligent than the public investigator. It is simply an affair of bread and butter."

The case that inspired these comments concerned the Brooklyn Museum of Arts and Sciences. One of its prizes was a small watercolor drawing made by one of the greatest of American artists, John Singer Sargent. His painting was a study of Benvenuto Cellini's famous bronze, Perseus with the head of Medusa.

The painting had hung for years on the Museum walls and had been seen by countless thousands. Suddenly the frame yawned vacant. The painting had been neatly slashed out. Ray was called in and set to work with absolutely no clue to start on. He began with his usual study of the landscape and investigation of all the inhabitants.

In reading of such a case one must imagine the drudgery and the trudgery, the questions asked of innumerable people, all getting nowhere, all the tasks necessary to eliminating everybody but the guilty one. For the sake of brevity and anonymity the names are given here merely as letters. The most striking thing about this appalling report is that none of these persons had anything whatever to do with the purloining of that painting.

B-2 reports:

Talked with museum executives A and B; then C, curator fourth floor, and D, chief attendant, fourth floor, were called in. Secured all information they had regarding theft, then looked over the ground in company with C and D.

D, chief attendant, personally dusts all pictures on fourth floor on Tuesdays, Thursdays, and Saturdays. On Saturday, May 9th, he dusted the Sargent about 9:30 a.m. He had a bulletin-board frame to put up nearby, and this took him till 10 a.m., which is the last time he saw the picture. He and an assistant then worked on the hanging of a large picture the rest of the morning. When D started for lunch at 1 p.m. he happened to glance at the wall and missed the Sargent. As the museum has been having a great deal of copying and photographing done lately he assumed the Sargent had been removed from its frame for this purpose. About 3 p.m. he began to grow suspicious owing to the long interval of time elapsed and reported the matter to Director A and Suprintendent B.

Art students from the XYZ Institute under Instructor E visited the gallery in a body Thursday and Friday.

On Saturday there were 1380 visitors to the museum, all having access to the picture. C states he noticed quite a few Italians in this particular gallery.

There is an artist, F (address given), who has been making copies for C, but no one noticed him about Saturday.

The attendants on this floor are D, ten years with museum; G, seven years; H, ten years; I, six years. (All addresses given.) Museum officials say all are beyond suspicion.

J, with museum three years, was formerly attendant on fourth floor, but was transferred to the first. The curator on the first floor, according to Superintendent B, is a little hard on attendants. This curator has been away some time. J, fearful of having trouble when the curator returns next week, has been appealing to both his immediate chief and to Superintendent B to be transferred to the top floor again. His request was refused. J was formerly an attendant at the PQR Museum in New York. He left there under peculiar circumstances, but I was unable today to see Superintendent K of that institution to get the details.

The artist, F, was not to be found at his home when I called there at 4:30 p.m. and again at 8 p.m.

Spent the rest of the evening up to 10:30 trying to get in touch with Attendants G and H, but without success.

As a routine matter and to warn possible purchasers, photographs previously taken of the missing watercolor were reproduced in great numbers and sent to art dealers, art auction-houses, antique shops, and the better second-hand stores. Still there was no hint as to the thief.

The baffled detectives finally threw themselves on the mercy of the criminal himself and appealed to him through the press. They published an advertisement in all the newspapers including the Italian, because the Curator thought he felt the presence of a fine Italian hand in the deed. The advertisement was an abject admission of failure, and promised in return for the return of the picture: "No questions asked."

No questions were asked, and no answer was given. The theft promised to rival in a minor way the famous mystery of the Mona Lisa stolen from the Louvre.

Suddenly with a loud crash an accident intervened, a fatal accident. Perhaps all mysteries are solved by accidents at some point of the procedure. But this accident was a real one. It solved the riddle by posing a new one.

A huge room on the ground floor had been closed to the public for a thorough cleaning. It contained hundreds of glass cases filled with natural history exhibits of all sorts, stuffed animals, birds, and, among a myriad of other things, a collection of gold nuggets that had been loaned to the museum.

One of the cleaners mounted a tall stepladder to spray a pair of golden eagles in a lofty nest. He carried a hose attached to an ammonia tank. The tank exploded, shattering many of the exhibits, and injuring three of the cleaners, one of them fatally.

The whole museum staff ran to the room to extinguish the flames. Police, firemen, and ambulance men joined them. But the public was carefully excluded.

In the final restoration of things to their places, it was found that the broken glass case containing the gold nuggets no longer contained all of them. There was only the mark of a thief's hand in the dust to show how he had hastily swept up a clutch of nuggets. No fingerprint was visible. He had doubtless stuffed his loot in his pockets unnoticed in the excitement of the fire.

Ray Schindler was sent for again. He saw no reason to cast suspicion on the policemen or the firemen. He felt sure that some member of the staff had been unable to resist the lure of the gold spread before him for the mere taking. Ray went on the assumption that the nugget-theft was just as plainly an inside job as the theft of the painting had been the work of some one among the multitudes of outsiders who had filed past it. While his staff was still combing the general population for the Sargent watercolor, Ray took upon himself the combing of the staff.

He secured the consent of the officials to a general psychological test to be conducted in installments, group by group, neglecting nobody: attendants, guards, elevator and repair men, engineers, typists, and doormen.

This was back in the days just before World War I broke out in Europe; and fingerprinting was still a new fashion, looked upon as something of a mystery by the general public. Ray announced a series of lectures on the art. The whole force was invited, and expected, to attend.

The apparatus was so little understood that Ray could make it look most complex and elaborate. He took along an impressive array of machinery. He began each lecture with a perhaps pardonable bit of deception. He held up a fragment of broken glass and announced that it was a part of the nugget-case, and carried the fingerprints of the thief. To this fable he added a pious belief that the theft was the act of a moment of thoughtlessness and the thief would doubtless be glad if the nuggets had been left where they lay. For that reason, he said the officers of the museum were willing to give the thief a chance to redeem the false step of a moment by returning the nuggets. For that reason, too, Ray promised to take no further steps for twenty-four hours. If, at the end of that time, the nuggets were not restored, he would go through the entire list of employees with a relentlessness that would doom the thief to public exposure and long imprisonment.

To make his threat-promise more convincing, he then launched into a discussion and demonstration of how infallibly fingerprints betrayed those who wore them. He picked out a little group and said:

"Here is a plain water glass. I will turn my back while one of you just picks up this glass and sets it down again. Then I will identify that person by selecting his or her fingerprints from the complete record."

Nowadays this would be accepted and expected by the merest child; but, in that day, all the spectators were awe-struck, and one of them was greatly amused when Ray picked out a tittering stenographer as the glass-lifter.

Ray exonerated her of guilt, but announced that he was going to spend a week, if necessary, taking the fingerprints of every employee without exception—unless the thief took advantage of the one day's grace and sent in the nuggets. He asked the members of each group to describe what he had shown to other employees and thus spread the gospel of repentance before it was too late. He added the ominous warning that, even if the thief tried to escape giving the fingerprints voluntarily, it would be easy to get them anyway, since anything that anyone touched would preserve and deliver to his apparatus the telltale prints. Wearing gloves would conceal the fingerprints, but it would attract all the more attention.

The very next morning a special delivery letter with a hand-printed address was delivered to the superintendent. Inside was a bit of paper on which the culprit had cautiously printed a promise that the nuggets would be returned by mail.

That afternoon a tobacco can arrived with every nugget enclosed, each wrapped in a piece of newspaper.

The next mail brought a large flat package containing the long-lost Sargent watercolor of the Cellini "Perseus."

The lettering of the address on both parcels was plainly from the same hand. On the flat package containing the Sargent picture the sender had conscientiously printed the words "Don't bend—handle with great care."

There were fingerprints on the package, but Ray had promised not to subject the staff to fingerprinting if the loot were restored. Instead, he called the employees back in groups and made a simple demand:

"I want each of you to print, not write, at the top of the paper given you, his name and address. Next, please print these sentences as I dictate them to you."

Then, while his operatives were carefully watching faces, expressions and unconscious mannerisms, he read off these disarming lines:

"Take good care of your teeth."

"Don't ride on the handle-bars."

"Bend and you won't break."

"It's great to be healthy."

The lines contained, of course, every one of the words lettered on the package, but Ray felt sure that even the thief would not notice this. Yet, to clinch the matter, when all the sentences had been printed, he dictated the line:

"Don't bend—handle with great care."

When every employee had done his stint, all the examples, together with the original wrappers, and the note, were turned over to the most famous handwriting expert of the day, Albert S. Osborn.

It was easy for Osborn to identify the guilty printer. The man was called in; and his fingerprints, when taken, proved to be identical with those on the wrapper. A search of the shabby rooms where he kept his wife and two children disclosed a bottle of ink and four different penpoints, but no wrapping paper.

He held out for two days before he confessed his guilt, though he could not explain why he had done what he did. Can anybody ever explain just why he did what he did?

Since the Museum had recovered what it had lost, the thief was not prosecuted but merely dropped from the roll of employees.

Since he had won his success by a series of bold pretenses, Ray calls this case an example of the success of psychology, a most important technique in detective cases when all other measures fail.

In another case of purloined art, the police were called in and worked hard for months without success. Ray merely dropped in, and hazarded a guess that was instantly acted upon and proved correct. It also confirmed Ray's theories as to subtle differences between masculine and feminine methods and motives in committing crimes.

The ancient and wealthy family of Daniel E. Sickles lived in a big suite in the Savoy Plaza Hotel. They had an art collection noble enough to include Gainsborough's "Black Boy" valued at $80,000. During their absence from the hotel one summer the paintings were covered with linen as usual. On their return in the Fall the coverings were removed and two masterpieces were missing, one of them, "The Black Boy." Both canvases had been cut out of their frames.

The police were called; and decided at once that some thief, knowing the great value of the masterpieces, had made off with them and would try to sell them for at least a part of their immense value. So the police not only exhausted every method of tracing the thief, but issued warnings to every imaginable dealer, pawnbroker, fence, or other likely purchaser in this country and abroad. And they kept looking everywhere for months.

Since Lloyds Limited had insured the paintings, they finally called in Ray Schindler. He went to the hotel and with him was Leonarde Keeler, inventor of the lie detector. They arrived at eleven in the morning.

Ray examined the empty frames which had never been desecrated with any other canvas; and gave the edges a careful study. Then he said:

"These canvases were slashed by a woman. A man would have taken a sharp knife and drawn it straight down each of the sides and straight across the top and bottom. This canvas was ripped off in little trembling zigzag gashes—an inch or two at a time. A woman did it."

The huge apartment had been serviced by many maids, and other women employees had had access to it. Also the Sickles family had maids of their own, among them an old German woman who had been with the family for fifteen years and had helped raise the children.

Ray wasted no time on the men who had had access to the apartment. When Keeler had set up his polygraph, Ray called in the women to go through the psychic ordeal one by one.

The old German woman was among the first he brought up, though Sickles was sure it was a waste of time, since, as he insisted, not only had the elderly Fräulein been a devoted servant for years, but she had been frequently questioned by the police.

She was a bit defiant at first. When she was asked if she knew what had become of the paintings she answered stoutly:

"Nein!"

But the lie detector said "Yes!"

She was told that she had answered falsely. She broke forth at once in a fury and rather boasted than confesed that she had taken the pictures. She was proud of the ir-retrievable vandalism. She told how, during World War II, the family had often spoken with anger and horror of the atrocious deeds of the German troops. The old woman's love for her Vaterland overcame her ancient loyalty to the family.

Furthermore the Sickles family had fought in the Revolutionary War and in the Civil War; and now she saw the head of the house in a Captain's uniform, making ready to fight her dear Hitler. She lost all control of her ᴌatred. She only waited her chance with a witchlike malignity to destroy the dearest things the family possessed.

She had gone to the beloved paintings and snipped and stabbed at the canvases till the pictures came free of the frames. Then she had wrapped up the priceless canvases, taken them to the summer home on Long Island, put them in the incinerator and secretly watched them burn—gloating over them with all the fanatic joy of a true follower of Der Fuehrer.

Ray had solved the mystery in three hours. But the solution left the almost mystic grief one feels when a seemingly immortal masterpiece is forever annihilated. Added was the impossibility, as well as the futility, of meting out a punishment worthy of the awful crime.

It was Ray's womanly intuition—that is, his intuition of womanliness—that had answered that riddle almost instantly. Another case where instinct whispered to him, "Cherchez la femme!" did not concern paintings, but it can be hung on here as a sort of jewelled pendant.

A prominent executive of an airplane company and his wife lived in a New York apartment hotel. One day they learned that some thief had robbed them of nearly all their jewelry. The loss was great in money costs, and greater in sentimental values; for their collection had been building from many years of travel about the world. Many heirlooms were included.

For over a year, police and detectives used all their arts in vain to find the thief or the jewels. One day the executive, who was a warm friend of Ray's, met him in a club and mentioned the loss and the vain hunt. He sighed:

"I wish I'd called you in."

"Was nothing ever recovered?" Ray asked.

"Not a thing. At least not by the police or the detectives. But the thief did send back my wife's wedding ring. It had an inscription on it and I suppose it touched even his hard heart."

"His?" said Ray. "You mean hers? A man thief wouldn't be touched by anything sentimental about a wedding ring. But a woman! Did the police or the insurance investigators look for a woman especially?"

"Not at all. They were sure it was a man's work."

"Let me talk to your wife," said Ray.

He called on her and questioned her closely till she suddenly recalled that about the time of the robbery she had been ill and attended by a nurse. Such a nice woman! Nobody could suspect her!

But Ray set his office force to work and they soon found that, during the past year the nurse had been living in a luxury she had not been accustomed to. Also she was wearing a good deal of jewelry. And she was not the type of woman that men throw diamonds at.

Under pressure she surrendered such of the jewels as she had not already pawned. And, since heirlooms and sentimental gems are hard to hock, the family got back most of its losses.

While we are on the subject of those three close relatives, women and jewelry and sentimentality, we might attach here the account of a most unusual technique employed by Ray in the recovery of an emerald bracelet valued at $50,-000.

A wealthy couple came to Ray and confessed that they had been innocent enough to play cards for high stakes with a charming couple of strangers on a trans-Atlantic steamer. In spite of all the warnings that have been lavished on this folly, and all the "Beware!" placards put up on the steamer walls, they had played.

As usual the ingenuous millionaires had begun to lose, after the usual preliminary winnings that are used for bait.

In the course of the exciting evening, the husband had lost $5,000, which he paid off with a check; the wife had lost $21,000, which was more than she had in her bank account. So she persuaded the other woman to accept her $50,000 emerald bracelet as security for the debt of honor till she could get ashore and dig up the cash. The sweet lady consented and gave her address as a big hotel.

Once ashore, the repentant wife acquired the $21,000 in cash and called at the hotel. The charming couple was unknown there.

In dismay she called in Schindler and gave so detailed a description that Ray's people, by checking the steamship records, cab stands and nightclubs, finally located the couple and tailed them to an apartment house.

Arresting them for stealing the bracelet would have been as fruitless as the publicity would have been embarrassing to the woman for whom the bracelet had a sentimental as well as a financial importance. But Ray's office kept the pair under observation till they discovered that the wife, or at least the woman, had left her husband, or at least her man; and taken an apartment of her own.

She began to appear everywhere with a new man of evident wealth. One night two of Ray's operatives took the table next to hers and began to talk in boisterous tones about a woman who, according to one of them, was "the cleverest woman crook on land or sea." He proved it by telling how easy and cleverly she and her boy friend had finagled an emerald bracelet worth fifty grand. The woman was manifestly uneasy but she sat it out.

The next day the gambleress and the same man lunched together expensively at another restaurant. Two entirely different operatives from Ray's staff happened to take the next table. One of them just chanced to tell in long distance tones about the amazing skill of "the cleverest woman crook on land or sea," and how she "got an emerald bracelet worth fifty grand for nothing net."

The woman finished her lunch in a hurry and left the place with her squire. While he waited for his hat, two operatives in riding breeches were discussing "the cleverest woman crook on land or sea." They marvelled aloud at her easy way of picking up an emerald bracelet worth so much.

This thing went on till the pretty swindler felt unable to find any place in town where she and her latest prospect could eat without having the air filled with the praises of the cleverest woman crook and her stolen emeralds.

The climax came in the Ritz-Carlton restaurant. Even there the next table was occupied by three Schindlers at once, Father John and his two boys, Ray and Walter. Even they were talking of a certain woman and certain emeralds.

By now she was desperate enough to tell her escort that those men over there were maligning her. Gallantly he went to the table and demanded satisfaction. The venerable ex-clergyman, John F. Schindler, protested that they were merely discussing one whom they considered the cleverest woman crook on land or sea. He asked how could that refer to the lady over there?

The escort apologized and went back to the table to explain to the frantic creature that it was all a mistake.

"They are merely discussing the cleverest woman crook on land or sea, and how she picked up a very grand emerald bracelet."

If you have ever had a popular tune run through your head till it threatened to drive you mad, you will not wonder at the desperation of that unfortunate woman. That night the woman cowering in her apartment was called to the telephone by Ray Schindler. In his most irresistibly dulcet voice he murmured:

"Had enough?"

She screamed: "Yes! What will it cost me to have you call off your wolves?"

"A certain emerald bracelet that cost you nothing," said Ray.

She shucked it off as if it had been a green snake, and had it in his hands as fast as she could get it to him. And as soon as he could get it to the woman who had lost it at cards, the homesick emeralds were once more coiled about her wrist.

There are ways and ways of regaining stolen property. A successful detective must know them all.

# 17.

## HE BUILDS A RAILROAD

If you wanted to catch a crooked architect Ray Schindler would build a cathedral for you if necessary. It would be a good cathedral, too; and would serve its purpose of saving souls.

Didn't he build a railroad?—a small one, but still a real railroad—to catch some crooks who were stealing millions? And didn't that bit of railroad pay his clients a handsome profit? The answer is Yes.

One day an eminent railroad lawyer sent for Ray and asked him:

"Do you know anything about rock ballast?"

"Not just now," said Ray. "But by tomorrow—"

"All right. Bone up on ballast."

He went on to explain that among his clients was a famous firm which had best be disguised here as the Rollins Syndicate. It owned a controlling interest in a railroad that had better be camouflaged here as the Monongahela and Pacific. The road carried vast quantities of coal from the mines to the customers, and, like any other growing railroad, it used vast quantities of rock ballast to keep its tracks solid and steady. It transported the ballast from the rock-quarries to wherever it was needed. One of the divisions demanded rock ballast in such enormous quantities that an accountant with a nose for figures thought he smelled something burning. It smelled like stockholders' money burning.

This man did some snooping and some computing and, as he added it up, though a foundation of rock ballast eight inches thick was considered enough even for the heaviest

261

traffic, this particular division was buying enough of it to make a foundation nearly twice as deep. Those rocks were costly by the ton and they had to be loaded and hauled hundreds of miles.

The accountant passed his findings along on up, and the Rollins people felt that they were being bled of their legitimate profits, and bled white. But this was a difficult thing to prove. They called in their lawyer. He called in Ray Schindler. So Ray learned all about ballast and enough about railroad building to build a young railroad.

The first thing that had to be learned was the actual number of carloads of ballast shipped from the quarries. For every car a card was filled out by the foreman of the shovel gang that filled the car with rock. These cards were kept in one of the company offices. How could a stranger get at them without exciting suspicion?

An ingenious story was cooked up for this purpose. One of Ray's detectives from New York passed himself off as a detective from Texas. His disguises were a drawl and a dialect. He said he had been sent up Noath among the damyankees to look foh a suttain cullud pussun who was wanted foh murda, and he reckoned the nigra mout have picked up a job as a gang-fo'man loadin' railroad caws at one of the rock quawwries.

The "Texan" carried with him a printed "Wanted" circular showing the side face and full face portraits of an ominous looking negro, with a description of his appearance and his crime, also a sample of his handwriting and his signature.

The detective said he would be mighty much obliged if the railroad people would let him go over all the loading cards as he thought that he might trace his man that way. It might have seemed more natural for him to go about among all the loading gangs and study their features; but he was given access to the files.

Every day he went to the offices and took his midday meal with him in a huge lunchbox. Nobody noted that every afternoon at closing time he carried away with him as many selected loading cards as his lunchbox would hold. He brought them back the next morning under his sandwiches and hardboiled eggs.

Nobody noted that at secret places an accountant worked all night on those cards and other records, copying from them such figures as proved the immense excess of loadings over the reasonable amount. In this way incriminating records were made at the seat of the thievery.

At the same time the high officials who ordered the buying and hauling of so much broken rock were under separate espionage. The detective covering them did not pretend to be a cowboy constable. He posed as a capitalist of limitless means.

The hotel men of Atlantic City had engaged the Burns bureau to rope in the Atlantic City supervisors who were paying public money for excessive and unused ballast for the highways. It has already been told now the hotel men had advanced $100,000 in cash for bribe-money and had not only received nearly all of it back but had put a stop to the nefarious practice.

The Rollins people put into Ray's hands a far larger sum to play with and not only ended the robbery but gained a handsome profit. Ray used this same clever roper for the railroad president, the chief engineer and several other high officials who were pocketing what ought to have been dividends for the stockholders.

This delicate task was entrusted to Edward Reed, who was an alumnus of Columbia University, and well trained in law. He looked like the million dollars he pretended to have. In the city where the president of the railroad lived, Reed took expensive rooms at the best hotel, and eased himself into the golf club through his unlimited hospitality to the monied aristocracy.

The Monongahela and Pacific people were about to build a railroad spur sixteen miles long to link up certain desirable territory with the main trunk and, incidentally, to furnish a new excuse for spending big money from which they would skim off the cream. They had advertised for bids, and counted on a deal with a crooked contractor who was secretly in business with them. His daughter was the wife of one of the railroad barons.

The Rollins company was able to furnish Ray with the exact amount of the lowest dummy bid; and, since it was oversize, it was possible to submit a lower bid that would still do the work and show a fair profit for the contractor.

But who was to put in such a bid and carry out the contract? The answer was Edward Reed.

He was not a contractor, of course, but it was not hard to find one and take him into an improvised firm. This man had to be an efficient builder and an honest one, just as the engineer who made the plans for the Atlantic City Board Walk had to be a real engineer and an honest one. In both cases it was thought best that the man selected should have no reason to suspect that he was being used for a secret purpose.

There was in a neighboring town a contractor of undoubted ability whose opportunities thus far had been limited to modest tasks. One day he was visited by the impressively gorgeous Edward Reed, who asked him if he cared to enlarge his business. This man may be called Tom Swinnerton and his answer was, in effect, Would a duck swim if he had a chance? All a duck needs is water; all that Swinnerton needed was capital.

Reed was the capitalist of his dreams. He proved it by depositing in a local bank $25,000 as a nest egg for the new firm of Swinnerton and Reed. The new firm put in a bid far below the amount proposed by the contractor in cahoots with the executives.

This caused them much dismay until the genial Edward Reed managed to make it evident to them that he was willing to grease the rails even more generously than their old crony. Incidentally, through these conversations and Reed's reports, Ray was enabled to secure proof positive of the dirty work that had been previously done by the expansive contractor. Ray learned that one of the devices was this: the railroad purchased ballast at the quarry, sold it to the contractor at cost price and then hauled it three hundred miles without expense to the contractor, but at the expense of the innocent and ignorant stockholders. The saving on the price of material and haulage was large enough to divide up into neat amounts for all concerned.

How the crooked contractor felt about being edged out of his easy profits by the upstart firm of Swinnerton and Reed is unknown and unimportant. The railroad men let him do his own worrying as they basked in the generosity of dear old Eddie Reed, and the efficiency of Tom Swinnerton, who was a wizard at laying tracks swiftly and well.

In the meanwhile, the investigation of car-loadings at the quarries was still being carried on by the indefatigable Texan, who showed a typically Southern laziness about overtaking that fugitive murderer.

At the other quarry, the loading cards were being ransacked by another operative, Charles Severance. He used a different approach. Instead of pretending to be a sleuth in search of a killer, he played the lady-killer. He squandered his charms on a girl who worked in the files of the quarry, and he managed to get hold of her office-key long enough to make an impression of it, and have a duplicate made.

With this he entered the office every night and, while two other operatives stood guard and helped him out, he went through the loading cards and filled a large burlap bag with them every night. This he and his two associates lugged to a distant building where a staff of expert accountants worked over them all night. Then Severance took them back to the office and restored them to their places before daybreak. In the course of ransacking the files, Severance was also digging up many incriminating documents, and these were being photostated before they were put back.

What the girl he had paid court to thought of Charlie Severance as an absentee suitor is not recorded; but perhaps it ought to be said at this point that all these acts of burglary and deception were entirely legitimate since they were authorized and paid for by the representatives of a majority of the stockholders, who had every right to make sure of the integrity and efficiency of their high-salaried employees. The president of the railroad was merely the highest-paid, but no less a trusted servant of the true owners of the property and the business.

Night after night, Severance and his assistants, Russell and Parsells, toiled at the files in such dim light as they dared to employ: the faint radiance of three flashlights held downward lest the night watchman should be drawn to them by any glow in the windows.

The watchman who patrolled the grounds at regular intervals was named Henry Kohler.

Ray Schindler is a sort of night watchman, too; and he patrols his battle lines incessantly. And so one night, as luck would have it, he went with Severance, Russell and Parsells to see how well they were getting along.

The four were squatting on the floor winnowing the files in little patches of light, and finding especially interesting material in a batch of letters. Abruptly they were half blinded by a big flashlight in their faces, and stunned by a thunderous voice that roared:

"What goes on here? Get up!"

Perhaps it was Charlie Severance who stammered the embarrassing introduction:

"Mr. K-K-Kohler, this is M-M-Mr. Schind-l-l-ler. Mr. Schindler this is Mr. Kohler, the night watchman!"

Anyway, Ray said something to this effect:

"Mr. Kohler, you and I and all of us are employed by the M & P Railway. You are a kind of detective, and so are we. We were sent here by the Rollins people, who really own the railroad. You and we are all in this together."

"Baloney!" said Mr. Kohler.

Ray made a more personal approach:

"Now look here, Kohler, I suppose you're a married man with a family. If you are, you'd better realize that your real boss is Arthur J. Rollins, who controls most of the stock. It's not controlled by the officials he hires to hire you."

The name of Rollins elicited a grunt of recognition if not of awe from Kohler, and Ray went on:

"I have a letter from Arthur J. Rollins himself giving me full authority to do what I'm doing now or was doing till you horned in. If you don't believe me, I'll show you the letter. It's right here in my left-hand pocket.

"You're a brave and conscientious man and you know your job," Ray went on. "If you do as I say, I'll see that you get a raise in pay, and I'll speak to Mr. Rollins personally about how brave and alert you've been. A word from me will go a long way with Mr. Rollins. If you don't believe it, a look at his letter will open your eyes."

Cautiously Kohler circled Ray, keeping his eyes on the other three men. He took the letter from Ray's pocket, backed off, got behind a desk, opened it and read it with half an eye and half a belief.

"How would I know it isn't a forgery?" said Kohler. "Why didn't your Mr. Rollins give you a letter to me?"

In growing desperation Ray thought up a new way out:

"Look, Kohler, you can easily learn if we're on the level. You can call Mr. Rollins on the telephone. I can give you his number."

"That's an idea. There's a phone right here on the desk."

Rollins did not relish being pulled out of bed at that ungodly hour, but when Ray explained to him the purpose of the call, he readily reassured Kohler, which seemed to please him very much. His full cooperation was obtained from that time on, making Ray's job much easier.

When at long last everything was in readiness and the documentation complete, the guilty officials were called together and confronted with the proof that their long reign of corruption was over.

It seemed undesirable in many ways to expose the railway's finances to the public eye by bringing the dozen prominent bloodsuckers to trial. They were permitted to resign and were glad of the privilege. The only announcement was that a general reorganization had been made.

When Ray wound up his work for the Rollins Syndicate, he was able to turn over to the company sixteen miles of excellent and solidly ballasted railroad. The firm of Swinnerton and Reed came to an end, with an equal division of their profits. Reed's share was $77,000, which he turned over to the Rollins Syndicate, which had backed him. The whole investigation had cost the Rollins Syndicate $52,000 and their net profit was about $25,000 in addition to a well-built spur of track and a thorough housecleaning.

It was high time that the purge was made; for the company had already been robbed of more than two million dollars, of which the high-handed marauders made restitution of less than one million. But had it not been for that sharp-scented accountant and the labors of Schindler, the company would not have had that and might still be staggering along, bleeding slowly to death. Corporations may not have souls, but they have systems whose health is vitally important to the public and to countless needy stockholders.

# 18.

## VANISHED WEALTH

One of the greatest mistakes that can be made—and the wisest people seem to be the most apt to make it—is to look for a certain logic in human conduct, to expect criminals to act according to a certain criminal logic; to expect some sort of reasonableness in human nature.

Why people do what they do is an everlasting mystery; and in no field more baffling than where the problem is, Why do people do what they do with money?—and for money?

Here is a true story in which the principal character was saved from a life of crime by stealing ten thousand dollars at the first try and without being even suspected. The story also includes the fantastic paradox of a bank teller who was spending far more than he earned—and on an actress of all people. And yet he was honest!

It is a short story that never got any publicity.

One day Ray was called over to a small city in New Jersey. A Bank President told him that ten thousand dollars had suddenly disappeared. It might have evaporated so far as any explanation was available; but it was in bills, and paper is not volatile, except metaphorically.

The wealth in question was part of the bank's reserve. It was in one of twenty or more canvas bags each containing ten thousand dollars in bills, and so labelled. These bags were piled up in the vault.

On a certain morning when the Cashier went in to take out the day's supply of change and bills, he gasped to observe a gap in the row of money bags. When Ray Schindler arrived he was told that only the President, the Cashier, and the Paying Teller had access to the vault. Each averred that when the vault was closed the night before the row had been complete.

The bank was an isolated building, two stories high in the front, and three stories high in the rear. In the lowest of the three floors lived the Janitress, a widow with a seventeen-year-old son.

The President told Ray that he wanted above all things to avoid publicity, and promised full cooperation. Ray brought in two of his men and they searched the building from top to bottom against the chance that the thief, having removed the bag from the vault, had concealed it elsewhere till he could find a safe occasion for carrying it off. There was not a trace of it.

Ray questioned all the employees thoroughly and felt that two of them might well be kept under observation: the Paying Teller, and the Bookkeeper. The Bookkeeper was shifty-eyed and sharp of speech, unpopular and crusty to his fellow employees, subservient to the President. The man who tailed him found him a tame and most monotonous person. His only recreation seemed to be endless games of Kelly pool in a highly respectable billiard parlor.

The Paying Teller was in full contrast, the son of well-to-do parents, a college graduate, a bachelor and a bon vivant. On the third day he dragged his "tail" to New York, where he went to a hotel and spent an hour in an upper room, whence he emerged with a very handsome young woman who proved to be a successful Actress.

In those Prohibition days, speakeasies were illegal, and this couple visited one for cocktails, then dined at an expensive restaurant, after which the Paying Teller escorted his companion to a stage door; left her there, went to the box office, saw the performance, returned to the stage door and took the actress out to supper.

The tailer had the dubious pleasure of watching this performance repeated two or three times a week; but he was unable to get close enough to see if any of the vanished bills were used.

It was, however, easy to compute that each of these outings cost the Paying Teller many dollars. At the rate of three dinners a week for a month, he was spending—and on the Actress!—about $240 a month out of a monthly salary of $175.

One Sunday he rented a handsome automobile and took his charmer for a long drive up into Westchester County. He ended the day with a banquet including champagne.

The champagne induced Ray to report to the Bank President the costly goings-on of his Paying Teller. But the President hated to take any positive steps, and the Paying Teller's outings continued.

On one occasion, while Ray was in the Bank President's office, he noted that the Janitress was inside the vault mopping it up. Her access to all that treasure was news to Ray, and he suggested that she be questioned. The President protested. The Paying Teller was so plainly the culprit. Ray insisted. He called on the Janitress in her basement quarters, and questioned her as to any hearsay or gossip that might have come her way.

She told him that most people disliked the Bookkeeper, especially her boy, who had said he wouldn't trust the man an inch. When Ray asked how the boy came to know the Bookkeeper, the janitress said that her son often carried the heavy buckets for his mother's scrubbery.

When Ray asked where he might see the boy, he was referred to a school. Ray called on the lad, there, and found him in a state of nerves. But when Ray asked him if he had ever been in the bank vault, instead of showing any of the usual signs of guilt, he went into a rapture of relief, and blurted out the fact that he had taken the ten thousand dollars, and was overjoyed to get the confession off his chest.

On the afternoon of the robbery, he had gone to the vault to replace a bucket of dirty water with a clean one. He noted the long row of money bags. He was no psychiatrist and could not even imagine why or whence the impulse had come to him; but he had been mystically impelled to dump one of the bags into the bucket of dirty water. He had not read the label, but had supposed that the contents were pennies, nickels or small bills.

He carried his loot to the basement, and studied it. He nearly fainted when he saw that he was the terrified possessor of ten thousand dollars. He had no ambition to be a pirate, and he was petrified with fright by the astounding success of his first thievery.

The thought of carrying the money back upstairs and returning with a confession was too appalling for his immature brain to conceive. He stuffed the bag in a closet and took a bucket of clean water upstairs without saying a word to his mother or anybody else.

That night, while his mother was away, he dug a hole in the back yard and buried the money—all but one hundred dollars which he was unable to resist lifting. He went to another bank and changed the bills into small paper without exciting suspicion; for no one in town outside the bank employees had yet heard of the loss.

He tucked ninety-eight dollars into the pages of a book in his room at school and kept two dollars for a spree. The investigation had been going on for three weeks by this time and he had still hardly broken into that two dollar treasure trove.

Ray Schindler is convinced that if the stolen sack had been filled with pennies, the boy might have been encouraged by his easy wealth to devote his life to thievery. But too much success is as discouraging to some souls as too little. This boy, aghast on the brink of crime, fell back from the abyss and hailed the detective as a savior.

He went with Ray to his mother's back yard and the two

of them unearthed the vanished fortune. Then they restored to the bank president his ten thousand dollars minus the boy's three weeks of high living, which had aggregated about forty-six cents.

There still remained the mystery of the Paying Teller's access to all the money he was wasting on wine and woman. Instead of tailing him farther, the President resolved to confront him with the evidences of his spendthrift ways. He called the Paying Teller into his office and turned him over to Ray Schindler, who startled the man by giving him an exact account of his doings on his excursions for the last three weeks. The Paying Teller was dumbfounded at first, then he began to smile:

"My God, what a case I was building up against myself!"

The President in an agony of affectionate anxiety pleaded:

"But where did you get all the money?"

Here again the solution of a great mystery was one that no self-respecting or reader-respected author would stoop to using. The Paying Teller's explanation was disgustingly simple:

"My father's only sister died and left me about three thousand dollars in cash. Just before the money was paid over to me, I met this actress, fell in love with her and became engaged to her. When I came into that money, I felt that I could afford to spend a little on my courtship, especially as my fiancée is making good money, too, since she is playing in a success. The date of our marriage depends somewhat on the length of the run of the play."

Could anything be more disappointing? It is disgracefully respectable. When ten thousand dollars vanish in a mist, and a Paying Teller is discovered to be squandering money on an Actress, everybody concerned has a right to expect something better than the fact that a scrublady's son carried it away in a pail of dirty water but was afraid to spend it; and that the Paying Teller, instead of embezzling the money, inherited it from a doting aunt and spent it on his fiancée.

This case has value chiefly as an example of the unexpectedness that a detective can expect, and the importance of questioning everybody, and everything.

# 19.

## A RAID ON FAIRYLAND

Things that were once more practiced than preached against are now more spoken of than practiced. The once-unmentionable is now a favorite topic of conversation and publication.

A century ago even trousers were called "unmentionables." If the legs inside them had to be alluded to, they were rendered a little less shocking by being called "limbs" or "nether members."

People suffered and perished in multitudes from certain diseases that were never alluded to in polite circles, however prevalent there. Now, the awful words are printed everywhere; heard from pulpits and discussed gravely and without snickers by nice adolescents.

There is another ancient curse that is now quite frankly discussed. Whether it is a vice or a disease, or both, homosexuality has always been one of the concomitants of civilization as well as of barbarism. It is denounced in the Bible. It was a raging plague during the Holy Crusades. It is mentioned in the court records of the Pilgrims and Puritans of Massachusetts. It is found in the court martial reports of our Revolutionary forefathers and in the army and navy files ever since.

Of late it has found wide treatment in literature. Proust and Gide have given it the highest stylistic treatment, and so have a number of English and American novelists. It pops up on the stage, usually but not always as a signal for laughter. The cult of Oscar Wilde gave it perhaps its first flare of general publicity, and his own cruel fate, along with his undeniable ability, gave it such a tragic aura that in certain circles it is taken as almost a sign and a proof of genius, rather than degeneracy.

From ancient Grecian days on down, it has been a most useful weapon of blackmail. Many a man would carry his head almost proudly after being compromised by a woman, but would commit suicide to escape exposure if involved with a man. And that form of blackmail is, of course, the easiest possible trap to set and spring for the innocent as well as the guilty.

But, however it may be regarded, it is "a condition not a theory," and a source of incessant problems. Americans touring the lower levels of Paris society often visit gathering places, largely supported by tourist curiosity, where homosexuals convene. They could easily be found in America and at times have been quite openly permitted.

Such assemblies are naturally avoided by normal men; and, now and then, some place of popular resort has been ruined for normal patronage by an invasion of abnormal congregations.

This fact brought Ray Schindler his most peculiar commission; and he had to solve it in an extra-legal way. He could not follow his usual procedure of finding out who committed what crime. And homosexual practice, in spite of the protests of many psychiatrists, is legally a crime in most states. But merely being, or seeming to be, a homosexual is not a crime. And that was what made Ray Schindler's problem a problem indeed.

The time was during World War II, just before women invaded the saloons with such a vengeance. The foot on the bar-rail is now likely to have a high heel for a better grip; and the rear ends perched on the high stools are more apt to be female than male.

World War II brought about another strange phenomenon. The army and navy had long refused enlistment to men of known homosexuality; but when World War II set the draftboards to sifting the whole population in order to secure twelve million recruits, the number of those rejected for questionable traits was great enough to turn out an army of respectable size if not of respectable quality.

Like other sects, the homosexuals enjoy congenial companionship and are apt to congregate. And so it was that the famous barroom at the—let us call it the Hotel Taverne was gradually taken over by an elfin host to such an extent that the heterosexual males were crowded out and became conspicuous by their absence. Mere presence in that bar was damaging to one's reputation.

Pretty boys and older men thronged the place, and the bar was losing money as well as prestige. The police could not be called in; for none of the curious customers misbehaved himself in public.

In desperation, the proprietor called in Ray Schindler and told his sad story. He was watching his income dwindle; and his hotel was acquiring a name that would soon drive away all but the most depraved. He begged Ray to cleanse the place, but he had to move with extreme caution since he had no legal weapon to invoke, and a misstep might involve the hotel in ruinous publicity and libel suits.

The crowded hour was between five and six, when the brokers, bankers, lawyers, and merchants had stopped in on the way home for cocktails and highballs.

After much thought, Ray recruited a number of his friends, all of them of robust build and led his little troop into the contaminated resort shortly after five, and they elbowed their way to the bar with an unmannerly roughness that the very gentle gentlemen found annoyingly rude.

Sprawling over the bar and monopolozing it, Ray's friends talked to one another in tones as loud as their manners were uncouth. Ray shouted down to a friend as the farthest end of the long bar:

"Hey, Bill, did you notice what a lot of pansies there are around here? You can smell 'em a mile. They're giving this place a bad name. But don't you quit coming here. In a week or two it will be the fairies who'll be giving this place the go-by. I'm going to chase 'em out of here for keeps."

"A damned good idea!" his friend howled back. "This place is lousy with 'em. They're smelling it up till a he-man can't breathe."

After half an hour of such stentorian warning, Ray and his gang bustled out. But the warning was wasted; or rather, it brought the boys out in a determined effort to defend their stronghold.

A week later, Ray arrived well ahead of the five o'clock rush. Now he had with him only three of his operatives. But they set up an elaborate fingerprinting apparatus on a table at one end of the room.

This time Ray said nothing, made neither threats nor promises. He just sat quietly at the table. But there was consternation among the flowery customers when they noticed that, as each of them finished a drink, the barkeeper took the glass to the end of the bar and handed it over to one of Ray's three men.

What was still more startling was the way the barkeeper handled the glasses. In every case, instead of taking one up in the usual way, the barkeeper put his first and second fingers inside and spread them so that they lifted the glass from the inside without touching the outside. Ray's helper repeated the performance; and set the glass on Ray's table. Then Ray carefully dusted the spot where the drinker's fingers had clasped the glass. He then laid on the dusted spot a piece of tape and removed it, plainly lifting the fingerprint. This he numbered carefully.

Now there was a tempest among the pansies. Some of them dropped their glasses and backed away from the bar. The girl in the hat-check room reported that she had seen at least three young men make a hasty exit with their glasses in their hands. They took them out in the street and broke them in the gutter.

Finally, after a hurried and almost hysterical conference, an elderly man of very dainty attire and sirupy voice approached Ray and said:

"I am a lawyer and I wish to warn you that you have no legal right whatever to take the fingerprints of my clients."

To this Ray replied:

"I am not asking your clients to give me their fingerprints, but after they have left them I have a perfect right to examine them. The police have given me a number of fingerprints of crooks they are looking for. These crooks happen to be known to be fags, and I don't know any better place to look for fag fingerprints than in this barroom which you and your clients have taken over. I will continue to take fingerprints from the glasses as fast as the customers leave them. Try to stop me!"

The lah-de-dah lawyer did not try to stop him. There was a general exodus from the barroom, and trade fell.

But, a week later, the place was still haunted by too many fragrant customers. Now the fingerprinting apparatus was missing, but a more fearsome engine was erected. At one end of the long bar was a big camera on a tripod so tall that the photographer stood on a table.

And now, whenever a little knot of boy-friends gathered at the bar with their boy-friends, Ray Schindler would edge up close to the group and wave to the cameraman, who would promptly flash a big light-bulb and ostentatiously take a photograph.

After a few of these explosions, the same indignant lawyer demanded what new deviltry Ray was up to, and how dared he photograph people without their permission? With a maddening grin, Ray answered:

"I'm not having their pictures taken, but I love to have my own pictures taken in a swell place like this. I want them for souvenirs. If other people happen to be in them, that's not my fault, is it?"

Immediately there was manifested a most unflattering unwillingness to be caught in Ray's vicinity. A quiet panic soon practically emptied the room. One of the exquisites called at Ray's office and made an effort to purchase the negative in which he thought he appeared. When Ray insisted on name and address he walked out.

That was his last battle in that barroom, for the place was abandoned by the violets. Still, like swarming bees, they found other lighting places, and Ray had further appeals for help in evicting such peculiar people.

There was one quaint after-effect of this strange eviction and recapture. Ray spread the warning to the owners of various cocktail bars in the neighborhood to beware of letting such people settle down in numbers and to deal drastically with the first-comers. In one of these places, Ray met a friend for a conference. When they moved up to the bar and ordered drinks, the barkeeper said:

"I'm sorry, Mr. Schindler, I can't serve you."

"And why not?" Ray demanded indignantly. He had only himself to blame for the answer:

"We are not allowed to serve drinks to two gentlemen unless they have a lady with them."

That is a rather startling evidence of the profound change that recent years have made in American *mores*. Before Prohibition a woman in a barroom would have excited stares of horror, and nobody would have called her a "lady." Now in self-protection from a certain type of "gentleman," couples of men were refused service unless they were chaperoned by a lady!

To the Schindler bureau many cases have come in which perverted persons are concerned. Though they excite extreme pity or disgust, they must be handled with a combination of extreme delicacy and extreme brutality.

In one instance, a rich man appealed to Ray to save him from being bankrupted by a wife who was squandering fortunes on re-decorating and re-re-decorating his house, to the enrichment of a certain interior decorator, whom the husband suspected of being her paramour. Ray's investigations disclosed the existence of a really indescribable triangle composed of the wife, and two mutually devoted decorators. Ray had to rescue the husband from this inescapable trio by collecting evidence against the two men that drove them away without spreading the noisome mess before the public nostrils.

Another almost more sickening situation concerned a woman of enormous wealth who had been duped into marrying a handsome young fortune-hunter. After they were sealed in holy matrimony, she discovered to her horror that her husband was a homosexual and was keeping a mister. Nauseating as such a situation may be even to mention, imagine what it must mean to a young wife? Ray has had at least a dozen such cases brought to him by wives who cannot bear the thought of publicizing their degrading plight.

In the state of New York a divorce can be secured only by proof of adultery. But a husband whose infidelity involves another man is not breaking the Seventh Commandment—or the Sixth as the Catholics number it. The law gives absolutely no release to the pitiable wife. Nor does it give release to a husband when, as not infrequently happens, his wife proves to be one of that accursed cult.

Many nice people will feel that such situations should not be even mentioned, but the monumental researches made by Havelock Ellis, Professor Alfred C. Kinsey and others have proved that they are far more horribly numerous than the average mind imagines. Even one such case is a multitude too many.

# 20.

## GRAND (SOAP) OPERA

Politicians and others who make a big business out of their enmity to big business always pretend to believe, or really do believe, that all big-businessmen stick together and form monopolies or trusts to destroy little-businessmen and maintain their own immunity to failure.

As a matter of fact, big-businessmen cut one another's business throats with the keenest pleasure and most fatal rivalry.

One of Ray Schindler's most spectacular cases took him into the lofty jungle where the biggest and fiercest moguls fought one another to the death.

The giant corporation that called Ray to come in and save it from other giants was one of the chief manufacturers of soap. It had developed a special kind of cleanser and deodorizer and had given each cake a special kind of shape, weight, color, smell, look and label. Huge advertising had made its name a sort of household word.

It had developed such a vast sale for the soap that its rivals decided to get on and ride. Several of them put out a soap with a name resembling the original and with every ingredient the same. The copyists could sell their soap much lower since they did not spend a penny on publicity. They let the innovator do all the advertising, and arranged with department stores and other retailers to display their soaps alongside, and price-mark them a few cents below. The housewives and other soap-seekers, seeing how close was the similarity, naturally bought the cheaper cakes.

The firm that originated the commodity naturally suffered anguishes as the profits vanished and their own advertising enriched their rivals. Yet when the originator asked lawyers to sue for damages and get out injunctions and drive the imitators out of business, the lawyers said, "No soap!" There was no law to give the originator a monopoly of a certain composition, color, scent, or form.

With soap, as with songs, sonnets, novels, dramas, or other manufactured articles, a close resemblance is not forbidden, unless there is a direct and evident "colorable imitation" and a definitely proved effort to profit by the creations of some-one else.

For instance, there was the famous Baker's Chocolate. For generations it had sold its wares under a certain trade mark. Numberless other people sold chocolate without interference. But along came a man named Baker, who decided to get rich quick by putting out a chocolate with his name on it. "Oh, no!" said the court, and forbade Mr. Baker to make and vend a Baker's Chocolate, since he was trading on the prestige built up by another commodity of the same name.

And so it was with this particular soap. Big lawyers said that the originators could sue the imitators only if they could prove a direct intent, an exact duplication, or a conspiracy to make profits out of the success of the original. The lawyers also pointed out that proving such a conspiracy was practically impossible.

It certainly looked so. How would you yourself set about getting inside the minds and secret conferences of the directors of an immense manufacturing company to find positive evidence convincing to a court that there had been a dark plot afoot?

It will save labor and dissipate fog to state outright that this story concerns the Lever Brothers and their pet baby, Lifebuoy Soap—the soap that made "B.O." famous as an expression, and made the populace B.O.-conscious after centuries of personal indifference to the twitchings of other people's nostrils.

Lever Brothers felt a natural distaste for continuing to

spread the gospel of smellessness at tremendous cost in order to build up the business of commercial rivals. So they cut their advertising appropriations for that special soap to a minimum.

This brought a wail from the firm that handled their advertisements, Ruthrauff and Ryan. They called on their lawyer to prevent this loss, and he thought that a conspiracy might be provable, provided Ray Schindler could be engaged to ferret it out of the guilty minds of the manufacturers feeding on the Lever Brothers' profits.

As Ray thought it over, he realized the practical impossibility of breaking into the brains of the rivals and dragging out their secrets. They must be induced to deliver their own damnations. But how was he to get hard-headed men to confess their sins on paper?

In the radio world, serials are often called "soap operas"; and this fact may have suggested to Ray an idea for a radio show as a bait. He did not propose to build up a rival soap-factory as he had once built a railroad or a boardwalk, opened a bank, or a second-hand bookstore, or some other institution. But he did develop an imaginary radio show that would offer cakes of soap as prizes, and give them in such numbers that he would need half a million cakes to start with; and more anon.

He kept the names of the imaginary backers of this show a secret; but gave them two agents, his manager, Shelby Williams and Arthur Parsells, of Ray's own staff. Ray provided these two ropers with a handsome suite at the Biltmore Hotel and furnished it with ten hidden dictographs.

As the first victim to be roped in, he selected a minor manufacturer in Brooklyn who was selling so much Lifebuoy-like soap that he had had to enlarge his plant. The roper approached this soaper and asked for a meeting in a Fifth Avenue bank. The soaper found the roper in conference with one of the vice-presidents of the bank. From there they went to the office of a friend of Ray's, the famous comedian, Charles Winninger, who also managed a theatrical agency.

Charlie had expensive offices on Madison Avenue where he tried out talent for radio shows, and he was placing such well-known artists as Ethel Merman.

Ray's manager, Shelby Williams, arranged to take the soap manufacturer to Winninger's office, as pre-arranged, at a time when Winninger was trying out some excellent talent. The soap man sat and listened to the various performers so that Williams, who was sitting with Winninger, could decide whether or not he wanted that talent on the proposed program. Winninger put on a most effective show for the benefit of the soap man.

But the roper said he needed bigger names than those on Winninger's list, and led his prey to his own suite in the Biltmore for further discussion.

There the roper called in those famous partners Bourbon and Water, and Scotch and Soda. The soaper was soon fizzing with pride over the big joke he was playing on the Lever Brothers. He boasted that they had merely invented and advertised Lifebuoy, while his own perfect imitation rode in on the Lever Brothers' backs to huge success.

The roper said at this point that his sponsor was seriously thinking of making use of the genuine Lifebuoy soap as his give-away. But the Brooklyn man pointed out how foolish that would be since he himself could make exactly the same soap and sell it to the sponsor at vastly less.

The roper said he would talk it over with his sponsor. He arranged for another session to give his victim time to seethe to a boil. At the second meeting, the roper said his sponsor was afraid the Lever Brothers might sue him for infringement. The Brooklyn man produced a letter from his own lawyer guaranteeing immunity. The roper said the sponsor was afraid the substitute soap could not be as good as the Lifebuoy. The Brooklyn man insisted that he had paid a high price to an eminent chemist to analyze the Lifebuoy ingredients, find out its formula, and copy it with such minute accuracy that no expert could tell it from a cake of Lifebuoy.

All this was duly recorded by dictograph. It was just what the doctor ordered: a detailed and complete confession of downright imitation—something the best lawyers had declared impossible to obtain.

With this man's bids in his possession, the roper next approached many other big soap-makers and asked for competitive bids. They all fell into the trap and the dictograph faithfully took down their damning confessions.

Only one of these cheated cheaters seemed to be suspicious. He would not walk into the roper's parlor and talk. He insisted on the roper's visiting him at his own hotel. But finally after a lengthy delay, the ropers succeeded in getting him into an apartment where a dictograph had been installed.

When the confessions of all the soap plagiarists were engraved on rolling discs they were privileged to hear their own voices rolling out their own self-exposures. Then Ray's operatives and his roper carried their traps to other cities and caught other travellers on the Lever Brothers' backs.

Since the wholesale piracy of the Lifebuoy methods was made possible by chemists, Ray published advertisements calling for trained men to work on health commodities and asked for their qualifications and experience in such work. Numbers of them frankly stated that they had succeeded in probing the secrets of Lifebuoy and making a synthetic duplicate of it. One chemist produced the very commission from a big manufacturer who had paid him to "tear down Lifebuoy" and build it up again for reproduction.

After a few months of such raids on the pirates' dens, Lever Brothers brought many suits calling for injunctions and cease-and-desist edicts by the courts. The trials were like auditions and the courtrooms resounded with phonographic cylinders parroting the very words of the executives in their very ears.

There is a harrowing difference between the mellow sound of one's own voice when he is burbling boastful confessions of his clever trickery over an *nth* highball in a private suite, and the ghastly sound of that same voice when it crackles forth the very same words in a court of justice with a judge frowning and one's own lawyer blushing.

The United States courts issued cease-and-desist orders, and the offending soap companies got together and drew up a working agreement with Lever Brothers.

The upshot of the matter was a complete victory for Ray's clients. Here again the vital importance of the private detective is shown in protecting properties where the police would be entirely without either jurisdiction or power.

# 21.

## HE PLAYS SANTA CLAUS

In the theater and in the pinker pictures a banker is always an icy-eyed miser, and the flat-footed detective is a little worse than the criminals he pursues. But here is a case where a banker and a detective combined forces to act like a twin Santa Claus. It was a case where, instead of some lucky wanderer finding a pot of gold at the end of a rainbow, a poor family stayed at home and the rainbow came to them bringing a hogshead of gold.

Once, when Ray was delving into a California crime, his brother Walter telephoned him from New York.

"Fly to Cuba at once!"

Ray's errand was to find a lost family there and dump a pile of gold on its doorstep.

The case was brought to the Schindler office by a bank in heartless Wall Street. The bank had on hand a very sizable fortune. If it could not find an heir to receive it, the money must be turned over to the State. The bank officials felt it their duty to spare no effort or expense in search of an heir.

It sounds like an impossibly sweet fairy story to tell about all that money wandering about hunting for somebody to accept it, but the Schindler bureau was commissioned to run down the heir, whose only guilt was his ignorance of the wealth that was calling for him.

It began as far back as 1885, when a certain young Señorita Sazarac from Cuba entered this Wall Street bank, and presented a letter of introduction from a Cuban bank. Her parents had recently died leaving her about $100,000 in cash and securities. She did not want to live longer in Cuba, and she asked the Wall Street bankers not merely to accept her fortune as a deposit but to invest it for her so as to bring her a living income.

This the bank did with such fidelity and intelligence that she had all the money she seemed to need. For nearly forty years she lived off her hundred thousand without diminishing it. In fact the sum kept on growing while keeping her fed and clothed. Her wants were simple, and she never married.

Early in the 1920's Miss Sazarac decided to treat herself to a pilgrimage in Europe. She settled in Paris and lived in the South of France for nearly a score of years. Then World War II sent her back to New York and she took rooms in a hotel where she dwelt until she died.

When the bank learned of her death, it looked about for a swarm of heirs to appear and fight over her money. No will turned up and neither did a single, solitary heir. The officers who had accepted her deposit over fifty years before had gone wherever it is that good bankers go. Nobody in the bank knew anything about Miss Sazarac except her name and address. The hotel people knew no more. So long as tenants pay their bills regularly, hotels ask no questions.

So here was the bank with not even the hint of an heir to notify and with a white elephant on its hands. For the $100,000 that little Cuban spinster had left with them in 1885 had not only supported her in comfort but had grown to a total of no less than $280,000. It would have gone on growing to half a million by the accretions of compound interest.

All the Schindlers had to do was to ransack the world and find some one of the little woman's kith and kin who did not even know enough about her or her money to send a message of polite condolence.

Since Ray was busy in California, the burden fell on Walter Schindler's broad shoulders. He questioned the employees of the bank and finally found an ancient one who vaguely recalled that Miss Sazarac had lived in a family hotel near Gramercy Park before she left for her twenty-year stay in Europe. He also vaguely remembered that she had a number of women friends whom she saw often and telephoned to constantly. But he could not even vaguely remember any of their names.

This hotel was so conservative that it had not taken the trouble to throw away its old telephone slips. These had piled up in the cellar till there seemed to be tons of them. So one of the unfortunate Schindler operatives was assigned to the staggering task of sifting those dust-encrusted papers.

It took him only two weeks of toil to find several numbers charged to Miss Sazarac's room. He took these to the telephone company's office and called for the telephone books of those years. The books were still kept on file and as a reward for all this labor one of the numbers was found to belong to an elderly woman still living on Riverside Drive.

This was vastly encouraging, for the old lady remembered Miss Sazarac, and remembered that she had originally come from Cuba, where she had left a sister. The old woman knew that the sister was married but could not remember her name, or even whether or not she were still alive.

The pursuit had now narrowed down to Cuba. Since the population of Cuba was only a little over four million, the rest was easy for a man with the eyes of an Argus. So Walter called up California and found Ray there, and told him to fly to Havana and get busy.

Fortunately, not everybody in Cuba was named Sazarac. Ray found people in Havana who knew of a Miss Sazarac. She dwelt in the suburbs of Havana. She had married an American, and given him two girls and a boy. Contrary to foreign expectation, this American was very poor. In fact he and his wife had made many sacrifices to give their children a good education, and the boy spoke English well.

Ray learned that the family had long since lost touch with the Miss Sazarac who had gone to New York. They had not even heard of her death, and had no idea that she had had more than barely enough to live on.

Imagine, if you can, their pleasant stupefaction when the handsome stranger who introduced himself as Ray Schindler made the amazing statement:

"I have come to turn over to you the sum of two hundred and eighty thousand *pesos.*"

What that kindly old witch did for Cinderella when she turned a pumpkin into a coach and rats into horses and rags into silk and scorched shoes into crystal slippers was almost nothing compared to what those wizard bankers did for that poor but honest family of Americo-Cubans.

It was a pleasant change for Ray Schindler, too. Instead of running down his quarry and throwing it into jail or worse, he came down in that humble cottage the way Jupiter came down to Danaë, in a shower of gold.

# PRETEXTS AND THE
# PASSION PLAYERS

One of the most important accessories of the detective's art is the Pretext. The best detectives rarely use disguises. They may have to employ fingerprint-lifting tapes and powders, cameras, chemicals, dictographs, lie detectors, and the devices of the handwriting expert.

But they must never appear anywhere without a good Pretext. At any moment someone may pop out with the questions, "Who are you? and what are you doing here?" An answer must be ready without hesitation.

When a strange man is seen loitering about a house at all hours of the night or during a blizzard; when he is found examining door-numbers or hotel registers; when he enters a strange town and barges into strange offices; when he spends days and nights, perhaps weeks and months, in a town where he has no apparent business and no visible means of support, he must be ever-ready with a quick explanation.

The story has already been told about how Ray's operatives pretended that they were going to change the famous Board Walk in Atlantic City to a concrete pavement. This was a mere pretext, of course, for roping in the thievish city fathers. The railroad he built was only another pretext for intricate dealings with a crooked railroad president and his crooked staff.

On three separate occasions the Schindlers pretended they were about to build a golf course. Their actual purpose was to learn the real value of certain lands and their exact owner-ship. Once it was necessary to have the tract surveyed and a golf course mapped. Once, wide publicity was given alleged attempts to secure one of the leading golf champions as the professional teacher for the imaginary golf club. Ray actually signed up a famous man for one of his mythical clubs.

To secure certain important information for one of the big automobile companies in Detroit, the Schindler bureau leased and ran for a whole summer a huge hotel at Put-in Bay on Lake Erie.

The Schindlers once had to put up a pretence of conducting a commercial enterprise in Paris in order to carry on a very delicate investigation. They went into the corset business.

There was a preface to this activity at home. The advertising firm of Ruthrauff and Ryan had built up a vast business with a slenderizing device known as the Madame X Corset. It was heavily advertised and the enormous sales attracted numerous imitators. The firm engaged Ray to track down these copyists and put an end to their imitation.

When, later, a complicated case required a long stay in Paris, Ray used the Madame X Corset as a pretext for his underground work over there. He posed as the European representative of the Madame X company and opened an office, which he kept going for two years. One half of the year Ray was in charge; the other half of the year his brother Walter conducted affairs. They had also a branch office in Brussels, and business prospered so that Ray's Parisian friends thought that his entire interest was in corsets, rather than in their contents. At the end of this disguised detective work the Schindlers sold their business to the local staff.

In Florida they went into real estate development and helped build Davis Island in Tampa. Ray acted as sales manager in Miami and Saint Augustine. Incidentally, Ray made a sizable fortune, most of which he left in Florida when the boom collapsed. But the real estate business was only incidental as a cover for detective work.

The book and magazine publishers and a leading bookstore once engaged Ray to look into certain underground industries that were robbing them of large sums of money. They knew that certain dealers were securing a big supply of books and magazines outside the regular channels without paying for them.

Ray accomplished what he could by shadowing suspects; but he was finally driven to opening a bookstore on Madison Avenue as a subterfuge. By pretending an interest in the black market, he was able to discover that the thieves were securing their wares for almost nothing through crooked deals with crooks in shipping departments.

Magazines usually make use of the "return privilege." They send a dealer a larger number of periodicals than he is sure of selling, and he has the right to return all the unsold copies. To save the expense of bulky shipments the dealer is permitted to clip the top of the front covers from each unsold magazine, return that and destroy the magazines.

But the thieves took these clipped copies, pasted on the covers a slip stating that the magazines were to be shipped overseas, and sold them abroad at a hundred percent profit since the magazines cost the dealers nothing but the freight.

Ray discovered the warehouses in Boston and Brooklyn where the stolen magazines were handled. As a result of his findings two of the dealers went to jail and their fraudulent work was stopped.

The bookstore Ray founded went out of business, after serving as a pretext for dealings with these dealers. It had not only achieved its purpose but had also returned a small profit to the clients.

On occasion Ray's office sold metal shoe laces, and insurance; sent out book agents, operated filling stations on Long Island, and even pretended genealogical research.

But the strangest of all his strange pretexts and one that had the most far-reaching and unforeseen results concerned the Passion Players of Oberammergau.

Various reasons arose for Ray's remaining in Europe over a prolonged period in 1922. He had a will case to investigate and also a political affair to clear up. It was partly a Governmental affair and involved certain foreign diplomats. After the defeat of Germany in World War I, the Passion Play at Oberammergau was not produced until 1922, thus breaking the decennial schedule that had been maintained for hundreds of years. In 1930 the Passion Play resumed its every tenth year appearance, but a second World War made impossible the 1940 production.

As most people know, the little village of Oberammergau has made the Passion Play its almost sacred and sole function. The children of the town are trained to take part in it as they grow up. The players earn their livings humbly and really live for the festival every ten years. They make their own scenery and costumes and are constantly in rehearsal. The actors are a kind of priesthood.

The belated revival of the Play in 1922 awakened the interest of Hollywood, and several producers visited the town with offers so glittering that they bedazzled the good citizens, who were promised not only the lure of wealth from a tour of the United States, but the ultimate glory of a motion picture immortality. To the amazement of the screen kings the humble players finally declined both the screen cash and the screen credit.

One of the agents for a big company told Ray of the hundreds of thousands of dollars he had dangled in vain before the pious actors. Ray went down to look things over, purely as a pretext for lingering around Bavaria.

He was put up at the home of the famous Anton Lang, who played the part of Christ in 1910, 1922, and finally in 1930. Lang's wife spoke English perfectly, which was a help since Ray did not speak German at all. But he became well acquainted with everybody concerned in the Passion Play and all the other leading citizens of Oberammergau.

In the winter the main product of the valley was snow and the transportation was skis. Ray had learned to ski as a boy, and this served as a further excuse for dallying. He began to work out a deep dark plot.

At that time the German mark was doing a bit of skiing on its own. It took about a million marks to buy a newspaper. Oberammergau was in a state of unusual poverty even for Germany. The town's one real industry was wood-carving and nobody was buying any wood-carving.

While piety had led the almost starving citizens to scorn the profane allurements of Hollywood, Ray began to instill in them the idea that it was their solemn duty to go on with the plans for the 1930 production of the Play. He solved the problem of how they were to keep alive till then by agreeing to furnish employment for all the wood-carvers in town. And he imported the wood for them to carve. He paid them, also, four times the daily pay they were asking. This amounted to but a few pennies apiece, yet it was princely to them.

All this while Ray was also preaching to them the idea that it was their missionary duty to carry their religious message to the United States and to make a tour of that benighted but begilded nation.

His winning ways overcame their last scruples and he collected a hundred of the principal people at a meeting and gave them a banquet of food imported from Munich and elsewhere. He even introduced them to the virtues of American whiskey. He had found several cases of it lying neglected in the hotel cellar for lack of purchasers. In fact, he bought out the entire cellar, including many bottles of twenty-year-old wine at less than ten cents a bottle—though ten cents in American coin translated into paper marks brought the price up to fabulous heights.

The punch was mixed in a bathtub.

The night of the party there was so much snow that the

guests almost had to make their entrance on skis through the second windows. Ray says that he met the first couple to arrive and greeted them with the only German he knew, which was "Auf wiederseh'n!" So they went away at once. The second couple seemed to understand his intention and pushed in past him. That was probably one of the gayest nights ever experienced in Oberammergau. As Ray describes it: "It was a good thing that the hundred leading performers did not have to appear on the stage the next day. The Passion Play had finished its six-months' run in September. It took Oberammergau two or three days to recover from the party given in celebration of the contract they had signed with me."

In the meanwhile Ray had assembled a group of investors to pay for the tour and handle it. Fifty men and women Players were brought to America at good salaries, even in American money. They were also insured, and furnished with roundtrip tickets. According to the contract, the first hundred thousand dollars that came in was to go to the Players. After that, the profits were to be divided equally between the Players and the American syndicate.

Among the backers of the tour were John D. Rockefeller, Jr., Al Smith, George Gordon Battle, Keith and Proctor, the theater operators, and others of like prominence. The troupe reached America in the Spring of 1923 and was housed at the old Waldorf-Astoria. The opening performance was in Grand Central Palace and made a sensational success.

But first the Passion Players had to make acquaintance with the fine high spirit of American labor union bosses. The bosses forbade the use of the stage settings so piously made in Oberammergau and imported for the sake of authenticity. Under threats of calling a strike, the bosses demanded that union men be hired to paint a new set of sets at a cost of $20,000. As soon as this was paid over, the company was graciously permitted to throw away the American sets and make use of the originals from Oberammergau.

By the time the Players had appeared in eight American cities, all the backers had been repaid in full and there was a profit of nearly a hundred thousand dollars.

There were still six months to go when a brilliant idea occurred to Ray. The company was to begin a two weeks' appearance in Baltimore. So he arranged to have the entire troupe taken to Washington the day before and formally received by President Coolidge, his Cabinet, the Supreme Court Justices, and other high officials.

The Players were to stand in a semicircle on the White House lawn and there to be introduced by the eloquent lawyer, George Gordon Battle. Then the Players were to shake hands with the President while the cameras took pictures, and the newspaper men took notes.

At the last moment, a prominent millionaire, who had been born in Bavaria but had come to this country as a boy and grown rich, begged for the privilege of introducing his fellow countrymen to the President. This seemed to be a very happy idea at the time; and the request was granted. To the stupefaction of everyone, the plutocrat, instead of showing the expected courtesies, began a furious defense of Germany and her share in World War I. He grew so frenzied that he tore at his hair. He screamed at the President in such vicious terms that Coolidge turned his back on the fanatic and returned to the White House, followed by the other notables, leaving the speaker unheard and the Players unintroduced. The only important pictures obtained were of Coolidge's shoulderblades.

The newspapers naturally made headlines of the outrage, and since the Players were all Germans they shared the obloquy the speaker had revived against the Kaiser and all his Huns.

Immediately, the sponsors of the Baltimore engagement, which was to have begun the following night, cancelled their contract. Other cities vied with one another in slamming their doors in the faces of the dazed and now homeless Players.

There was nothing for Ray and his syndicate to do but ship the company back to Oberammergau. With them they took nearly $96,000 in profits. But the church in Munich seized half of this and the German government seized the other half. All the Players had for their reward was what they may have saved from their weekly salaries. All that Ray got out of it was experience. He did not get back his own expenses.

He had, however, accomplished the detective work that had taken him to Germany, and the Passion Players had served successfully as a pretext. But what a Pretext!

The next time you see a production of Wagner's four *Ring* operas at the Metropolitan Opera House, you might be pardoned if you suspected that it was all a pretext of Ray's to discover if one of the trombone players is issuing false notes.

# THE LIE DETECTOR

# DETECTS THE TRUTH

Lie detection began just after the first lying began. It is the oldest detection in the world.

The Chinese used for ages an ordeal test. They gave the suspect powdered rice to swallow. The rice powder was a form of saliva test. For various mechanical reasons the confronted liar finds his salivary glands failing and his mouth going dry. Rice powder needs moisture and chokes him.

The lie detector has often discovered white lies rather creditable than otherwise, and it has rescued many persons from convictions of guilt and some men from prison. One convict was released after thirteen years in the penitentiary. Once the lie detector proved two accused bank robbers innocent despite the positive identifications of five eye-witnesses. The guilty men later made detailed confessions.

The lie detector has also exposed the altruistic self-sacrifice of people who have confessed to crimes they did not commit in order to save others who did commit them.

For ages it has been recognized that emotional tensions are reflected in irregular breathing, irregular pulse, changed blood pressure and other reactions. Of late skin-electricity has been discovered, and brain storms proved to be really electric.

Many years ago Professor Muensterberg of Harvard introduced certain tests. But it remained for Leonarde Keeler to develop and perfect a complicated machine to such efficiency that it is doubted only by those who know little or nothing about it. It is so feared by people who have gone through its tests that the mere invitation to use it has often brought confessions.

Keeler preferred to call his apparatus a "polygraph," which might be translated as a "many-writer." It actually put several pens to writing on charts the various responses to questions asked in such a manner that the answer must be either Yes or No.

Like other delicate machinery, the polygraph can go wrong or break down when inexpertly managed. If the subject being polygraphed catches his breath at a confusing question, that is registered. If he holds his breath to deceive the instrument, the pen makes a level line; but the breath-holder soon betrays himself because he sets up a shortage of oxygen that must be compensated for by quick breathing later.

So it is with the other recordings. Self-control by effort in itself exposes a tension. In fact, the detector detects excitement rather than merely lies. Professional gamblers with poker faces often reveal almost hysterical internal flutterings when certain cards fall to them.

The polygraph works as well in tests of innocent deception. Thus, if you select a card, or a number between one and ten, and try to keep it a secret the inner machineries of thought and emotion are thrown out of gear or held in mesh with such will-power that the strain shows on the polygraph.

The clever deceiver who gets by successfully at the first trial is likely to show at the end such signs of relief or triumph that these betray the release of the brake.

Persons vary, of course, in their reactions to all sorts of stimuli. One person may receive the most tragic shocks with a numbness that is as far from indifference as the screams or swoons of another. So each subject must be subjected to very thorough preliminary tests and his or her standard of reaction established as a norm.

While the lie detector has won its fame by many spectacular exposures of criminals, or by discoveries of the burying places of victims or treasure, its chief activity has been in commercial institutions where its best successes have been kept from public notice.

Like every other step in human enlightenment and progress it has been ferociously opposed by those whose conservatism is a vice. So the lie detector has been ignored in most communities while put to the fullest use in others. Particularly in Chicago, where Dr. Keeler lived, it is depended upon by bankers, personnel officers, institutions of every sort, the State of Illinois, and the police. Some judges ask for it on occasion. Keeler had an annual retainer from the Governor of Illinois.

One of the polygraph's chief values is its power of elimination. When several are suspected, the polygraph will ordinarily acquit all but one or two of suspicion, and thus save unlimited waste of labor and investigation.

In banks and other institutions where its use is insisted upon at regular intervals, the percentage of dishonesty has been known to fall to almost nothing. Some insurance companies, including Lloyds of London, give a reduction in insurance rates to firms that use a lie detector to test their employees.

The polygraph draws a dismal picture of average human nature, since thousands of cases establish the fact that, where people are in a position to make petty thefts without much danger of discovery, 62% of them do so. In one chain of retail stores the first tests proved that 76% of the employees had pilfered. The next time the tests were made, only 3% confessed. The fear of the machine compels a certain fear of dishonesty. Even people in charge of charity drives are hardly above the average in peculations, on the theory perhaps that charity begins at home.

So the polygraph has preventive value. One man connected with safe deposit boxes was thrown into such agitation by the test that he blurted out a future plan to duplicate the key to a certain box and remove the $50,000 it contained.

In innumerable cases, persons suspected of one theft or other crime have confessed to many more that had never been known of.

But this is not the place to yield to temptation and retail the all-but-innumerable victories it has gained over the human will to deceive and the habits of dishonesty. Nor is it the place to describe its exact mechanisms. The point here is that, from the first, Ray Schindler saw its value and not only made use of it but went into close alliance with Dr. Keeler for its improvement and the enlargement of its field. He calls it "the most important contribution to crime detection of the last generation." He allied himself with Dr. Keeler, Dr. Le-Moyne Snyder, the medico-legal expert, William W. Harper, the forensic physicist, and Clark Sellers, the famous handwriting expert, in forming the complete crime investigation service incorporated as "Scientific Evidence, Inc." whose resources and experience are available to anyone faced with a difficult problem involving crime or the suspicion of it.

An example of the effectiveness of the polygraph is seen in Ray's experience with a young man accused of having stolen cameras and quantities of film from his employer at a time when war needs gave them high value. He had a wife and two children and his record had been blameless hitherto.

After Ray had made the necessary investigations he confronted the young man with the evidence he had accumulated, and soon wrung from him a frank confession that he had stolen merchandise valued at no less than $11,000.

The exactness of the sum and Ray's experience that men rarely confessed their entire guilt, led him to put the man through the lie detector. Within fifteen minutes he tripled the total of his thefts. The reason he had stopped at $11,000 was that he knew he could raise that amount by selling his home and such securities as he had. He thought that the restitution of that amount would clear him.

His employers had never dreamed that his peculations

had reached the handy sum of over $35,000, and, at Ray's suggestion, they decided not to take an expensive revenge by sending him to the penitentiary but to let him pay back gradually what he had carried off.

The constantly amazing thing is the discovery every day that institutions where incessant watch is kept over employees are often unaware of a constant drainage by veteran employees. Not long ago a woman who had been awarded a medal for faithful and honest service extending over twenty years was caught by a little slip-up and confessed that she had abstracted a grand total of $180,000 during those unsuspected years.

In almost unnumbered cases men and women put through the test only because such a test is being made of everybody on the force are bewildered into confessions of startling depravity. Incessantly, the employee who is sent through the mill because a thousand dollars is missing comes through with an admission that he or she has really stolen much more.

Now and then a subject has made an hysterical attack on the apparatus itself as if it were a fiend of uncanny and diabolic power. But, ordinarily, the victim's skull becomes a seething caldron of such bafflement, turmoil, and resourcelessness that the long-held secrets are expelled in desperation. They grow spiritually seasick with the churning motion the relentless, unpredictable questions set up in their souls, and find their only relief in doing as other seasick wretches do, vomiting up the indigestible contents of their queasy consciences.

While Ray Schindler makes constant use of the lie detector, one of its most dramatic successes was scored in Los Angeles in 1946. It chanced that Dr. Keeler and Dr. Snyder and Ray had visited the city for a vacation. It became a busman's holiday; for, when they took a friendly luncheon with Ray Pinker, the brilliant chief of the Los Angeles Crime Laboratory, Jack Donahue, chief of the Homicide Squad, and various other friends, the three Easterners were taken for a ride.

The police had been brought to a standstill by a murder case in which they were certain of the guilty man, but could not prove his guilt and could not even prove that a crime had been committed. All they knew was that Mrs. Hills, the wife of a well-to-do horticulturist, had disappeared. She and her husband had quarrelled frequently and noisily and, finally, according to the husband, she had decided to leave him and go back to her mother farther East. She had two sons and a daughter by a previous husband, but throughout the case they sided strangely with their step-father.

Now, the missing Mrs. Hills had a set of false teeth. She often removed them; but, whenever the doorbell rang, she always scurried about to find and replace them. Two or three days after her alleged departure, her daughter, cleaning up her room, noted something faintly glowing far under the bed. Dragging it out it proved to be the grinning ghastly false teeth of her mother!

Since Mrs. Hills would never even go to the door without them, it was dazing to find that she had gone so far away for so long and left them on the floor.

Word of the find was promptly reported to the police and Mr. Hills' plausible story of her departure was suddenly bitten in two by a denture. He simply said he could not explain why his wife should have forgotten so important a part of her wardrobe; but there it was.

With a sort of divining rod made for that purpose, the ground on the Hills property was searched for days by driving that rod into the ground to see if a body could be located. The police had dragged neighboring ponds and lakes with no more success.

Hills had visited the police headquarters frequently for over six months importuning them to find his wife, and the police radio had blasted out her description and asked the public for information regarding anyone remembering Mrs.

Hills. The police, therefore, had Hills in their mind as the number one suspect. But there was no corpse and no evidence of a crime.

It was while Keeler and Ray were lunching with Ray Pinker, Jack Donahue and others that they were told of the Hills case. It was suggested that Keeler put Hills on the lie detector.

Since the submission has to be voluntary, it was necessary to persuade Hills to take the treatment. He called his lawyer, who vigorously advised him to avoid it. But the three Easterners talked to him, told him how bad it looked to refuse to be questioned about his absent wife, how little an innocent man had to fear, and assured him that, in any case, the lie detector would not appear in court.

At last he consented. He entered the room where Keeler applied the various instruments to him. He never guessed that Ray Schindler and others were studying him from a darkened room.

The first questions Keeler asked him were meant to overcome his natural uneasiness and to adjust the machine and its calculators to his individual scale of tension. He began to feel rather foolishly at home when the dreaded inquisition amounted only to such foolish questions as made him giggle with their silliness:

"Do you live in Van Nuys?"

"Yes."

"Did you have breakfast this morning?"

"Yes."

"Are you wearing a green tie?"

"No."

"A red tie?"

"Yes."

After an easy and easing while of this, Keeler's soft voice suddenly murmured:

"Did you shoot your wife?"

"No!!"

"Did you stab her?"

"No!"

"Did you push her over a cliff?"

"No."

"Did you choke her?"

"N-no."

The unseen pens were palsied by that question. But Keeler's tone and manner were unchanged:

"Did you throw your wife into the ocean?"

The pens calmed down as he answered:

"No!!"

"Did you throw her into a fire?"

"No!!!"

"Did you bury her?"

The pens shivered before he could answer with a dry throat:

"No."

Still Keeler made no sign that he suspected any of the answers to be revealing. After a few more idle and calm-restoring queries, he began:

"Did you bury her on your property?"

"No!"

"On your neighbor's property?"

"N-no."

Finally, when Hills was limp and more afraid of himself than of that inhuman machine, Keeler disengaged him and called in the others. The lie detector had told Keeler that Hills had strangled his wife and buried her. Now he was told:

"Let's go dig up your your wife and give the poor thing a decent burial."

"Of course!" he said, and led the police, Keeler and Snyder to a spot just over his line in a large cabbage patch on the neighbor's property. There the spade was applied.

Five feet underground they came across a fur coat, and beneath that the body of the wife. She had been choked to death. Her husband had killed her in a furious wrangle, carried her out of the house in the dark, dug her grave, given her a grisly funeral, shovelled the earth over her, and disguised the places as best he could.

He might never have been convicted if the police had not done what they could, especially about those poor teeth of hers. Even so, he might have escaped if the lie detector had not winnowed his thoughts and shaken out the grain of truth. The lie detector was not introduced in the Los Angeles County Courts, but the results of its work were there. The jury found Hills guilty and the judge sentenced him to death in the lethal gas chamber at San Quentin. In February of 1948, the Governor of California commuted his sentence to life imprisonment.

By an odd coincidence, I happened to be visiting that penitentiary the very day the Sheriff's men delivered him there with a commitment letter from the Judge instructing the Warden to keep him safe until a certain date, then put him to death.

This sentence was never carried out. Strangely, the man's stepchildren and the wife's own sisters clung to the murderer, kissed him, wept over him, pleaded for him. Murderers are apt to be such nice people—otherwise.

The devotion of the stepchildren and other testimony as to Hills' character made a strong argument that he had not killed his wife by cold premeditation, but had been driven to a frenzy by her temper and had slain her in a sudden flare of helpless anger. So Governor Earl Warren yielded to many appeals, in which the stepchildren and the sisters-in-law joined. He commuted the sentence to life imprisonment.

Ray Schindler feels that this action was just; for, after the body was recovered, he had a long talk with Hills and with the dead woman's children, and he was convinced that the slaying was not done with cold calculation and premeditation.

The Moral here would seem to be that wives should not deal too harshly with their husbands. There are murders enough by wives to make the same advice applicable to husbands.

# 24.

## THE LOST GIRL

The modern emancipation of women and the opening to them of a whole world of opportunity has meant also the emancipation of girls. Opportunity is also temptation, which many of them have resisted everything else but.

Up to the Twentieth Century it was the boys who ran away from home; girls rarely left except in an elopement with some man. Now and then in the past some freakish lass would break away into a life of such adventure as made "the Spanish nun" an almost fabulous character; and there have been a few women pirates and soldiers more or less disguised—though a man's clothes are less of a disguise than an emphasis of a normal female form.

In our century, however, girls began to run away in swarms. The stolen automobile and the pick-up of the hitch-hiker enable the fugitive to escape at a rate hard to follow; and the multitude of ways of earning a living in big cities offer the runaway a perfect concealment with a means of support.

Along with this new freedom came a multiplied array of perils not only to morals but to life itself. Whether sex-crimes are more numerous now in proportion to the population than before may be a matter of doubt; but there is no doubt of the enormous increase of population in the last century, and the raper and the murderer have immensely increased opportunities for speed of attack and escape.

When, then, a young girl vanishes nowadays, her parents have reason to fear what is called a fate "worse than death," or even death itself. The runaway boy faced such danger, too, and the life of the tramp and the hobo with its camps in the jungle subjected the lad to moral dangers as well as physical. But a boy was supposed to be able to take care of himself and to run the gauntlet of dangers without permanent harm. This was not always true by any means, as the horrible increase of juvenile delinquency keeps proving. Still, there are peculiar terrors surrounding the fate of a girl or a young woman who disappears.

The story has already been told of Ray Schindler's long and complicated labors in discovering what man raped and beat to death the little child in Asbury Park who vanished on her way home from school along a short straight road. Her hideous fate was all too soon discovered though it took nearly a year to find the guilty man and prove his guilt.

This is the story of a girl who walked out of school and disappeared as completely as a soap bubble that floats away. In this case all Ray's toil and skill were unavailing. Paula Weldon was born and raised in Stamford, Connecticut. Ed McCullough, the Editor of the *Stamford Advocate*, who helped to finance the investigation, was responsible for enlisting Ray's services.

She was eighteen years old and in her second year at Bennington College in Vermont. She also worked in the dining room. On December 1, 1946, a Sunday, Paula Weldon put on her old slacks and went for a walk, saying that she would be back in time for supper. She did not take her pocketbook.

She did not come back for supper. She did not come back that night. Anxiety gave way to alarm. Search was begun. Then the town police were called in. When they failed they called in the State Police. Next, the Connecticut State Police were asked to help. At last the F.B.I. joined the hunt on the chance that it was a case of kidnapping, in which field the F.B.I. has authority to act. Again and again the wooded mountains above Bennington were ransacked.

The girl's family lived in Stamford, Connecticut, where the father worked for a large corporation. At last, after many months of hunting and wasting, the corporation asked Ray Schindler to help, and offered him a modest fee.

He spent far more time than he was paid for and far more money than he was paid. He used every scientific device and left no part of the mountains and the forests unsearched. So thorough was the combing of the terrain that they found another body, that of a man who had vanished months before. But there was no clue to Paula.

Ray was convinced that he had traced her several miles from the college. She had begged a ride on a small truck driven by a man of good reputation. The trouble here was that, though he described Paula perfectly, he insisted that the girl who rode with him to the city limits wore a brown jacket. Yet it was known that the jacket Paula wore was red.

This baffling contradiction was finally solved by a simple test suggested by Shelby Williams, Ray's office manager. The truck driver's vision was examined and it was found that he was color-blind. All red objects looked brown to him.

But this was the last success they had in the case. And this ends the story. No trace of the girl has ever been discovered. The story is told here only as a proof that failure always threatens the most zealous detective, and not even Schindler always succeeds.

# 25.

## WHO WAS THE RED KILLER?

One of the ugliest features of life in our beloved America is the difficulty of convicting the most vicious criminals. A still uglier feature is the fact that, despite the uncertainty and rarity of such punishments, now and then some perfectly innocent person is caught in the toils of circumstantial evidence and made to suffer for a crime he did not commit.

Instances have already been given of how Ray Schindler's zeal for saving the innocent vies with his zest for overtaking the guilty.

One of the battles which most interested him was waged in cooperation with Erle Stanley Gardner, who is not merely a writer but an international institution. His millions of readers are really subscribers. They demand his work so regularly and so often that he is a periodical as well as a personality.

Erle Gardner has called Ray and his brother Walter "the leading detectives in this country." He was reporting the de Marigny case when Ray was working on it and was greatly impressed by what he called Ray's "uncanny ability."

A busy lawyer before he became so superhumanly popular as a writer, Erle Gardner's utmost endeavors were given to the defense of victims of the law. On one occasion he became so interested in the case of a man who had been sentenced to death for murder, and his investigations led him to intervene so successfully that every juror retracted his verdict, the Governor issued a pardon, and the condemned man went forth to lead a useful life.

At the full tide of his success as a story-maker, he wrote a

313

letter to Governor Earl Warren of California pleading with him to postpone the execution of a man convicted of murder. The Governor had won his first successes as a prosecuting attorney, and advanced to the post of Attorney General of his State, thence to the governorship. He was so far convinced by Gardner's arguments that he commuted this death sentence to a life sentence and declared himself open to persuasion of the man's complete innocence on the presentation of proof.

This is a case where disproof of guilt is exceedingly difficult. All the detective work had to be done in reverse. Instead of moving from the mystery of a crime toward the discovery of the culprit and the proof of his guilt, he had to start with the conviction, work backwards and try to unravel the fabric of the proof; and so release the innocent.

The crime was a hateful one, and the victim of it a young girl who was outraged and slain. Gardner in his version of the atrocity went so far as to say that his careful study of the adduced evidence convinced him that it was not sufficient for a conviction. He believed that the actual murderer had not yet been found, and in this opinion he had the complete support of Ray Schindler.

Very briefly told, this is the story of the crime: On August 18, 1943, three sisters, Barbara, Willa Mae, and Jackie Hamilton were swimming in the Feather River in northern California. They lived with their father, mother, and another sister in a camp close by. When she had finished her swim, Jackie went to a boathouse on the bank, changed from the old dress she wore for a bathing suit into other clothes and returned to the home camp two hundred yards away. She left her sister Willa Mae in the water. A little later Jackie, who was only thirteen years old, took a soft drink, then left the camp and walked toward the river to wash her feet. When she did not return, a search was made and her raped and battered little body was found in a clearing further down the river.

A young sheepherder, Guino Fillipelli, had sat under a tree on the opposite bank and watched the sisters while they swam. He testified that he had seen a red-headed man walking up and down the river bank, brandishing a stick all the while the girls were swimming. The sisters saw the man, too, and Willa Mae saw him there after Jackie had left the water.

Later, according to the sheepherder, when Jackie reappeared from the house and walked toward the river, the red-headed man came out of the willows and the bushes and attacked her. The sheepherder saw her fall.

Now it so happened that there was a red-headed man named William Marvin Lindley living in a boathouse not far away. He had been living in his boathouse before the Hamiltons built their camp there. He had done odd jobs for the people living thereabout and they spoke well of him as quiet and likeable, though not an intellectual giant.

So "Red" Lindley was arrested by the officers who were summoned. They took the sheepherder's word for it that Lindley was the murderer, though they made no effort to take fingernail scrapings from the dead girl or make any of the other routine investigations.

Erle Gardner says that the witnesses summoned "tell the most amazingly contradictory stories I have ever encountered in a murder case. These contradictions are so numerous that they seem to have attracted little attention."

That latter sentence reads like a sort of Irish bull, but the matters overlooked really strike the later student as almost the most conspicuous features of the case.

Because of his vast popularity, Gardner is accustomed to receiving so many appeals to intervene on behalf of convicted persons that he hardly has time to read the letters. But his secretaries drew his attention to letters from Lindley's lawyer, Al Matthews, and these impelled Gardner to send for and to study for several evenings the full transcript of the testimony. The contradictions and oversights appalled him.

For one thing, he discovered that there was another red-headed man in the case and he had duped a friend into providing him with an alibi that was a deception. He had appeared with his face bearing such scratches as a frantic girl might have inflicted on an assailant. Shortly after the hour of the crime he had appeared in a store and was so nervous and excited that he could not pick up the change from the bill he had laid on the counter. His comments on the crime later had so offended his fellow-workers that they had stopped speaking to him.

He was not arrested.

But Lindley was arrested and eventually convicted, though the dead girl's father testified that he himself was with Red Lindley until about five minutes before Jackie reached the camp after she finished swimming. Another man named Owens had confirmed this testimony. He and Jackie's father and Lindley had been out in an automobile for an hour.

But, as Gardner points out, the red-headed man was in the willows all the time the girls were swimming and so he could not have been Lindley. As Gardner puts it:

"Obviously, the testimony in the record itself, instead of proving the defendant guilty beyond all reasonable doubt, proves him innocent beyond all reasonable doubt."

The man who was convicted had been with the girl's father and another man until five minutes before the murder of the girl, though the red-headed man in the willows had been there continuously for at least half an hour, watching the young girls splashing about the water in the clinging old dresses they used for bathing suits. And that was the man who attacked Jackie in view of the man who was herding sheep near by. Thus, as Gardner emphasizes, the very man who described the murder, "the most biased, bitter witness in the entire case gives the defendant an ironclad alibi."

The other man was never arrested. So far as the evidence shows, he was never even sought for.

The police pounced on the nearest red-head they found and he was convicted. Thus far the case reminds one of the Asbury Park rape and murder of a little girl. In that case a drunken ex-convict Negro was discovered near the scene of the crime, and he would undoubtedly have been executed if Ray Schindler had not been called in by two men who doubted the air-tight conclusiveness of the evidence against the Negro. Only by the most complicated detective work was it possible to save the bewildered Negro by eliciting a confession from the young German gardener who really killed the girl and was willing to let the innocent Negro die. The Negro had a bad name. He was an ex-convict.

So Lindley had a previous conviction against him, but there was nothing in his record to indicate a tendency toward sex-crime.

Lindley is accused of having confessed twice that he had murdered the little girl. But one of those who testified to the confession had himself been convicted of a crime and the details of the alleged confession are in conflict with the facts known about the murder. Such alleged confessions are suspicious, as Gardner notes, when reported by prisoners, since they often pretend to have heard such confessions in order to win release from jail themselves.

The second alleged confession was merely a vague admission said to have been made to the sheriff who was taking Lindley to San Quentin after his conviction and sentence.

There is another curious twist to the case. After his arrest and before his trial, the court appointed psychiatrists to examine Lindley and they reported him insane. He was put away in a state hospital for a year, then adjudged sane and put on trial.

Yet, as Erle Gardner insists and as the evidence stands, the murderer "could not possibly have been the defendant . . . it proves irrefutably that William Lindley is innocent . . . that he was convicted on false testimony."

After Gardner had made his expert summing up of the

case, three members of the California Supreme Court expressed "grave doubt" as to Lindley's guilt. On their recommendation Governor Warren stayed his execution and gave him commutation to a life sentence. But, if Lindley was innocent and his trial bungled, a life-sentence is only a lesser outrage than a death-sentence.

If it had not been for the unselfish devotion to justice, the painstaking analysis of the evidence and the eloquent ardent intervention of Erle Stanley Gardner on behalf of a total stranger, "Red" Lindley would now be dead. Ray Schindler's enormous experience and his minute study of the case led him to join his friend Gardner in a determined effort to save Lindley from the living death of lifelong incarceration. Neither of these men asked for other remuneration than such ease of conscience as can come from devotion to the cause of sacred justice.

We are all apt to grow as impatient as Hamlet did with "the law's delay." We are apt to denounce the endless difficulties placed in the way of convicting criminals on the assumption that they are innocent till proven guilty. Yet now and then a case arises like this of Red Lindley where, by some complex conspiracy of events, a man of the most apparent innocence is railroaded to prison or to execution, and must rely for his rescue on the rare chance intervention of some stranger who happens to take an interest and the rarer chance that he will persevere till the rescue is complete.

It was William Lindley's fate to suffer the last injustices, to endure the bewilderment not only of being accused of a murder he could not have committed, but of being convicted and being sentenced to death for it. Then came commutation to life-long imprisonment. No wonder his overwrought mind gave way and he went insane. He is still kept behind prison walls, and there seems to be no hope of his recovering either his intellect or his liberty.

From the martyrdom of this humble soul has risen an institution of high nobility. It is called The Court of Last

Resort. It was founded by Erle Stanley Gardner with the splendid cooperation of Harry Steeger, who has given it wide public recognition and encouragement in *Argosy Magazine*.

The beautiful purpose of this Court Beyond Courts is to look into the histories of persons convicted of murders and sentenced to life terms in spite of their innocence. Of course, numberless guilty people protest their innocence to the last; but there are others whom circumstances have conspired against with merciless success.

Erle Gardner and Ray Schindler have travelled thousands of miles, spent thousands of hours and thousands of dollars investigating such cases, interviewing persons, and, when convinced of innocence, appealing to the authorities to release the victims of twisted evidence.

They have had success in three cases already. Clarence Boggie was "pardoned" after thirteen years of false imprisonment and seven months of the hardest work on the part of Gardner and Schindler. William Keys was released after eleven months of toil on the part of The Court of Last Resort. He had spent fifteen years of confinement in a penitentiary. Louis Gross, after seventeen years imprisonment, has been promised a new trial.

Two brothers, John H. and Coke T. Brite, are still hoping for the success of their strange friends of the Court. And there are twelve other convicts whose life sentences are under investigation by the tireless Samaritans of the Court.

This may well be the note on which to end this study of the life and works of Ray Schindler. The cases selected from his long and infinitely varied career have shown something of his problems and the methods that a great detective uses for their solution. They show also how important it is for a detective to have not only a head but a heart also.